Rails-to-Trails

NEW YORK

"A wonderful and long overdue guide that uncovers New York's special and hidden places. New York trail users will love this practical and entertaining guide, regardless of their mode of travel."

—Anne O'Dell, Author of *Ride New York: 35 Horse and Multiple-Use Trails in the Empire State,* and former chair of the New York State Trails Council

"There aren't better spokespersons for the rails-to-trails movement than Craig Della Penna and Tom Sexton. They help you feel the magnetic pull of New York's rail and canal trails as they carefully reveal their history, their beauty and their many hidden secrets. . . . There isn't a better guide than this one to set you on your way."

—Betsy Russell, Founder, Ontario Pathways

"I'll never look at a rail trail the same way again! Coupled with fascinating local histories, precise directions, and . . . extensive knowledge of the natural world, this is an indispensable resource for those who want a rewarding learning experience while enjoying the scenic beauty of New York State."

—Fran Gotcsik, Executive Director of the Genesee Valley Greenway

"The accurate maps and interesting text make it easy for people to enjoy the extraordinary greenway and rail-trail system in New York."

—New York Parks & Conservation Association

Help Us Keep This Guide Up to Date

Every effort has been made by the authors and editors to make this guide as accurate and useful as possible. However, many things can change after a guide is published— trails are rerouted, establishments close, phone numbers change, facilities come under new management, and so on.

We would love to hear from you concerning your experiences with this guide and how you feel it could be improved and kept up to date. While we may not be able to respond to all comments and suggestions, we'll take them to heart and we'll also make certain to share them with the authors. Please send your comments and suggestions to the following address:

The Globe Pequot Press
Reader Response/Editorial Department
P.O. Box 480
Guilford, CT 06437

Or you may e-mail us at:

editorial@globe-pequot.com

Thanks for your input, and happy travels!

Great Rail-Trails Series

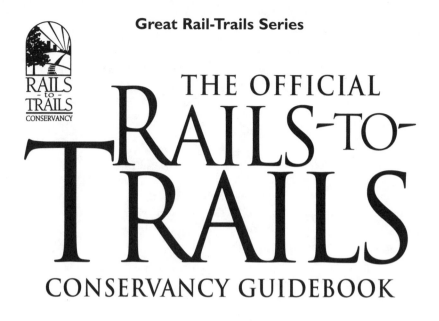

THE OFFICIAL
RAILS-TO-
TRAILS
CONSERVANCY GUIDEBOOK

The Definitive Regional Guide to Multi-use Trails

New York

by
Craig Della Penna
and Tom Sexton

The
Globe
Pequot
Press

GUILFORD, CONNECTICUT

Text design: Lesley Weissman-Cook
Maps: Tim Kissel/Trailhead Graphics, Inc., copyright © The Globe Pequot Press

Photo credits: pp. xiii, 1, 7, 9, 10, 11, 123, 143, 144, 185, 187, 190: Matt Vuolo; p. xviii: Mark White; pp. xxi, 111: The Westchester County Department of Parks, Recreation & Conservation; pp. 17, 35, 36, 38, 59, 60: Karen-Lee Ryan; pp. 50, 51, 52: Catskill Revitalization Corporation; pp. 73, 76, 79, 83: Fran Gotcsik, Friends of the Genesee Valley Greenway; pp. 98, 105: David J. Shufelt, Harlem Valley Rail Trail Association; pp. 135, 136: Betsy Russell; p. 157: Rails-to-Trails Conservancy; all others by the authors.

ISBN: 0-7627-0450-0

Manufactured in the United States of America
First Edition/First Printing

*To the many local rail-trail volunteers
who are helping to make
New York a better place to live.*

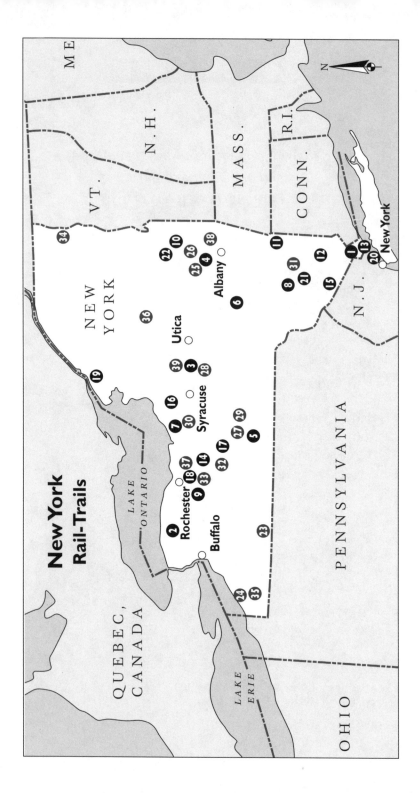

New York
Rail-Trails

CONTENTS

ACKNOWLEDGMENTS

No non-fiction book is a work by one person, or even two. We're going to attempt to list, in no particular order, the folks who encouraged us, gave us inspiration, and helped us in some small way:

New York Parks and Conservation Association; New York Department of Transportation; New York Canal Authority; New York Office of Parks, Recreation and Historic Preservation; Trolley Museum of New York; New York State Snowmobile Association; New York State Trails Council; Matt Vuolo; Fran Gotcsik; Betsy Russell; Ron Foley; Lisa Lyon; Robin Dropkin; and David Inman Adler; Nick Lagai; Rod Fargo; Doug Dingman; Glen Heinke; Al Massey; Jason Piquette; Wilbert Chillis; Sissy Danforth; Aaron Vogel; Chris Dillenbock ; Jim Fincher; Richard Miga; Les Johnson; Norm Gollnitz ; Jeff Olson; Eric Ophardt; Mark Grainer; Dan Kelly; John Dimura; Robert Reinhard; Jim Bachorz; Alane Ball; J.D. Wood; Evan Jennings; Kim Meade; Stephen Allocco; Kevin McClaughlin; John Pilner; Judy Anderson; Cliff Patrick; Brian Goodman; Sue Frampton; Bill Sepe; Jeff Johnson; Anne O'Dell; Cosmo Kramer; John Nehrich; Jill Marshall; Bill Masalski; Barry Liebowitz; Dave Schufelt; Dick Hermans; David Delucia; George Danskin; Sheldon Quimby; Brad Barclay; Kip Grant; Len Kilian; Howard Halstead; Steve Marsh; Steve Feeney; Dave Riordan; Joe Higgins; Sue Poelvoorde; Jay Schissell; Larry Carpenter; Rich Caraluzzo; and Dave Morgan.

ABOUT THE AUTHORS

Craig Della Penna is the New England Representative for the Rails-to-Trails Conservancy. He has written two other books on rail-trails. He lives adjacent to the rail-trail in Northampton, Massachusetts, with Kathleen, his wife of thirteen years, and Governor, his yellow Labrador retriever. He has visited and cataloged the railroad archeology of more than 250 rail-trails and on the weekends he can be found exploring old railroad corridors throughout New England.

Tom Sexton is head of the Northeast Regional Office of the Rails-to-Trails Conservancy and has been with RTC since 1991. He has helped launch several rail-trail projects and has bicycled a few thousand miles of rail-trails. He is also the author of *Pennsylvania's Rail-Trails* currently in its seventh edition. He lives with his wife and young son and daughter in central Pennsylvania and looks forward to bicycling across the United States on one long rail-trail.

INTRODUCTION

This book contains exciting journeys for you to explore, journeys on old railroad corridors. These corridors were created or owned by some of the country's most famous names in steam railroad transportation: the Delaware & Hudson Railroad; New York, Ontario & Western Railroad; Delaware, Lackawanna & Western Railroad; Erie Railroad; Pennsylvania Railroad; New York, New Haven & Hartford Railroad; Lehigh Valley . . . why, there are even a few trolley lines in here, as well as a bike-path corridor built along a road or two. In addition, we cannot forget the Erie Canal Trail—a forerunner to rail transport. All the trails in this book, however, were built to different engineering specifications to meet the individual terrain and the different levels of resources available to the builders. Let's talk a bit about how those differences came about.

A Short History of New York's Railroads

A short history of New York's railroads simply has to revolve around the New York Central System (NYC). The NYC was the largest operator in the state and the first railroad company to become a player on the national scene, with immense amounts of capital available to it—both monetary and political capital. Indeed, in 1967, just before the NYC merged with Pennsylvania Railroad to become that ill-fated entity known as Penn Central, NYC was, in terms of mileage, the country's largest railroad—almost 10,000 miles.

NYC System was a huge company in its prime years. The focus should be on the *system* part of the name. It included the New York Central, which obviously was mostly in New York, but also four other separate (to differing degrees) corporate entities: the Boston & Albany, the Toledo & Ohio Central, the Michigan Central, and the Cleveland, Cincinnati, Chicago & St. Louis Railroad—Big Four for short. NYC also owned minority shares in some other connecting roads.

In the Beginning

It all began in 1825 when the Erie Canal opened. Though the canal was a vast improvement over other means of transportation, there was always a traffic jam between Albany and Schenectady. This 40-mile stretch had a large number of locks to bring the canal boats down from the higher Mohawk River at Schenectady to the Hudson River at Albany. In response, a transloading operation was initiated, moving freight from boat to horse-drawn wagon and back to boat. This involved a 20-mile stagecoach route, however, and while it was somewhat faster than canal travel, it remained cumbersome. The bottleneck created the demand for the newfangled technology of the day, a railroad, to bypass the problem area.

In 1826 the appropriately named Mohawk & Hudson Rail Road was incorporated. It was open by 1831, and the first locomotive was named De Witt Clinton, after the governor who was in office when the project was commenced. Clinton was the man most responsible for the creation of the canal, so it was somewhat ironic that his name would appear on the first locomotive of the railroad that would make the canal largely obsolete.

In ensuing years more and more railroads were incorporated, capitalized, and built to connect, end to end, to the Mohawk & Hudson. These lines collectively competed directly with the canal, and since they operated very close to the canal in many places, the state legislature initially forced them to pay tolls to the state-owned canal corporation. These early railroads became collaborators in an attempt to have the tolls rescinded; they succeeded in 1851. In 1853 these ten short railroads were combined into a single corporate entity known as the New York Central Railroad.[1] The mainline east-to-west route became known as the water-level route, a reference to its proximity to the Mohawk River and the Erie Canal.

Around the same time these east-to-west oriented railroads were being built and operated, a couple of other railroads were being constructed north-to-south along the eastern bank of the Hudson River, emanating from New York City. The strongest of these companies was the Hudson River Railroad. The weaker railroad, the New York

---

[1] The origin lines of the NYC were the Mohawk & Hudson, Utica and Schenectady, Syracuse & Utica, Auburn & Syracuse, Auburn & Rochester, Tonawanda, and Attica & Buffalo. These seven, along with three more—the Schenectady & Troy, Buffalo & Lockport, and Rochester, Lockport & Niagara Falls—made up the original ten lines that were merged to form the New York Central Railroad.

Along the Orange Heritage Trail's segment in Goshen, you will encounter an active rail line adjacent to the trail. This is called "rail-with-trail"—a dual-use corridor.

& Harlem—which had lines constructed the length of Manhattan— became the interest of one Cornelius "Commodore" Vanderbilt. In 1857 he bought enough stock to become the controlling party. He then improved the bottom line enough that by 1863, he was able to purchase control of the Hudson River Railroad. In 1867 he purchased a majority share in the NYC, and in 1869 he merged his earlier rail- roads into the NYC. He continued acquiring logically connecting roads for a number of years, folding the four major entities (Boston & Albany, Toledo & Ohio Central, Michigan Central, and Big Four) into the New York Central System.

One of the more interesting sidebars to the rail wars of the late nineteenth century happened when a new railroad was being laid out along the western shore of the Hudson River to reach Albany and points west. The NYC's line along the eastern Hudson was an obvious target for this upstart new railroad. Vanderbilt suspected that the proponents of the West Shore Railroad were merely a front for the Pennsylvania Railroad—the archenemy of his NYC.

In response, then, Vanderbilt—with help from two other big names of the day, Andrew Carnegie and John Rockefeller—set out to build a railroad across Pennsylvania that would be a shorter route to Carnegie's steel mills, with more favorable grades, than the Pennsy's route. Thus, each major eastern railroad was building a line in the other's territory to spite and damage the other.

J. P. Morgan—another famous name—was called in to broker a truce. After lengthy negotiations on Morgan's yacht, the NYC ended up owning the West Shore Railroad, and the Pennsy ended up owning the South Pennsylvania Railroad. The NYC's West Shore Railroad has now largely been abandoned west of Albany, but the north-to-south segment on the western Hudson River is still operating today.

Pennsy, however, never finished the South Pennsylvania Railroad project, and later sold the corridor (along with several semi-constructed tunnels) to the state of Pennsylvania. The state then used the alignment to construct the Pennsylvania Turnpike—which ironically would take much freight traffic away from the Pennsylvania Railroad.

The Name Trains

As the railroad industry matured, the NYC became synonymous with plush, streamlined long-distance passenger trains. Some of the more famous names on the NYC's roster included the Twentieth Century Limited, Pacemaker, New England States, Empire State Express, and more. The crown jewel of the company's passenger operations, though, was the Twentieth Century Limited.

The Twentieth Century Limited was a night train with overnight sleep accommodations and a transit time between Chicago and New York of only sixteen hours. In operation from 1938 to 1967, it was said to be one of the world's finest trains, and indeed, it was an experience like no other. Special signage, special uniforms for the train crews, and a huge custom-made red carpet emblazoned with the logo of the Limited greeted boarding passengers; when they sat down for evening dinner, a vase of fresh flowers was found on every dining table. Additionally, since the train was the fashionable way to travel long distance (before airlines), Hollywood celebrities regularly rode this train—along with their ever-present paparazzi. The train was even pulled by specially designed locomotives with "streamlining" details.

By the mid-1960s, however, with the airline industry blossoming and the interstate highways connecting most portions of the country, the railroad industry's passenger operations began to lose favor. In 1967 the New York Central ran the Twentieth Century Limited for the last time, just before it merged with the enemy Pennsylvania Railroad.

"Like Scorpions in a Bottle" [2]

How did such an improbable merger come about? With the loss of not just passengers but also freight to highways in the 1950s and 1960s, the railroad industry in general was hemorrhaging the red ink. Says Frank N. Wilner in his 1997 book *Railroad Mergers: History, Analysis, Insight:*

> Indeed, there were just too many miles of railroads to take care of and two few trains carrying freight. Just 10 percent of the nation's rail route-miles were carrying fully half of the railroads' total ton-miles, while 30 percent of the network carried less than 2 percent of all intercity rail-freight traffic. The cost of maintaining and servicing underutilized rail facilities was driving many carriers toward bankruptcy and discouraging outside investment in even profitable railroads. Meanwhile, excessive regulation capped many rail rates below what was needed to attract capital.[3]

Talk of railroad mergers and consolidations had always filled the air. Indeed, all the major railroads operating were the result of some merger or railroad war. One proposal, however, caused quite a stir.

In 1957 the NYC and the Pennsylvania Railroad entered into talks to merge. Most rail line mergers were end to end, creating a longer

---

[2] The phrase *scorpions in a bottle*—describing the principal players in the Penn Central debacle—is from chapter 10 of *Railroad Mergers: History, Analysis, Insight* by Frank N. Wilner (Simmons-Boardman Books, 1997).

[3] Wilner, page 120.

railroad; NYC and Pennsy were largely parallel lines, however, making for an unusual partnership. Moreover, a merger of these two roads would be akin to a merger of oil and water: The railroads had diametrically opposed management styles and operating cultures. The NYC "green team" tended to be more hard charging and had more energetic leadership, while the Pennsy "red team" was more conservative. Additionally, the intense and long-standing competition between the two roads had instilled a kind of hatred between them. Merging these corporate giants was not easy, but after ten years of talks, some dancing with other partners, and getting a government okay, the two finally came together on February 1, 1968.

The dominant "partner" in the deal was the Pennsylvania Railroad. That dominance became apparent to all the employees when the better management positions were held for former Pennsy employees. This caused many of the best NYC employees to leave.

> In addition to the problems of unification, the industrial states of the Northeast and Midwest were fast becoming the "Rust Bowl." As industries shut down and moved away, railroads found themselves with excess capacity. The Pennsylvania was worse than practically anyone else in having four or six tracks where one or two would do—tracks that were no longer needed but were still on the tax rolls. West of the Alleghenies Pennsy and NYC duplicated each other's tracks nearly everywhere. The PC merger was like a late in life marriage to which each partner brings a house, a summer cottage, two cars, and several complete sets of china and glassware—plus car payments and mortgages on the houses.[4]

On June 21, 1970, the Pennsylvania Central—sixth largest corporation in the United States—entered bankruptcy court. In 1974 it was determined that the PC could not be reorganized, and a new government-owned entity, Consolidated Railroad Corporation (CR), was created. CR took over operations on April 1, 1976.

---

[4] *Historical Guide to North American Railroads* (Kalmbach Books, 2000), page 327.

As an entity with 17,000 miles of track, CR was a major player, but its government ownership placed it under a lot of pressure to reduce costs and become profitable as quickly as possible. CR management thus set out to abandon 6,000 miles of unneeded or duplicate trackage. The money saved from consolidation and land sales would produce needed cash that could be used to repair the rest of the system.

But abandoning track was made complicated by old and constraining regulations governing rate setting. These rules, set by the Interstate Commerce Commission (ICC) during the years when railroads were flush with cash, needed to be relaxed.

Staggers and the Humpty Dumpty Wellness Act

To streamline rate setting for the railroads, the Staggers Rail Act of 1980 was passed by Congress and signed into law by President Jimmy Carter. One component of this law made it easier for railroads to abandon unprofitable branches. In the years prior to Staggers, it was a bureaucratic nightmare for a railroad to abandon lightly used branch lines. Before the ICC would grant permission for the formal abandonment, the petitioning railroad had to appear at a series of public hearings and present its case to the locals concerned about their loss of a railroad connection.

It was not uncommon for the ICC to deny abandonment because a single shipper (which in many cases had only minimal rail traffic) objected to the loss of service. Most times, the whole process took years to complete. After Staggers was enacted, however, it took railroads only months to dispose of unwanted and unprofitable branches. This opened up a huge new inventory of urban land—abandoned, neglected, and maybe slightly toxic, but also linear, connected, and historic—that could be adapted to new uses, such as rail-trails.

Staggers' streamlined process also allowed an additional option: instead of abandoning track, a railroad could sell it to a qualified shortline operator. Because of their hands-on, local management, shortlines could solve shipping problems quickly, and customer service became the order of the day.

In the early 1980s so many branches were being abandoned by railroads and so many of the corridors were being acquired and broken up by adjacent property owners or reversion clauses that Congress passed an amendment to the National Trails System Act. This one-paragraph provision (sometimes called the Humpty Dumpty Wellness Act) allowed the ICC to implement a step before final abandonment.

This step, called railbanking, allowed the corridor to be set aside for use in the future as a transportation corridor while being used as a trail in the interim. Without railbanking, many of the abandoned corridors would have disappeared overnight as legal entities, broken into so many hundreds of small segments that "all the king's horses and all the king's men" couldn't put them together again.

Railbanking is one of the major pillars upon which the Rails-to-Trails Conservancy rests. There are currently around 3,000 miles of railbanked corridor around the United States. The Rails-to-Trails Conservancy regularly monitors attacks by property rights organizations on railbanking regulations and steps in with technical assistance and sometimes friends-of-the-court briefs in key cases.

The Unmerging of Penn Central

Given all this new legislation, Conrail had become such a well-run and profitable company by the mid-1990s that it was bought by both CSX Corporation and Norfolk Southern (NS). These two suit-

A split-rail fence reinforces the rustic ambience along the Harlem Valley Rail-Trail.

ors bid up the price to $10.4 billion, the largest amount ever paid for a railroad in the United States.

A bit of background might be helpful here. Back in the late 1950s, when the NYC and Pennsy were planning to merge, the NYC actually explored joining with the C&O Railroad and others. A NYC and C&O merger would have actually made a lot of sense; the two had compatible routes, corporate cultures, and traffic base. Pennsy, meanwhile, had looked at a merger with the Norfolk & Western Railroad, which also matched up well with Pennsy's routes, cultures and traffic base. Neither of these preferred mergers happened, of course. Instead NYC and Pennsylvania merged—with disastrous results.

Flash ahead to 1998. When CSX and NS carved up Conrail, CSX—whose predecessor company was the C&O—acquired the NYC segments of Conrail. NS sought and acquired the Pennsy segments. It thus took thirty-five-odd years for the correct merger to finally take place.

Today CSX and NS are running well and beginning to get past their initial start-up jitters. Much capital is being spent on improvements to the mainlines, and long-haul truck traffic is once again being taken off the roads. At the same time, the lesser-density branch lines are operating as shortlines. These connector railroads, operating with local hands-on management, bring customers back to a railroad—those small customers that huge, faceless entities like CSX and NS cannot even begin to court. Major railroads have begun to realize that these low-scale operations are in fact major contributors to their success.

And as for the abandoned lines, scores of projects are currently under way in New York that will convert these to rail-trails. Some are nearing the construction phase, while others are only a gleam in a local official's, grassroots organization's, or trail neighbor's eye. Together they total another 350 miles for the citizens of New York. When all these projects are complete, New York will have in excess of 1,000 miles of rail-trails. Amazing.

A community's rail-trail project of today is a reminder of the same grand vision that created the railroads. Such a vision was well expressed in 1907 by Daniel Burnham, the architect who designed the Union Station in Washington, D.C.:

> Make no little plans; they have no magic that stirs men's
> blood and probably themselves will not be realized. Make
> big plans; aim high in hope and work, remembering that
> a noble, logical diagram once recorded will never die, but

long after we are gone will be a living thing, asserting itself with ever-growing insistence. Remember that our children are going to do things that would stagger us. Let your watchword be order and your beacon beauty.

Thus is that old cliché, the "romance of the rails," being reincarnated today as the "romance of the rail-trails" all over America.

The History of the Rails-to-Trails Conservancy

The beauty of the Rails-to-Trails Conservancy (RTC) is that by converting the railroad rights-of-way to public use, it has not only preserved a part of our nation's history, but also allowed a variety of outdoor enthusiasts to enjoy the paths and trails. Bicyclists, in-line skaters, nature lovers, hikers, equestrians, and cross-country skiers can enjoy rail-trails, as can railroad history buffs. There is truly something for everyone on these trails, many of which are also wheelchair accessible.

The concept of preserving these valuable corridors and converting them into multiuse public trails began in the Midwest, where railroad abandonments were most widespread. Once the tracks came out, people started using the corridors for walking and hiking while exploring the railroad relics that were left along the railbeds, including train stations, mills, trestles, bridges, and tunnels.

Although it was easy to convince people that the rails-to-trails concept was worthwhile, the reality of actually converting abandoned railroad corridors into public trails proved a great challenge. In 1986 the Rails-to-Trails Conservancy was formed to provide a national voice for the creation of rail-trails. The RTC quickly developed a strategy designed to preserve the largest amount of rail corridor in the shortest period of time. A national advocacy program was formed to defend the then-new railbanking law in the courts and in Congress; this was coupled with a direct project-assistance program to help public agencies and local rail-trail groups overcome the challenges of converting a rail into a trail.

The strategy is working. In 1986 the Rails-to-Trails Conservancy knew of only seventy-five rail-trails in the United States, and ninety projects in the works. Today there are more than a thousand rail-trails on the ground and many more projects under way. The RTC vision of creating an interconnected network of trails across the country is becoming a reality.

The thriving rails-to-trails movement has created nearly 12,000 miles of public trails for a wide range of users. People across the country are now realizing the incredible benefits of the rail-trails.

Benefits of Rail-Trails

Rail-trails are flat or have gentle grades, making them perfect for multiple users ranging from walkers and bicyclists to in-line skaters and people with disabilities. In snowy climates people enjoy cross-country skiing, snowmobiling, and other snow activities on the trails.

In urban areas rail-trails act as linear greenways through developed areas, efficiently providing much-needed recreation space while serving as utilitarian transportation corridors. They link neighborhoods and workplaces and connect congested areas to open spaces. In many cities and suburbs, rail-trails are used for commuting to work, school, and shopping.

Signage on many rail-trails, as here on the North County Trail, is similar to that found on highways.

In rural areas rail-trails can provide a significant stimulus to local businesses. People who use trails often spend money on food, beverages, camping, hotels, bed-and-breakfasts, bicycle rentals, souvenirs, and other local products and services. Studies have shown that trail users have generated as much as $1.25 million annually for a town through which a trail passes.

Rail-trails allow for the preservation of historic structures, such as train stations, bridges, tunnels, mills, factories, and canals. These structures shelter an important piece of history and enhance the trail experience.

Wildlife enthusiasts also enjoy the benefits of rail-trails, which can provide habitats for birds, plants, wetland species, and a variety of small and large mammals. Many rail-trails serve as plant and animal conservation corridors; in some cases endangered species can be found in habitats located along the route.

Recreation, transportation, historic preservation, economic revitalization, open-space conservation, and wildlife preservation—these are just some of the many benefits of rail-trails and the reasons people love them.

The strongest argument for the rails-to-trails movement, however, is ultimately about the human spirit. It's about the dedication of individuals who have a dream and follow that vision so that other people can enjoy the fruits of their labor.

How to Get Involved

If you really enjoy rail-trails, there are opportunities to join the movement to save abandoned rail corridors and to create more trails. Donating even a small amount of your time can help get more trails up and going. Here are some ways you can help the effort:

- Write a letter to your city, county, or state elected official in favor of pro-trail legislation. You can also write a letter to the editor of your local newspaper highlighting a trail or trail project.
- Attend a public hearing to voice support for a local trail.
- Volunteer to plant flowers or trees along an existing trail or to spend several hours helping cleanup crews on a nearby rail-trail project.
- Lead a hike along an abandoned corridor with your friends or a community group.
- Become an active member of a trail effort in your area. Many groups

host trail events, undertake fund-raising campaigns, publish brochures and newsletters, and carry out other activities to promote a trail or project. Virtually all of these efforts are organized and staffed by volunteers, and there is always room for another helping hand.

Whatever your time allows, get involved. The success of a community's rail-trail depends on the level of citizen participation. The Rails-to-Trails Conservancy enjoys both local and national support. There are currently 5,500 RTC members in New York State. By joining the RTC you will get discounts on all of its publications and merchandise while supporting the largest national trails organization in the United States. To become a member, use the order form at the back of the book.

RTC works with many different trail-building partners. The lead state-wide organization for rail-trails is the New York Parks & Conservation Association. For more New York trail information or for technical assistance, you can write to the NYPCA at 29 Elk Street, Albany, NY 12207. You can also call them at (518) 434-1538 or visit their Web site at www.nypca.org.

How to Use Rail-Trails

By design, rail-trails accommodate a variety of trail users. While this is generally one of the many benefits of rail-trails, it also can lead to occasional conflicts among trail users. Everyone should take responsibility to ensure trail safety by following a few simple trail etiquette guidelines.

One of the most basic etiquette rules is "Wheels yield to heels." The figure below indicates the correct protocol for yielding right-of-way. Bicyclists (and in-line skaters) yield to other users; pedestrians yield to equestrians.

Generally, this means that you need to warn the users to whom you are yielding of your presence. If, as a bicyclist, you fail to warn a walker that you are about to pass, the walker could step in front of you, causing an accident that could have been prevented. Similarly, it is best to slow down and warn an equestrian of your presence. A horse can be startled by a bicycle, so make verbal contact with the rider and be sure it is safe to pass.

Here are some other guidelines you should follow to promote trail safety.

- Obey all trail rules posted at trailheads.
- Stay to the right except when passing.
- Pass slower traffic on the left; yield to oncoming traffic when passing.
- Give a clear warning signal when passing.
- Always look ahead and behind when passing.
- Travel at a responsible speed.
- Keep pets on a leash.
- Do not trespass on private property.
- Move off the trail surface when stopped to allow other users to pass.
- Yield to other trail users when entering and crossing the trail.
- Do not disturb the wildlife.
- Do not swim in areas not designated for swimming.
- Watch out for traffic when crossing the street.
- Obey all traffic signals.

How to Use this Book

The main rail-trails featured in this book include basic maps for your convenience. It is recommended, however, that street maps, topographic maps such as USGS quads, or a state atlas be used to supplement the maps in this book. The text description of every trail begins with the following information:

Trail name: The official name of the rail-trail.

Endpoints: The beginning and ending points of the trail.

Location: The counties through which the trail passes.

Length: The length of the trail.

Surface: The materials that make up the rail-trail vary from trail to trail. This section describes each trail's surface. Materials range from asphalt and crushed stone to the significantly more rugged original railroad ballast.

Uses: What kind of activities are appropriate for each trail.

To get there: The book will provide you with directions to the rail-trails and describe parking availability.

Contact: The name and contact information for each trail manager is listed here. The selected contacts are generally responsible for managing the trail and can provide additional information about the trail and its condition.

Accommodations: If you're interested in turning your rail-trail journey into a multi-day trip, these inns and B&Bs are conveniently located near the trail.

Bike repair/rentals: Some of the rail-trails have bicycle shops nearby. This will help you locate bike rentals, or a shop in which you can have repairs made if you have a problem with your equipment.

Campgrounds: If you'd prefer to experience the rail-trails of New York over a period of several days, pack your sleeping bag and pup tent. These campgrounds are nearby and convenient for an early morning start.

Description: The major rail-trails include an overview of the trail and its history, followed by a mile-by-mile description, allowing you the chance to anticipate the experience of the trail.

Key to Map Icons

 Parking   Rest Rooms

 Information

Note: All map scales are approximate.

Rails-to-Trails

NEW YORK

New York's

TOP RAIL-TRAILS

---

1 Bronx River Pathway

Endpoints: Valhalla, Bronxville.

Location: Westchester County.

Length: 11.55 miles.

Surface: Asphalt with some short cinder sections. *Note:* About 2.6 miles of this trail are on neighborhood roads. Some sections are very busy, with intricate pedestrian and bike crossings.

Uses: All nonmotorized uses.

To get there: The trailhead is at Kensico Dam Plaza Park, which is located at the intersection of the Taconic State Parkway and the Bronx River Parkway.

Contact: David DeLucia, Director of Park Facilities, Westchester County Department of Parks, Recreation and Conservation, 25 Moore Avenue, Mount Kisco, NY 10549: 914–864–7070.

Bike repair/rentals: Bronx River Bicycle Works, 6 North Bond Street, Floor 1, Mt. Vernon, NY 10550-2551; 914–667–7417; bronxriverbicycle works@msn.com.

Most of the trails in this book are either former railroad corridors or canal towpaths. The Bronx River Pathway is an exception. It lies in the corridor with, and alongside, the first automobile "parkway" in the United States. A *parkway* is usually defined as a scenic road with much greenery adjacent to the travelway, with careful thought having gone into making it a visual pleasure.

Although the Bronx River Parkway was designed as a scenic roadway connecting Westchester to the Bronx, it had some visionary transportation design features. Using entrance and exit ramps, it was the world's first example of the design concept known as a limited-

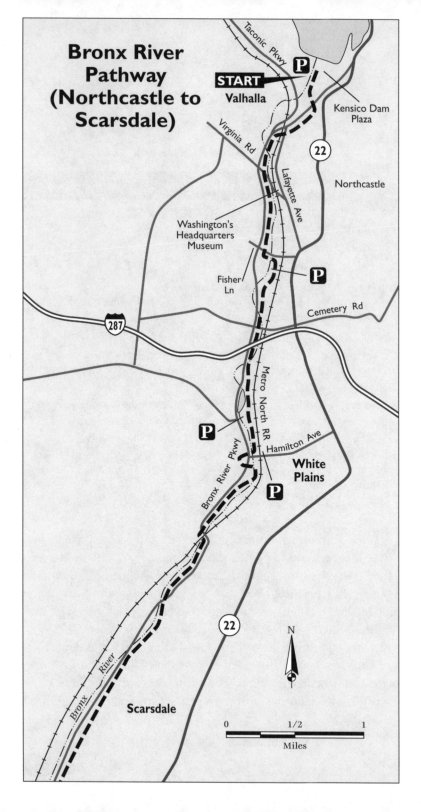

Bronx River Pathway (Northcastle to Scarsdale)

Taconic Pkwy

START
Valhalla

P

Kensico Dam Plaza

Virginia Rd

Lafayette Ave

22

Northcastle

Washington's Headquarters Museum

Fisher Ln

P

Cemetery Rd

287

Metro North RR

P

P

Bronx River Pkwy

Hamilton Ave

White Plains

P

22

N

Scarsdale

Bronx River

0   1/2   1

Miles

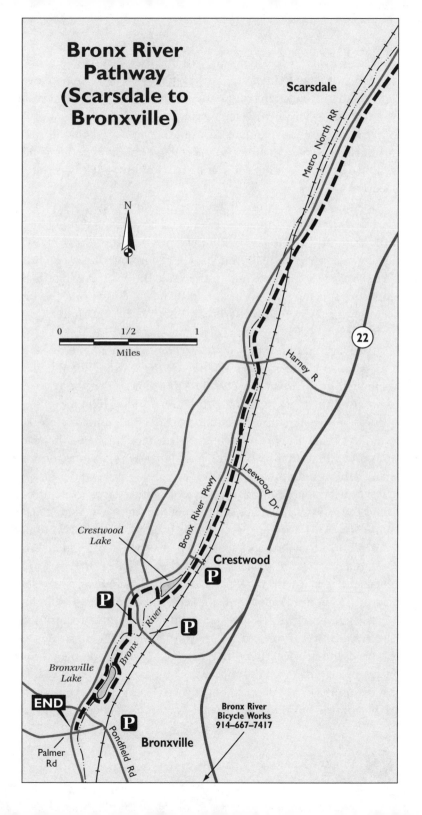

Bronx River Pathway (Scarsdale to Bronxville)

Scarsdale

Metro North RR

22

N

0   1/2   1
Miles

Harney R

Bronx River Pkwy

Leewood Dr

Crestwood Lake

Crestwood

P

P

P

Bronx River

Bronxville Lake

END

P

Pondfield Rd

Palmer Rd

Bronxville

Bronx River Bicycle Works
914–667–7417

access highway. It was also built with the then-little-known concept called landscape architecture, making this road facility an enjoyable journey. Parkways don't allow trucks; they usually have lower and, in most cases, visually pleasing bridge structures.

Another unique characteristic of this parkway is that it was not primarily designed to enhance the transportation experience of the motoring public, but instead was an early attempt at environmental cleanup.

In the early years of the twentieth century, it was widely understood that pollution along rivers was a substantial problem, but little was done to mitigate it. But here, just outside of New York City, local government actually undertook to improve those conditions. In 1905 a sewer pipe was laid in alongside the river. Previous to that, conditions in the river were so bad that the lakes within the Bronx Zoo—which were fed by the Bronx River—were becoming a threat to the animals.

Also around that time a plan was commissioned to build a highway—not so much to move the burgeoning automobile population as to acquire a "greenway corridor" on each side of the river, thus protecting the waterway for future generations. The project organizers knew that using eminent domain or condemnation to acquire land for a roadway corridor would be accepted by the public, but using condemnation for environmental purposes would be controversial; there would probably be court battles.

With all the politics going on, it took twenty years to acquire and build the parkway. In fact, it was held up for a few years because some New York City elected officials tried to have the entire parkway law, together with its governing body's power of condemnation, declared unconstitutional. They failed. Their efforts in trying to stop the parkway came to embody that old saying, "There are three stages of truth: Ridicule, Opposition, and How did we ever live without it?"

A huge amount of effort went into the natural restoration of the area. In the 1910s and 1920s, more than 12,000 oak trees were planted, along with 11,000 maples, 7,000 pines, and over 140,000 shrubs. Recently, with the approach of the new century, the Westchester County Parks Department invested heavily in even more varieties of tree plantings: dogwoods, crab apples, beeches, and some new species of pines, among many others. Another recent addition is a series of call boxes in key areas near grade crossings or near underpasses. These devices, when activated, summon emergency personnel to the location.

In 2000 the Bronx River Parkway Reservation celebrated the seventy-fifth anniversary of its opening. The popularity of this path will be evident when you get under way.

* *

MILE BY MILE

0.0 mile: Kensico Dam, which was completed in 1915, was built just below the old dam that formed Lake Kensico. The dam is 300 feet high and 1,830 feet long; it creates a pool of water 13 miles long containing more than 30 billion gallons of water. The headwaters of the Bronx River are at a small wetland in the town of New Castle, just a few hundred yards south of the intersection of Bedford and Whippoorwill Roads. From the wetland, water flows south through two small private lakes and into the Kensico Reservoir. The water then flows 23 miles to its mouth at the East River in New York City.

The parking facilities, pavilions, and mobile band shell for numerous summer and fall events—along with a spectacular view of the imposing dam—makes this park a destination in itself. There are rest rooms here.

The trail pathway is at the east side of the dam's face and heads south, away from the dam. One of the first things you'll notice on this trail is its narrow width—6 to 8 feet, as compared to today's standard of 12 to 14 feet on busy trails.

0.48 mile: Pass a ball field on your left while the trail meanders around the

The Kensico Dam provides an imposing backdrop to the start of the trail.

interchange of ramps for the Taconic and Bronx River Parkways.

0.65 mile: Crossing over Washington Street, you'll be traveling parallel to Lafayette as you also cross over the Valhalla Bridge over the Metro-North Commuter-Rail (which will be nearby for the entire journey). The bridge was built in 1925 as part of the parkway development. It features a plaque commemorating the occasion and congratulating the foresight of the Parkway Commission in undertaking the cleanup of the Bronx River and restoring natural beauty to the area. Head steeply down right after the bridge.

1.1 miles: Grade crossing at Virginia Road. If you take a detour and go left here, you'll shortly come upon the Miller Farmhouse, which was one of George Washington's headquarters during the American Revolution. This is where the American commander planned the battle of White Plains during the 1776 New York campaign. Back on the trail and shortly ahead is an access road to a Metro-North locomotive repair facility.

1.56 miles: You'll find a call box and a park 'n' ride lot here at Fisher Lane, where you'll cross over the Bronx River before turning south again. The trail is discernible if you follow Fisher Lane and then, just before the railroad overpass, take a right, placing the guardrail for the parking lot to your right and the railroad embankment to your left. This narrow corridor is the trail.

2.0 miles: Still in the commuter rail parking lot, you'll see a pedestrian tunnel to your left under the tracks that lead to the train station. Turn right here, away from the railroad corridor, and you'll see the trail heading west. The unusual trees here are yellow twig cottonwoods.

2.2 miles: The trail turns south again, and you'll cross the Bronx River once more.

2.35 miles: After a grade crossing at Cemetery Road, you'll come upon the pump station for the Tennessee Gas Pipeline. The natural-gas pipeline and the trail share the corridor in this area.

2.4 miles: Pass underneath I–287, which crosses here.

3.28 miles: The separated trail ends here. You go out onto a short service road, passing by a natural-gas pump station. To your left you'll see a 1913 concrete tunnel for the road to cross under the railroad tracks. This is where things get a bit confusing. Still head-

This impressive arch bridge, seen at 1.55 miles, carries Thompson Avenue over the Bronx River.

ing south, you'll come to Hamilton Avenue; take a right, go west for one block, cross at the pedestrian signal, and then head south for one block. Then turn left and go east for a block. The trail will be to the southwest side of the exit ramp for the Bronx River Parkway. It's between the exit ramp guardrail and the embankment above. This confusing jog in the trail has been made because there is no safe off-road route; this route is the only one where a pedestrian-activated light is available.

3.71 miles: You'll see another call box in this area, and then a bridge over the Bronx River.

4.14 miles: Cross under the Woodland Viaduct on the Bronx River Parkway.

4.21 miles: The trail takes a sharp left here, passes over a wooden-deck bridge spanning the river and then quickly dips under the railroad.

4.35 miles: The trail surface turns to stone dust for a short distance.

4.71 miles: Another call box is found here. Then you'd better be careful because the trail turns sharply and crosses under the parkway. There isn't much headroom—you may even need to duck while on a bike.

5.0 miles: A residential neighborhood is to your left, and the river is still adjacent.

5.14 miles: A dam here creates the pool of water in the river.

5.2 miles: The Westchester County Tennis Club is seen here.

5.29 miles: This is the beginning of the trail's other challenging section. Right after this, you'll come out onto a neighborhood road with a Presbyterian church just ahead. Turn left and travel on roads here for about 1.62 miles. When you get to the top of the hill, turn right onto Walworth Street. In one block this will become Fox Meadow Road. Follow this south and bear left at the fork, still on Fox Meadow Road. Continue to follow the road until you reach the T intersection at Crane Road, where you turn right and then make a quick left onto East Parkway, which in three blocks becomes Scarsdale Avenue. Follow Scarsdale Avenue all the way to Harney Road and turn right. Cross over railroad tracks; just before Harney leads out onto the parkway (in one block), head south across Harney on the crosswalk. You'll find that the trail starts south again.

From East Parkway and Scarsdale Avenue to Harney Road is about 0.1 mile. You'll be traveling largely in downtown Scarsdale; many shops and stores provide myriad services, including a huge park 'n' ride lot for the ever-present commuter rail.

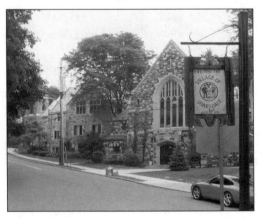

The Bronx River Pathway includes a short stretch through Scarsdale.

Reset your odometer to 0.0 at the Harney Road trailhead.

0.86 mile: Another call box is here, along with a grade crossing of Leewood Drive.

1.02 miles: Travel right along the river in a very rural section.

1.47 miles: Head out onto a small access road to a parking lot with another call box.

As seen at the 1.93-mile mark of the trail, Crestwood Lake is maintained by a small dam. This rural vista belies the lake's urban/suburban neighborhood.

1.55 miles: The Thompson Avenue arch bridge over the river and the General Facilities Building for the Westchester County Parks Department are found here, along with Crestwood Station.

1.93 miles: This is Crestwood Lake, which unfortunately has an overabundance of Canada geese, but there are also lots of ball fields, benches, and places to watch the passersby. At the south end is a waterfall. Here you'll cross to the west side of the river by way of a small bridge.

2.97 miles: Grade crossing at Garret Avenue. Shortly ahead you'll return to the east side of the river. There's another scenic lake, Bronxville Lake, which has a path on either side of it.

3.11 miles: Another call box.

3.4 miles: Grade crossing at Pondfield Road.

3.65 miles: Grade crossing at Palmer Road. This is effectively the end of the trail.

2 Erie Canal Heritage Trail (Erie Canal, Western Section)

Endpoints: Palmyra, Lockport.

Location: Wayne, Monroe, Orleans, and Niagara Counties.

Length: 85 miles.

Surface: Crushed stone, asphalt, dirt.

Uses: All nonmotorized uses.

To get there: *Palmyra:* Take exit 43 off the New York Thruway, I–90. Drive north on NY Route 21 for 6 miles, then west on NY Route 31 for 0.75 mile to Aqueduct Park. The trail is west of the park entrance. *Brockport:* Take the New York Thruway, I–90, to exit 47 (Leroy). Take I–490 east 4 miles to exit 2, then head north on NY Route 19 for 9 miles to Harvester Park. The trail is accessed across the lift bridge. *Lockport:* Take the New York Thruway, I–90, to exit 49 (Depew). Head north on NY Route 78 (Transit Road) for 15 miles. Turn right onto NY Route 31 and continue east for 2.5 miles. Take a left onto Cold Springs Road and drive 0.5 mile to parking. The trail is accessed across a high bridge over the canal.

Other trail access points are found near canal locks or lift bridges in Fairport, Pittsford, Henrietta, Rochester, Spencerport, Albion, and Medina.

Contact: John DiMura, New York State Canal Corporation, 200 Southern Boulevard, Albany, NY 12209; 518–436–3034.

Accommodations: Adams Basin Inn, 425 Washington Street, Adams Basin, NY 14410; 716–352–6784; halya@adamsbasininn.com; www. adamsbasininn.com. Country Cottage Bed & Breakfast, 7745 Rochester Road, Gasport, NY 14067; 716–772–2251; www.countrycottagebandb.com. Liberty House Bed & Breakfast, 131 West Main Street, Palmyra, NY 14522; 315–597–0011; fax 315–597–1450; info@libertyhousebb.com; www.libertyhousebb.com. Twenty Woodlawn Bed & Breakfast, 20 Woodlawn Avenue, Fairport, NY 14450; 716–377–8224; conniebf@frontiernet. net; www.nycanal.com. The Victorian Bed & Breakfast, 320 Main Street, Brockport, NY 14420; 585–637–7519; sk320@aol.com.

Bike repair/rentals: Bicycle Outfitters, 45 North Main Street, Brockport, NY 14420-1648; 716–637–9901; fax 585–637–8909; fattirejunkie@ aol.com; www.bicycle-outfitters.com. Freewheelers, 1757 Mount Hope Avenue, Rochester, NY 14620; 716–473–3724. RV & E Bike and Skate, 40 North Main Street, Fairport, NY 14450; 585–388–1350; fax 585–

377–4510; rvebike@frontiernet.net; www.rvebike.com. Scooter World, 3752 South Main Street, Marion, NY 14505; 315–926–0707; fax 315–926–0415; scooter@rochester.rr.com; www.scooterworldonline.com. Sugar's Bike Shop, 2139 North Union Street, Spencerport, NY 14559-1261; 716–352–8300.

The western section of the Erie Canal Trail is the most complete, and it also offers the best services for bike tourists. It passes through an interesting mix of rural countryside, small villages, and cosmopolitan urban areas.

Many people equate Governor De Witt Clinton with the canal, but interestingly, the original spark for the project came from a Geneva businessman named Jesse Hawley, who transported flour to markets. While in debtor's prison (apparently he went broke trying to move goods without a canal), he wrote fourteen essays on the subject of a canal. These were published in the *Genesee Messenger,* a local newspaper of influence in western New York in the early years of the nineteenth century.

Around the same time, in 1808, a survey was done to determine if a canal was indeed possible. The answer was yes, but the canal would have to rise 500 feet from the Hudson at Albany to Lake Erie. Debate ensued. Some wanted the canal to terminate at Lake Ontario north of Syracuse, rather than go all the way to today's Buffalo area. The cause of a canal was then taken up by the mayor of New York City, De Witt Clinton, who ran for governor on a "pro-canal" platform. Following his election, construction of the Erie Canal began in 1817.

Though the builders started in the easiest section, they knew that they had four major difficulties ahead of them in western New York: Great Cayuga Swamp (today's Montezuma Wildlife Refuge), the Irondequoit Creek Valley, the Genesee River Valley in what is now Rochester, and the Niagara Escarpment.

To get through the Great Cayuga Swamp, thousands of Irish immigrants were employed to dig the canal by hand. So many were felled by malaria and other mosquito-borne diseases, however, that

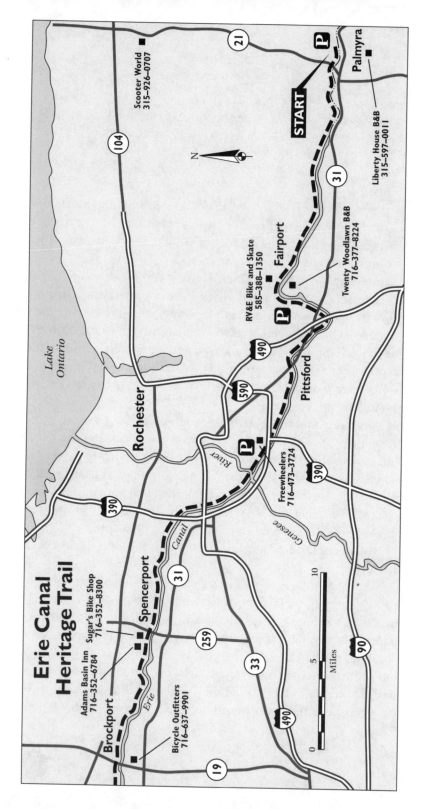

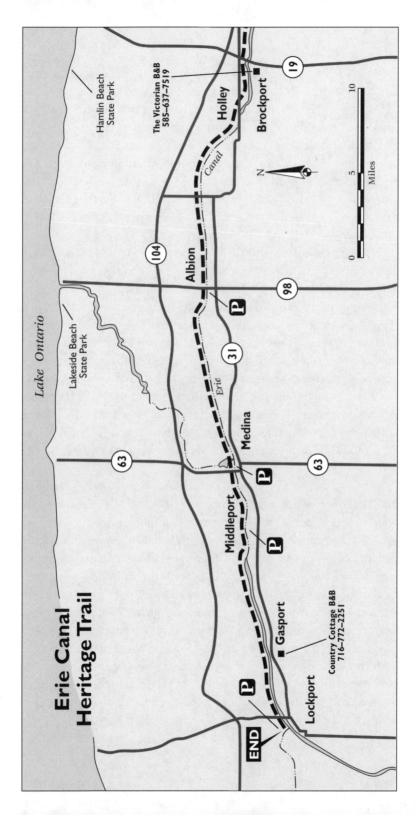

they decided to dig this area in the winter. Huge logs were driven into the soft mucky soil to ensure that the banks of the canal held.

At Irondequoit Creek, a huge fill was constructed to carry the canal over the floor of the valley. When finished, it was 70 feet high and about a mile long. It is still known today as the Great Embankment. The only comparable fill in the mid-Atlantic region is the Lackawanna Cutoff in northwestern New Jersey, which is about 15 miles long and upward of 125 feet high. It's noteworthy that Great Embankment was built with hand tools and wheelbarrows, while the Cutoff was constructed with steam shovels.

The Genesee River cut through the center of what would be the future city of Rochester. In order to span both the river and what would become a business district, the builders needed to construct a bridge to carry the canal across the river and the adjacent plain. They built an eleven-arch, 8,000-foot stone bridge—the largest aqueduct in the world. It served thousands of canal boats. When the canal was later relocated south of downtown Rochester in 1928, the aqueduct was filled and became Broad Street, still in use today.

To get over the 50-foot sheer cliff at Lockport, the builders constructed a five-step combined lock system chiseled out of the face of the cliff. They actually constructed two sets of locks here—one for eastbound traffic, another for westbound. This prevented traffic bottlenecks.

When completed in 1825, in the amazing time of only seven years, the canal opened upstate New York to growth and development. Shipping costs dropped 80 to 90 percent. Even more amazing, there were virtually no professional engineers involved in the project. Many of the supervisory personnel went on to became pioneers in that next big wave of transportation development, the railroads.

Derided by many of his contemporaries, Governor De Witt Clinton was a visionary who knew the economic development potential that the canal would bring. William Stone summed it up perfectly when he said, "They have built the longest canal, in the least time, with the least experience, for the least money, and to the greatest public benefit." As you traverse the old sections of the Erie Canal on the towpath, you will see these amazing monuments, some of the region's most impressive relics of industrial archaeology.

The restored building on the left is Putnam's Store, which is found alongside Lock 28 on the Erie Canal.

One of the more interesting side routes to the Erie Canal is Route 31. Also known as Bike Route 5 or simply "Bike 5," this is a well-maintained state road that offers low traffic and wide shoulders for much of its route. Bike 5 also parallels most of the canal towpath in this section of western New York.

Palmyra

This canal town is the birthplace of Mormon Church founder Joseph Smith. The Smith house and other sites associated with the Mormon Church are here.

Every September the town celebrates Canal Town Days. Crafts fairs, flea markets, and a well-respected antiques show are the highlights. At Aqueduct Park, a stone arch aqueduct (hence the name of the park) offers good photo opportunities from Route 31.

Fairport

Here's a true-to-life canal town: In fact, Fairport calls itself Princess Port. Fairport and the town of Pittsford are making a real effort to capitalize on tourist dollars by providing clean, bright downtowns full of interesting shops and services—more than 200 businesses are located there. Come by during the first week of June, for the annual Canal Days. Several hundred crafts vendors and dozens of food vendors greet the 75,000 visitors who come to sample life in small-town New York. This event is sponsored by the Fairport Merchant Association, which plows the proceeds from the Canal Days event back into the town by paying for holiday lighting, floral displays, benches, and many other improvements. This is reportedly the premier festival event in western New York. Fairport is 11 miles from Palmyra and 64 miles from Lockport.

Pittsford

As you head west from the Palmyra area, you will come to two places of special interest before you get into Pittsford proper. First up is the Great Embankment over the Irondequoit Creek Valley. This structure was built to allow the canal to span the valley, and when you traverse it you'll get a feel for just how spectacular it really is. Shortly after this comes Bushnell's Basin, a pond that is bisected by the canal. In the early years of canal operation, before the Great Embankment was built, Bushnell's Basin was the end of the canal. In later years a trolley line was built through here—the Rochester, Syracuse, and Eastern—and much freight was transferred here. Bushnell's Basin is 15 miles from Palmyra and 70 miles from Lockport.

Pittsford calls itself the Queen of the Canal Ports, not only because residents think of their community as the best along the canal, but also because the town was settled before the coming of the canal. Nearly all of the other small villages along the canal were by-products of the canal that didn't exist until the new waterway created a need for them. Pittsford, however, has an interesting history that predates the canal. In fact, Pittsford was the first community in Monroe County to have a school and a library; it also boasted the county's first doctor and, of course, the first lawyer.

Today Pittsford has many specialty shops and restaurants right on the towpath. There are even a few old industrial buildings related to canal transport still standing at Schoen Place. The old coal tower for the fuel dealer, now converted to a restaurant, is still photogenic.

This is a very busy area, with loads of sight-seeing tourists and local folks fishing the canal and just enjoying life. Cyclists should walk their bikes through here. You'll also find Locks 32 and 33 still functioning in Pittsford; they're about 3 miles apart. These are the last locks until Lockport, about 70 miles away. This stretch of the canal

The boardwalk at Schoen Place features specialty shops and restaurants right along the towpath. Note the old coal facility on the far left.

is called the Long-Level for that reason. Schoen Place in Pittsford is 18 miles from Palmyra and 57 miles from Lockport.

Rochester

When they think of Rochester, most people today think of the Eastman Kodak Company. In fact, Rochester was the first "boomtown" in the country—a boom created by the Erie Canal. In ten years its population exploded from 300 to 8,000. Though the canal was rerouted south of town in the 1920s, there are plenty of reasons to divert into Rochester. Genesee Valley Park, 0.5 mile north of the canal trail, was designed by Frederick Law Olmsted, the father of landscape architecture. The city rents canoes here for use in the Genesee River, and there's a great system of bike paths through the park (call 716–428-7005 for more information). Genesee Valley Park on the south side of Rochester is 24.5 miles from Palmyra and 61 miles from Lockport.

Spencerport

Nearly all the "port" towns on the Erie Canal were sited in their locations with reference to the distance to the next town, almost invariably 5 to 6 miles—the range of the mules that pulled the boats. Spencerport is another town that loves its canal heritage, and it shows in what residents have done to improve their canal frontage in the past few years. A new gazebo on the waterfront hosts regular concerts and is now a touchstone for the townspeople. Other recent infrastructure improvements include bike racks, picnic benches, walkway pavers, and a water fountain. Come by on a Sunday afternoon in July or August and you'll hear a live concert from the gazebo. July features an event called Canal Day. In addition to the usual fare for a community event, you'll see a paddling race using all sorts of vessels—conventional and unconventional. This is small-town America at its best. There is even a "Christmas on the Canal" event in December, featuring horse-drawn carriage rides and caroling by candlelight. Spencerport is 35.5 miles from Palmyra and 50 miles from Lockport.

Each year the New York Parks & Conservation Association holds a ride from Buffalo to Albany along the Erie Canal. Here are some participants from the 2001 ride. For information on how to take part in this event, go to www.nypca.org.

Brockport

Brockport, the midpoint on the trip, is a town with a plan. The recently completed master plan reveals the dedication of Brockport residents to make their canalfront even better than it is now. Recently completed segments include waterfront benches, landscaping, and lighting. This is a lively and cosmopolitan small town with a State University of New York campus, 9,000 residents, and a well-maintained and energetic downtown. The historic Victorian neighborhoods have pride written all over them.

History is footnoted here as well. Cyrus McCormick, inventor of the McCormick reaper that revolutionized farming, was invited to come to Brockport to tour some local manufacturing companies, and the Globe Iron Works in particular. The town hoped that McCormick would be so impressed with both the town and Globe that he would use Globe as a subcontractor in the manufacturing of his reaper. The Brockport boosters were successful, and in addition to reapers many other farm implements were manufactured right here, along the canal near Park Street at the site of the old Globe facility. Today a park on this canalside location memorializes the town's claim to fame. The center of Brockport at Route 19 is 40.5 miles from Palmyra and 45 miles from Lockport.

Holley

Holley is the first town in Orleans County that you encounter along the canal. One of the more unusual geological features of the area is the abundance of round cobblestones. Left over from eons of wave action pounding against the shores of the ancient and long-gone Lake Iroquois, they were a hindrance to early colonial farmers, who had to move them by the millions, but eventually they became a source of building materials for distinctive homes and civic buildings. When the canal came, moving the stones became much easier, and it's said today that there are more than 500 buildings all over upstate New York made of these stones.

One of the most distinctive features of the town of Holley is the new park along the canal. Holley was the first small rural town to be awarded a grant from the federal government's HUD Erie Canal Corridor Initiative. Geared toward the smaller communities on the canal, these grants can be used for improvements and upgrades to cultural and historic centers, trail construction, and bridge and main street restoration projects. Interestingly, these initiatives must also have a viable economic impact in order to be funded. There must be one new job created for every $50,000 of federal funding.

This trailhead facility and gazebo is at Holley, one of the many quaint and picturesque canal villages along the Erie Canal.

There is $100 million committed to this corridor, so these communities should expect at least 2,000 new jobs. In appreciation for its grant, the town named the new park for Andrew Cuomo, who was the secretary of housing and urban development when the funds were awarded. More recently, the National Park Service has designated the Erie Canal Corridor as a National Historic Corridor, making it eligible for special staff and funding for more improvements. The center of Holley is 45 miles from Palmyra and 40 miles from Lockport.

Albion

The county seat of Orleans County, Albion is famous for its tall, spired churches. The Presbyterian church has a steeple 175 feet high. The town was home to George Pullman, inventor of the upscale railroad passenger cars that bore his name. Albion is 54.5 miles from Palmyra and 31 miles from Lockport.

Medina

One of the more unusual places along the Erie Canal is found in Medina. Culvert Road, just east of town off Route 31, passes under the canal. The only road that passes under the canal, it is regarded as such an extraordinary achievement that it's been noted in "Ripley's Believe It or Not." This area is among the most rural segments of the canal. The center of Medina is 65 miles from Palmyra and 20.5 miles from Lockport.

Middleport

The town of Middleport was a pretty busy place for transportation in years past, with the railroad, a trolley line, and the canal all in close proximity. Such geographic convergence for all the transportation systems of eighty years ago meant that the town had extensive facilities for transloading cargo among the different modes of transportation. Today the town has some of the best facilities for boaters making the passage along the canal. The center of Middleport is 70.4 miles from Palmyra and 15.1 miles from Lockport.

Gasport

Gasport features one of the more interesting side-trips along this stretch of the canal—especially if you are traveling with children. Becker Farms is a family-owned, 340-acre fruit and vegetable farm that sells most of its products directly to the public. Besides fresh home-grown produce you can expect to find homemade fruit pies, homemade fudge, gourmet cookies, ice cream, drinks and souvenirs. Activities that are geared towards children include a visit to the petting zoo, hay rides, and pony rides. To get there: Start where the bridge crosses the canal in Gasport and head north to Slayton-Settlement Road (the first crossroad you encounter). Turn right (east) and go 0.5 mile and turn left onto Quaker Road. The entrance to Becker Farms is 1 mile down the road. The center of Gasport is 75.3 miles from Palmyra and 10.2 miles from Lockport.

Lockport

You'll find the fourth and most significant of the geological impediments to the creation of the Erie Canal right in Lockport—the Niagara Escarpment. Locks 34 and 35 each raised the canal 25 feet, one of the largest changes in elevation for a canal in the world. In the early years of the canal, this section was traversed by a five-step series of locks that brought a boat up to the level of Lake Erie. One set of these "famous-five" is still in place, but used only for controlling water overflow.

The town of Lockport was established to accommodate and house the workers who chipped away the rock to make the locks, giving the town its name.

Lockport offers many interesting canal boat tours that traverse the locks, and even an underground boat ride through an old power canal. There's also a trolley tour of the town.

This community is the western terminus for our purposes, but it should be pointed out that work is continuing farther west to bring together the missing sections so that the canal trail will be a contiguous off-road trip. Lockport is 85 miles from Palmyra.

3 Old Erie Canal Trail (Erie Canal, Middle Section)

Endpoints: De Witt, Rome.

Location: Madison, Oneida, and Onondaga Counties.

Length: 35.5 miles.

Surface: Mostly stone dust or crushed stone; there are some limited on-road sections.

Uses: All nonmotorized uses.

To get there: From I–481 near Syracuse, take exit 3 for NY Route 5/92 west. Take first right and head north onto Butternut Drive. In about 1 mile, the trailhead will be on your right. For a trailhead with more parking, go to the Cedar Bay Picnic Area: Take exit 3 off I–481 and head east on Route 5/92 for 1.2 miles to a left fork onto Lyndon Road. Follow this for 1 mile. The trail access is over the canal footbridge.

Contact: Kenneth Showater, Park Manager, Old Erie Canal State Park, New York State Office of Parks, Recreation and Historic Preservation, Andrus Road, Kirkville, NY 13082; 315–687–7821.

Accommodations: Beard Morgan House Bed & Breakfast, 126 East Genesee Street, Fayetteville, NY 13066-1302; 315–637–4234; fax 315–637–0010; beardmorgan@yahoo.com.

Bike repair/rentals: Wayne's & Meltzer's Bicycle Shop, 2716 Erie Boulevard East, Syracuse, NY 13224; 315–446–6816; fax 315–446–1156; dwv1218@aol.com; www.waynesbikes.com.

One of the best features at the beginning of this trail is the very interesting signage about the history of the canal. Be sure to read it before getting under way, as it will help make your journey more enjoyable. The first sign is at the very western end, so if you're starting at Cedar Bay, you must head west on the trail for about 0.5 mile to find it.

The section of the Erie Canal in Rome is the oldest part of the canal. On July 4, 1817, Governor De Witt Clinton wielded a shovel in a groundbreaking ceremony near today's Canal Village complex in Rome. The project was started here in the middle for both political and engineering reasons.

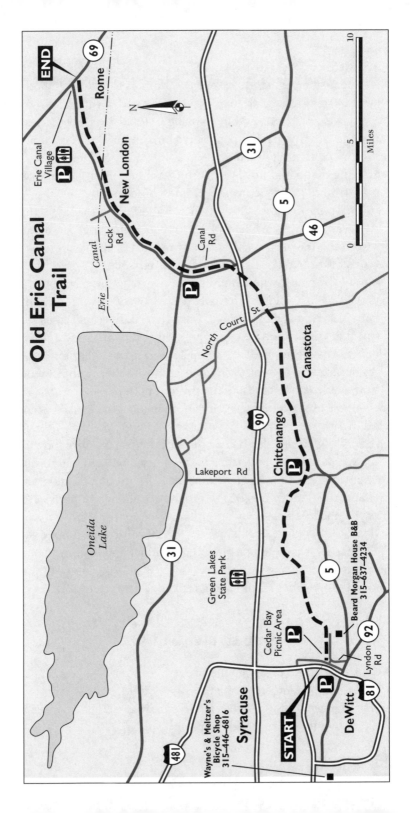

Just as most big transportation projects today weigh important political considerations, Governor Clinton's project was guided by political necessities: It had to get under way and to show significant progress as quickly as possible. Starting in Rome was advantageous because geography made it possible to build many miles of canal in this section without any locks.

Starting in the middle also meant that the "built mileage" would increase rapidly because the builders could use two crews, one headed east, the other west. Another consideration was that this area in 1817 was a pretty desolate place; the governor counted on support from the towns and shippers at the ends of the canal to expedite construction and finish as quickly as possible.

When completed, the canal was an overwhelming success. For years the state of New York actually derived its entire annual budget from the tolls received from canal boats. Indeed, the canal was so successful that it was quickly overwhelmed with traffic and required widening. This began in 1842, and a second major widening project was undertaken in the early years of the twentieth century. By then the railroads had taken most of the traffic, but the Erie Canal still saw considerable use. When the last major upgrade of the canal was completed in 1917, using a new alignment within Oneida Lake, the Old Erie Canal Trail was established on the abandoned portion of the canal.

Today this section of the canal looks pretty much as it did seventy-five years ago, and the towns along the way are quaint, quiet, and well kept. You'll enjoy this trip. A brochure put out by the New York Parks & Conservation Association, an advocacy organization based in Albany (518–434–1583), states: "The Old Erie Canal State Park Trail is a prime example of a great recreational opportunity gleaned from a historic transportation corridor. . . . The trail passes through some of the most beautiful rolling hills in central New York."

. . . .

MILE BY MILE

0.55 mile: Cedar Bay Picnic Area.

1.5 miles: Grade crossing at Burdick Street. Note that the trail also has signage telling you the grade crossing you're at. This is appreciated by more than a few people.

2.97 miles: Grade crossing at Manilius Center Road.

5.0 miles: Pass through Green Lakes State Park. This 1,700-acre facility offers camping, a nice beach, boat rentals, a series of meandering trails for hiking, and even an eighteen-hole golf course. Still, the main claim to fame here are the "Green Lakes"—significant geological anomalies. More than 200 feet deep and boasting a deep aquamarine color, they're very unusual and best seen from the road above the golf course.

7.1 miles: Grade crossing at Pools Brook Road. Rest rooms and parking are found here as well.

10.2 miles: Enter the Chittenango Landing Canal Boat Museum. Though not open all the time, this place is definitely worth a stop. In 1855 a canal boat repair and building company opened here; the complex included three dry docks, a blacksmith, and a sawmill. When the canal was relocated during World War I, this complex was closed down, the dry docks filled, and the buildings demolished. This entire restoration project is being driven by local volunteers who donate time, work, and money, and also serve as interpretive guides. Call them before you come to coordinate when they will be open (315–687–3801).

Food and other services can be found in town if you follow Lakeport Road south for 0.5 mile in Chittenango. All places have a claim to fame and Chittenango is no different: The town features yellow brick sidewalks. Why? Because L. Frank Baum, author of the *Wizard of Oz,* was born here. He grew up on NY Route 13 just south of the village. Each May there is an Oz Festival in the village.

16.0 miles: Turn onto State Street in the town of Canastota for about 0.5 mile, then back onto the trail.

19.28 miles: Reach North Court Street, where a short detour is necessary. Look for Canal Road on your right; the trail is adjacent.

21.1 miles: Turn off the trail at Cobb Street, and then turn onto Canal Road to climb up over I–90, the New York Thruway. Return to the trail on the other side.

22.1 miles: Grade crossing at NY Route 316 in Durhamville. The trail ends at NY Route 46 just ahead. A section of about 2 miles of on-road travel is at hand. Two options are available: Take Route 46 north or the parallel-running Canal Road. To get to Canal Road, go across Route 46 and onto Center Street. Take the first left onto Church Street, then left again onto County Route 89; passing by the Durhamville Fire Department, you'll come upon Canal Road. Turn right here and follow this north. All these turns are within 0.2 mile, so it's very hard to get lost. Follow Canal Road north for 2.25 miles.

24.6 miles: Grade crossing at NY Route 31. Turn left here, then make a quick right onto the trail again.

26.9 miles: Grade crossing at Higginsville Road.

29.3 miles: Grade crossing at Lock Road. Turn left and follow this for about 0.5 mile until you come to the new Erie Canal and Lock 21. This allows you to cross the canal and continue east.

34.1 miles: Grade crossing at Zingerline Road.

35.0 miles: Grade crossing at Fort Bull Road. Turn onto Route 46 for a short distance.

35.5 miles: Here's the end of the line at the Erie Canal Village, a fair representation of just what an old canal village used to look like. Bicyclists are welcomed; in the visitor center you'll find some snack food, refreshments, and bathrooms. There is even a mule-drawn canal boat tour on this section of the canal. There is a small fee to enter the museum. For further information, call 315–337–3999.

4 Mohawk-Hudson Bikeway (Erie Canal, Eastern Section)

Endpoints: Albany, Rotterdam Junction.

Location: Albany and Schenectady Counties.

Length: 36.5 miles.

Surface: Asphalt with a small segment of stone dust. There are 4 miles on city streets.

Uses: All nonmotorized uses.

To get there: *East end:* To start at Albany's Corning Riverfront Preserve at the eastern end of the trail, from northbound I-787, take Broadway and stay on this until you see the parking lot for Corning Preserve. From I-787 south, take the exit for Colonie Street and turn left at the end of the ramp; the parking entrance is ahead on your left. *Center:* To start at Colonie, approximately in the center of the trail, take exit 7 off I-87 to U.S. Route 9 North. In about 2 miles and just north of Boght Corners, take a left onto Old Loudon Road, then a quick left onto Schermerhorn Road. Follow this to the town of Colonie Park, where you'll find extensive parking and trailhead facilities. *West end:* To start at Rotterdam Junction on the western end of trail, from exit 26 off I-90 or exit 1 off I-890, follow NY Route 5S north for 3 miles to Scrafford Lane. Turn west; you'll find parking up here. However, at the time this book went to press, Guilford Rail Systems, owner of the railroad tracks just ahead, had taken steps to block this crossing, and the outcome is unclear at this time. A tunnel might need to be built here in coming years because the railroad is now so busy. Do not attempt to climb over a stopped train should you find one here. Instead, go back south on Route 5S and travel about 1 mile back to Mabie Lane; you may find a safe parking and starting point here. If not, then go another 1.5 miles back to Kiwanis Park.

Contact: Kathleen DeCataldo, Supervisor, Town of Niskayuna, 1 Niskayuna Circle, Niskayuna, NY 12309; 518-386-4503. Steve Feeney, Schenectady County Planning Department, 107 Nott Terrace, Schenectady, NY 12308; 518-386-2225. Friends of the Mohawk Hudson Bikeway, Howard Halstead, 141 Willow Creek Avenue, Schenectady, NY 12304-2235.

Accommodations: The Mansion Hill Inn & Restaurant, 115 Philip Street, Albany, NY 12202-1731; 518-465-2038; fax 518-434-2313; inn@mansionhill.com; www.mansionhill.com.

This trail is a testament to perseverance and dedication. Built through five towns and paralleling the beautiful Hudson and Mohawk Rivers, it's one of the most interesting and diverse trails you'll ever experience.

It also makes for an interesting study on how a completely integrated network of greenways, rail-trails, riverfront paths, and on-road connections creates a resource for all the communities along the way. This sort of network should be a model for other regions in New York and beyond.

One of the more unusual aspects of the Mohawk-Hudson Bikeway, however, is its unusual piecemeal construction using different standards. The management also uses such a fragmented arrangement. The different standards mostly apply to how the trail and roads come together at grade crossings; also, some of the curves are sharper than you'd expect. Some extremely steep grades were necessary, too, to get around modern office complexes that were built on the grade of the railroad. Most of these deficiencies would not be duplicated on a more modern trail.

Nearly every community along the trail calls it by a different name: Mohawk-Hudson Heritage Trail, Mohawk River Trailway, and Colonie Bicycle Path are some of them. No set mile markers denote its complete mileage. Some communities have mile markers, but they are built to different standards and only have that specific town on the marker. These relatively minor issues are being resolved.

The New York Department of Transportation, working in concert with the regional planning agencies of the communities hosting the trail, has produced a highly detailed, multipanel map of the entire project. This is free; simply call the contacts provided, and they'll send you a copy.

In Albany the trail starts at the Corning Riverfront Preserve, where you can warm up at the riverfront fitness trail. In Watervliet you'll pass by the nation's oldest continuously operated arsenal. In Schenectady, nicknamed Electric City for the General Electric Company's high-profile presence, the trail passes through one of the most interesting historic districts you'll ever see on a trail. This is called the Stockade District; some buildings date back to the mid-1700s. You'll also pass by the site of the old American Locomotive

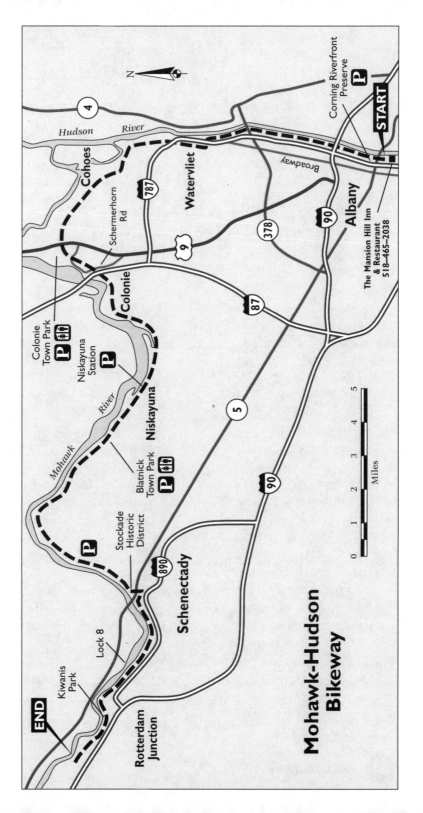

N

④

Hudson River

Cohoes

Schermerhorn Rd

787

Watervliet

9

378

90

Albany

87

Broadway

START

P

Corning Riverfront Preserve

The Mansion Hill Inn & Restaurant 518-465-2038

Colonie Town Park

P ♿

Niskayuna Station

P

Colonie

Mohawk River

Niskayuna

Blatnick Town Park

P ♿

5

90

P

Stockade Historic District

890

Schenectady

Lock 8

Kiwanis Park

END

Rotterdam Junction

Miles

0   1   2   3   4   5

Mohawk-Hudson Bikeway

Company's (ALCO) erecting sheds. This is where the world's best mainline steam locomotives were constructed. For more than a hundred years, the name Schenectady was synonymous with ALCO and locomotives. ALCO was profitable right into the diesel age in the 1950s; it was eventually combined with General Electric, which built the electric generators inside the locomotives. The ALCO site was shut down for this type of heavy manufacturing in 1969, but the faded name AMERICAN LOCOMOTIVE is still visible on the larger building. Finally, you'll pass by the Lock 8 of the Erie Canal and share the rural surroundings of the old towpath for the majority of the distance to Rotterdam Junction. Here the trail ends at the active railroad tracks of the Guilford Rail Systems Company.

. . . .

MILE BY MILE

Starting at Albany

0.0 mile: As you travel north with I–787 to your left and the Hudson to the right, you'll be mesmerized by the beauty of this special river. But don't forget to look back occasionally at the Albany skyline as it recedes. There's also a "par course" here along the Corning Preserve—a series of stations for doing various types of exercises or calisthenics.

1.4 miles: Pass under I–90; I–787 is still running parallel.

3.78 miles: Pass under NY Route 378, which crosses the Hudson at this point.

4.8 miles: Pass through a tunnel and cut under I–787, which leads you to the intersection of 4th and Broadway in the town of Watervliet. You now travel on city streets for about 4 miles.

5.0 miles: Head north on Broadway and in less than a mile, you'll go past the Watervliet Arsenal, the oldest arsenal in continuous use in the United States. Today the facility is mostly concerned with the manufacture and rehab of large-diameter artillery for the U.S. Army.

6.7 miles: After passing by many restaurants and other services, turn right (east) onto Lower Hudson Avenue, which curves around to the north and continues.

The Mohawk-Hudson Bikeway provides excellent outdoor recreation opportunities for families.

7.45 miles: Pass under NY Route 7.

7.92 miles: Turn left onto Tibbits Street.

8.2 miles: Turn right onto Cohoes Avenue.

9.24 miles: Cross under I–787 and then over Saratoga Street at a grade; do not follow Saratoga Street north as the BIKE ROUTE sign directs you. Instead, cross Saratoga Street and the railroad tracks on the other side, following the neighborhood street up the hill. This is Spring Street. Take this until it ends shortly as it bends to the left, then turn right onto Alexander Street. Continue a couple more blocks and you'll see the trail appear again.

9.56 miles: Turn right; you're now on the trail again.

10.6 miles: Grade crossing at Columbia Street.

11.51 miles: Grade crossing at Manor Avenue.

12.72 miles: Grade crossing at Route 9 near Fonda Road. This was the site of the old Crescent Station and the "top" of the great curve through Cohoes and Colonie.

13.35 miles: Grade crossing at Schermerhorn Road. This is the access point for Colonie Town Park.

13.74 miles: Pass by a housing development that's one of the first built in the Northeast to specifically include a direct connection to the neighboring rail-trail. It's been in the ground now for at least seven years and seems to be thriving and providing many trail patrons. Remember that old saying or highway advertisement?—"If you lived here, you'd be home by now"? It sure seems appropriate for a place that makes it easy to bike from home to work.

The trail offers up broad scenic vistas like this one in Colonie.

14.15 miles: Grade crossing at Dunsbach Road. Turn right here and bike on this residential neighborhood road for 0.2 mile until you reach Island View Road. This brings you under I–87, which has severed the railroad corridor.

14.85 miles: Take a left onto the bike path again. This is a short but steep uphill section. When you crest the top, you'll be taking a right to return to the old railroad grade.

15.15 miles: Travel on a short but pretty big shelf with a 30-foot drop-off to your right.

15.4 miles: Pass under a set of high-tension wires, then onto a big fill that stands perhaps 80 feet above the floor below.

15.73 miles: Pass a sewer treatment facility separated from you by way of a chain-link fence overgrown with grapevines.

16.15 miles: You're still in a very rural area.

16.85 miles: Travel very close to the river past the front yards of a number of houses.

17.05 miles: Pass over a small bridge that carries a stream to the Mohawk River. A set-off along adjacent River Road has some parking for a few cars, making for a mini trailhead.

17.55 miles: You're still along the Mohawk with its interesting wetlands.

18.65 miles: Parking available for five or six cars at another small trailhead found here.

18.75 miles: Reach the border with the town of Niskayuna. The adjacent road now becomes known as Rosendale Road.

19.03 miles: Head past an old rail-served building that was once a part of the railroad village at Niskayuna.

19.13 miles: Trailhead parking is available at the old Niskayuna Passenger Station. The trailhead facility itself is called Niskayuna Lions Park. The famous local resident George Westinghouse used to catch the train to Albany from this station.

19.23 miles: The trail traverses a causeway here that is a bird-watcher's paradise for those interested in waterbirds. Egrets are seen often.

20.25 miles: Cross over a culvert dated 1909 that carries water underneath the corridor.

20.45 miles: Farmlands line each side of the trail.

Views of the Mohawk River in Niskayuna are especially breathtaking.

20.62 miles: A stop sign for trail users alerts you to an agricultural grade crossing.

20.95 miles: Head into the woods, then descend a ramp to a road and climb steeply up to the railroad grade again.

21.0 miles: Another of the New York Central–built culverts is at the bottom of a 40-foot fill. Also near here is Lock 7 on the Barge Canal. Bathrooms are available here. You will also see a commemorative plaque dedicated to Margaret Lordi and Eleanor Brown for their stewardship of the Mohawk River and their leadership in establishing this bikeway.

22.0 miles: Here's an example of the power of nature. This retaining wall was built in 1909 by the railroad; today it's being pushed over, ever so slowly, by the hillside above. Also in this area are a few derelict ties left over when the railroad was scrapped back in the 1970s.

22.45 miles: A small box culvert is found here as well as some good vistas of the river. The trees have canopied the trail.

22.65 miles: Climb steeply uphill as the trail diverges from its original alignment to avoid a nuclear research facility.

22.71 miles: Head past the town's Blatnick Park, which has lots of parking as well as picnic areas, ball fields, and rest rooms. Shortly after the park, the trail has a short but steep downhill grade.

24.01 miles: There's a steep upgrade here in the vicinity of the GE research facility.

24.3 miles: The trail meanders into the woods.

25.75 miles: Pass through a canopied area with lots of moss growing on each side of the corridor.

25.85 miles: Travel on a bit of a fill only 8 feet high, then out of the woods into a residential neighborhood with a parking lot for trail users.

27.56 miles: Grade crossing at Maxon Road. Here the trail environs become more industrialized. Note the railroad bridge over the Mohawk; this is the old Delaware & Hudson Railroad. New York Central's Troy & Schenectady Branch junctioned with the D&H mainline here. The old freight office was used for dispatching operations on the D&H before Canadian Pacific Railroad took over and moved the jobs to Milwaukee.

28.43 miles: Follow a steep downgrade chicane to Nott Street. There was an interesting girder bridge through this section until about 1999, when the city—working in concert with nearby Union College— saw the removal of the bridge as a way to improve the neighborhood. If you head back up the chicane arrangement on the other side of Nott Street, the trail does continue southwest here for a few blocks to South Jay Street. If you're going all the way to Rotterdam Junction, however, it's best to diverge from the trail at this point and head right (west) along Nott Street.

28.66 miles: Crossing onto North Street and bear left here to continue in basically a westerly direction.

29.0 miles: You're now passing into the Stockade Historic District for the city of Schenectady. Check out the side streets.

29.5 miles: Turning left onto Washington Avenue will bring you to NY Route 5 (State Street). Take this north toward the river; just before the road crosses the river, look for the signs to Schenectady Community College. Take this access road, which will lead you back onto the trail.

30.2 miles: You're now in more rural areas. The trail hugs the river as you continue west.

30.88 miles: I–890 crowds the trail very close to the river at this location.

31.5 miles: The trail avoids the highway interchange here by way of a sweeping curve around the exit ramps.

32.01 miles: Nice overlook here.

32.55 miles: Lock 8. An interesting retaining wall is made of I-beams and 3-by-12 timbers near the approaches to Lock 8; it's a great place to stop and watch the passersby, both boaters and trail users.

33.6 miles: Curve around more highway interchanges, these between I–90 and I–890.

34.27 miles: Kiwanis Park.

35.16 miles: Cross Route 5S. Use care, because the cars approaching here are going pretty fast.

35.5 miles: Cross over Mabie Lane.

36.52 miles: Scrafford Lane is the end of the line—though you might have to go back to Mabie Lane to get to a road, because the crossing at Scrafford Lane has been shut down by Guilford Rail Systems. A tunnel under the tracks is being planned.

5   Catharine Valley Trail

Endpoints: Mark Twain State Park, Watkins Glen

Location: Chemung and Schuyler Counties.

Length: 12 miles (when completed).

Surface: Crushed limestone.

Uses: All nonmotorized uses, but horseback riding is restricted in part of the corridor, and hybrid or mountain bikes are recommended; fishing access.

To get there: The trail is easily reached by NY Route I–17, which runs through Elmira and the length of the state along its southern tier. Take exit 52N off Route 17 and travel north on Route 14. The trail runs adjacent to Route 14. Small parking areas have been established at the trailheads in Millport and Montour Falls.

Contact: Sue A. Poelvoorde, New York State Office of Parks, Recreation and Historic Preservation, 2221 Taughannock Park Road, P.O. Box 1055, Trumansburg, NY 14886; 607–387–7041; Sue.Poelvoorde@ oprhp.state.ny.us.

This trail is located 5 miles north of Elmira and runs north to the tip of Seneca Lake at Watkins Glen. It uses the abandoned Northern Central Railroad and the old Chemung Canal. At the time of this writing another short section of trail is planned to open, thus creating a 5-mile trail from Millport to Montour Falls. The trail will eventually connect Watkins Glen State Park and Mark Twain State Park to the south for a total of 12 miles.

When complete, the trail will have a wide range of uses, and inline skaters will be able to travel the asphalt section in Watkins Glen. Equestrians are relegated to a 1.5-mile section of state-owned trail between Pine Valley and Stafford Road, but this links up with existing horse trails in Mark Twain State Park. For those experienced bike riders who want to pedal NY Route 14, there are wide shoulders—but note that part of the road is signed at 55 miles per hour.

The trail is named for Queen Catharine, a Seneca leader of Native American and French ancestry who moved her tribe to the region from Pennsylvania after her father died in battle. Paralleling Route 14, this narrow glaciated valley is also historically referred to as Sullivan's Trail for the general who led a large scorched-earth campaign against the Iroquois during the American Revolution.

The Chemung Canal, opened in 1833 to Elmira, was 42 feet wide. Several of the forty-nine locks are still visible. While often damaged due to flooding, the canal was active up to the Civil War. The construction of the railroad line in the early 1850s actually exacerbated the flooding, and soon the Chemung Railroad became the dominant means of shipping coal northward from the mines of northeast Pennsylvania. Full train service in the valley was crippled after the 1972 Agnes storm, and the last partial service, to Montour Falls, ended in the early 1980s.

The trail passes several marshes, most notably the almost 900-acre Queen Catharine Marsh Wildlife Management Area—an important stop for many species of migratory birds. Geologically, the valley is important for a glacial moraine near Mark Twain State Park that reversed the flow of water northward into the St. Lawrence watershed. Some of the marsh's waters still drain south, however, into the Susquehanna watershed!

Like most of the Northeast, the open 5-mile section of trail was heavily lumbered in the late 1800s, but the trail now passes through a mature hardwood forest where oak, hickory, and maple abound. Some of the stone headwalls from the locks in this area are still in good condition.

Even in winter the Queen Catharine Marsh near Watkins Glen is a compelling landscape.

Exposed 100- to 200-foot-high rock cliffs on the western side of the corridor (especially the northern section) are geologically outstanding. These cliffs create several waterfalls, and

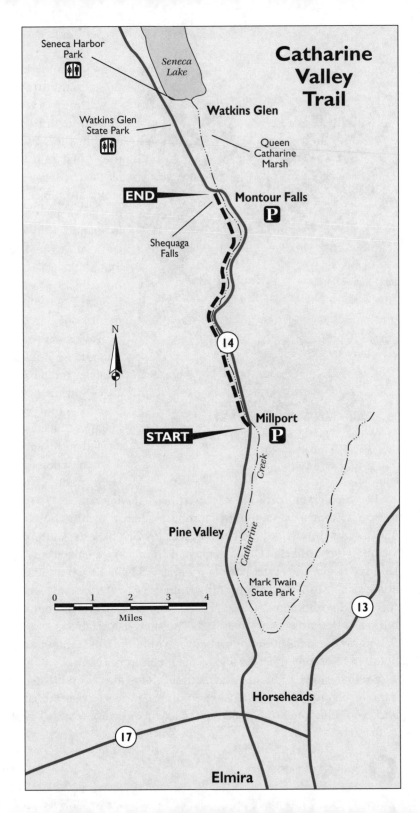

Catharine Valley Trail

Seneca Harbor Park

Seneca Lake

Watkins Glen

Watkins Glen State Park

Queen Catharine Marsh

END

Montour Falls

P

Shequaga Falls

N

14

Millport

P

START

Catharine Creek

Pine Valley

Mark Twain State Park

13

0 1 2 3 4
Miles

Horseheads

17

Elmira

One of several falls along the trail, the 156-foot Shequaga Falls is a must-see.

even some wonderful ice sculptures in the winter. Except for winter and fall season, the view of the falls may be blocked by foliage, so look hard. Since the trail uses some streets in Montour Falls, you can't miss the 156-foot Shequaga Falls. Actually, any visit to the area would be incomplete if you didn't visit these falls. The Louvre in Paris, France, includes a 1820 painting of the falls by King Louis Philippe. The falls are located at the corner of South Genesee and Main Streets.

Be prepared for some crowds on April 1—the opening day of trout season. Catharine Creek enjoys a robust rainbow trout population, and anglers throughout the Northeast enjoy this fishery. Adult trout swim up the Catharine Creek each year from Seneca Lake to spawn. Unfortunately, the creek has been impacted by both zebra mussels and erosion. In 1999, with funding from the New York State Department of Environmental Conservation, the creek bank has been stabilized; other projects are planned. The state has established seven fishing access areas off Route 14 between Millport and Montour Falls, but they're on the opposite side of the creek from the trail.

Several miles of ditches and potholes have also been created to benefit migratory birds and other wildlife. Grasses were established and are maintained on spoiled areas to encourage waterfowl nesting. These enhancements were made possible by the New York State Migratory Bird State Program, Ducks Unlimited, and the M.A.R.S.H. Program.

The trail will eventually end at Seneca Harbor Park overlooking Seneca Lake. It features a pier, rest rooms, a waterfront promenade, and bicycle, canoe, and kayak rentals. A few blocks away is Watkins Glen State Park Falls, a scenic wonder that includes a walk over the falls. It's also been the site of the famous NASCAR Winston Cup since 1986, and before that Formula One racing. The first race began in 1948 and was sanctioned by the Sports Car Club of America. It was the first closed-circuit race on public roads after World War II. Even the trains were held up for races. Races are no longer held downtown, but the trail route crosses the old raceway.

Endpoints: Bloomville, Grand Gorge.

Location: Delaware and Schoharie Counties.

Length: 19 miles.

Surface: Cinder.

Uses: All nonmotorized uses.

To get there: From exit 10 (Richmondville) off I–88, head south on NY Route 10 for 20 miles to Stamford. Turn southeast onto NY Route 23 and continue 0.3 mile, then drive west-southwest on Railroad Avenue for a very short distance. Ample parking is found at the old train station on Railroad Avenue. This is also the headquarters for the Delaware & Ulster Railroad, owners and managers of the trail.

Contact: David Riordan, Executive Director, Delaware & Ulster Railroad, P.O. Box 310, Stamford, NY 12167; 607–652–2821.

Accommodations: Boncranna Bed & Breakfast, 13 Maple Avenue, Hobart, NY 13788; 607–538–1129; boncranna@aol.com; www.boncranna.com.

The Catskill Mountains were formed by two moving forces: the glaciers of the Ice Age and the railroad. The first moved slowly over many millennia, the second required little more than a century, and both profoundly transformed the landscape. Glaciers carved a plateau into the mountains; trains turned the mountains, once accessible only to stalwart hunters, into a booming resort region.

The moving force behind the Ulster & Delaware Railroad was Hudson River steamboat magnate Thomas B. Cornell of Kingston, New York. Along with the rest of America after the Civil War, he caught "railroad fever." His entrepreneurial eye gleamed as it glanced at a potential road from Rondout stretching 109 miles northwest near Oneonta and two other rail connections, bringing rail freight right to his own backyard, to be towed by his boats down the river.

His railroad, to be called the Rondout & Oswego, was chartered on April 3, 1866, with Cornell as the principal stockholder. In May 1870 the first passenger train ran from Rondout to West Hurley; by the end of the following year, it stretched all the way to Roxbury.

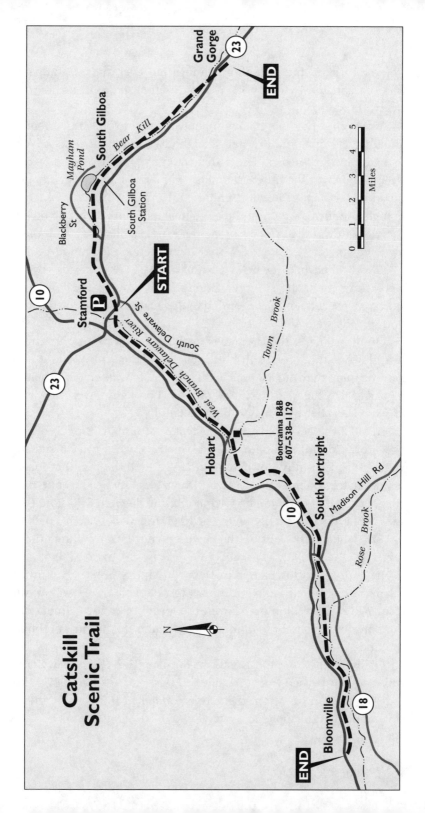

There were some financial shortcomings, however, and the company was reorganized twice by 1875, with its final name the Ulster & Delaware Railroad.

Meanwhile, hotels and boardinghouses sprouted like mushrooms all along the line, and ordinary farmhouses hung out signs advertising rooms for tourists. The resort boom had begun, fueled by the U&D's owners. Like other railroads, they published lavish promotional materials touting the "sanitary advantages" of summer spent in high altitudes away from the city's heat and polluted air. To divert vacationer from rival resorts in the eastern Catskills, they built their own showpiece for 450 guests, the Grand Hotel at Highmount.

City dwellers became believers and came by the thousands every week throughout the summer. Friday night brought the "husband specials," packed with men joining their vacationing wives and children for the weekend.

On return trips, the U&D took coal and Delaware County milk, cauliflower, and "gilt-edged" butter back to the city. By 1900 it was hauling more than 30,000 tons of milk annually. Passengers reached a peak of 676,000 in 1913. But World War I brought fewer travelers, and the U&D began slowly rolling downhill.

In 1932 the U&D became the Catskill Mountain Branch of the New York Central Railroad, and "Ski Specials" were run for several years, unsuccessfully, to revive traffic. By 1950 the line that locals affectionately dubbed the "Up and Down" was reduced to one passenger train daily that ran up to Oneonta and down to Kingston. Passenger service was finally halted in 1954; freight service limped on to 1976, when Penn Central, the newest owner, began selling rail for scrap.

In 1979 seven townships in Delaware and Schoharie Counties formed the Catskill Rail Committee to establish an excursion rail ride. With a $3-million grant from the local O'Connor Foundation, the committee bought a 45-mile rail corridor and began to rebuild the line.

On June 11, 1983, the Delaware & Ulster Rail Ride made its 4-mile maiden voyage from Arkville to Fleischmanns. By 1987, with ongoing track restoration, the ride extended 12 miles, stopping at several old U&D depot sites.

After an extensive effort in 1996 and 1997 to clear and debrush the right-of-way, the rail-trail component of the corridor is currently open for 19 miles; this will soon expand to 26 miles when a sewer-line construction project in the villages of Grand Gorge and Roxbury is complete. Interestingly, this is a project being called for and sponsored by the City of New York Water Department, which owns all the reservoirs in the area.

This trail has some impressive features: the friendly openness of the local residents; the firm, well-drained cinder surface of the trail; and the close relationship between the right-of-way and the West Branch of the Delaware River, which is its constant companion.

MILE BY MILE

East from Stamford Station

0.1 mile: First up is the old grain transloading and storage facility that is now the Stamford Farmers Co-Op. The facility is no longer rail-served but performs truck-to-truck transfer services.

0.21 mile: Grade crossing at South Delaware Street. Right after the street is an old building that seems to have once been used by the railroad; there's evidence of rail side doors and a siding.

0.36 mile: Grade crossing of Route 23. The trail then heads between some commercial buildings and residences.

1.53–1.58 miles: You'll see whistle marker and flanger signs at some of the village street grade crossings.

1.95 miles: Grade crossing of Blackberry Street as you enter the village of South Gilboa.

2.02 miles: Here's the first of a series of pressure-treated benches. They were designed and constructed by a local Americorps team; sited by a local Eagle Scout, who was doing his badge on this trail project; and finally installed by the D&U Rail Ride. As they say, it was a real team effort.

2.1 miles: Reach a modern cattle underpass built of poured concrete.

2.78 miles: Mayham Pond is seen off to your left; just ahead is a crossing of County Route 14. By the way, the stream that mean-

Expect rural surroundings and a well-maintained trail on the Catskill Scenic Trail.

ders in and out of view is the Bear Kill.

3.11 miles: Another of the ubiquitous benches is seen here. There's also a concrete mile marker with the inscription "K71"—Kingston, 71 miles.

3.16 miles: Grade crossing at Benjamin Road.

3.47 miles: The nice old passenger station of South Gilboa is found here. It certainly needs lots of work, but the D&U Rail Ride is considering buying it to restore for trail-oriented uses.

3.77 miles: Head into a nice cut that features trees overhead reaching out to create an arching canopy. Just beyond this look for a big red barn that's probably your mind's-eye view of exactly what a barn should look like. Then comes a concrete batch plant.

3.95–4.26 miles: Two through-girder bridges and one deck-girder get you over the Bear Kill. There are some large carp in this area of the stream. Look for the "K70" mile marker here as well as a bench.

4.66 miles: Grade crossing of Saccaro Road, then head back into farm fields. This also is the town line.

4.87 miles: Whistle marker on your right. With its expanded, slant-cut top, it looks much like the type you'd see on Delaware & Hudson corridors in eastern New York and Vermont.

5.05 miles: Another bench, with a "K69" mile marker.

5.13 miles: Here you'll find the remnants of an old cauliflower packing plant adjacent to the railroad.

5.47 miles: A whistle marker that faces west is seen here. Note the pedestrian bridge over the stream to the south.

5.98 miles: Head past mile marker "K68."

6.01 miles: A deck-girder bridge and another bench.

6.17 miles: Cross Bruce Korin Road. This is the last grade crossing and marks the last segment of the trail open for use.

6.21 miles: You'll see a tall bridge over the Bear Kill: only 20 feet long, it's about 25 feet above the water level.

6.4 miles: Head downhill into a cut and then out. The stream is below you.

6.65 miles: Reach the end of the currently open trail.

West from Stamford Station

0.1 mile: First up is an old creamery on the north side of the trail. It's a gentle reminder that the industry you'll find on this trail is dairy farming.

0.21 mile: A deck-girder bridge over the West Branch of the Delaware River is the first of many crossings, most on this same type of bridge.

On a hot day, one of the more pleasing attributes of a mature rail-trail is the canopy of leaves that stretches across the trail.

0.75 mile: Enjoy wide-open views of active dairy farms with an uphill slope to the north side.

0.87 mile: Reach the first of the pressure-treated benches on the western leg of the trail.

1.49 miles: Creamery Road grade crossing. This area's a real maintenance nightmare for the railroad, with ongoing minor washouts from a constant spring that has a penchant for flooding the right-of-way.

1.89 miles: Cross a small bridge over Bassett Brook; shortly after is another bench.

2.58 miles: Visible here are the stone foundation remnants of an old dairy barn; then the West Branch of the Delaware River comes in alongside the railroad right-of-way. Note that old railroad ties are stacked along the corridor in this area as well.

2.76 miles: You're in the village of Hobart. The major employer in this town is the Mallinckrodt Corporation, makers of pharmaceuticals including methadone. Its white-glove facility is just up the hill from the trail corridor.

Mountain biking is just one of the many activities that the trail supports.

3.42 miles: Grade crossing at Railroad Avenue near the Hobart Fire Department, where you'll find a town park along the river. There's an automatic teller machine at the nearby bank. Going out to the main street to the north, you'll find Leo's—good food. Cross Maple Avenue and then head into a wooded section of the trail with village houses on each side.

3.82 miles: Another of the ubiquitous benches is seen here along with a concrete mile marker inscribed "K78"—Kingston, 78 miles.

3.98 miles: Here's an 80-foot crossing of Town Brook. This bridge even has a center span and is the scene of some occasionally problematic flooding. Note, on the east side, the long-abandoned town swimming pool in this area. The right-of-way is straight as an arrow through here, and the panoramas of farms is scenic.

4.35 miles: Grade crossing of County Route 18 (Hobart River Road). This is at an oblique angle to the trail, so be careful crossing the highway.

4.76 miles: Another bench.

4.95 miles: Travel on a big, 25-foot fill as you curve around to the right.

5.1 miles: Notice here the large number of downed trees. In the summer of 2000, a storm took down many trees—a storm so severe that it was suggested it might have been a small tornado.

5.35 miles: Granite culvert crossing a small stream.

5.53 miles: Another small bridge similar to the one you just passed.

5.64 miles: Grade crossing of County Route 18 once again. Much like the previous crossing, this too is at an oblique angle.

5.92 miles: Another bench is available here as you travel through a hardwood forest into the village of South Kortright.

6.8 miles: An old creamery complex lies adjacent to the trail—a kind of ghost of the rural industry past.

6.9 miles: Grade crossing of Madison Hill Road.

7.2–7.3 miles: Here you'll find the railroad center for South Kortright; look for an old passenger station converted to a modern residence, a freight house converted to a mini warehouse, and a team track area that today holds grazing horses, as well as a nice view of Belle Terr. This large mansion is today part of the Phoenix House system of drug rehab centers. The other similar, but smaller, structures nearby were once part of the estate.

7.8–8.04 miles: You are now again very close to the West Branch of the Delaware River. You'll also notice the new construction work here—the river recently washed away part of the right-of-way. Public access to fishing is found here as well. Note the retaining wall along the other side of the river.

8.76 miles: At an agricultural grade crossing, there's an agricultural outbuilding, footings for a creamery, and a team track.

9.1 miles: Another bench, along with a deck-girder bridge about 20 feet long that crosses over Rose Brook.

9.5–10.2 miles: River crossings again—three, in fact, in this short stretch. First, the West Branch is crossed by a through-girder bridge about 70 feet long. This area is where both streams come together as well. Then similar bridges are used for the subsequent crossings, but the second one is a bit longer, at 80 feet.

10.6 miles: NY Route 10 is above to your right as the river meanders around to your left.

10.9 miles: Another bench is here, along with a cut-stone culvert that allows Kit Brook to pass under the right-of-way.

11.9 miles: The old Sheffield Creamery is found here. Being restored by a loving owner into a residence, this structure was originally the first place in the country to implement pasteurization of milk.

12.0 miles: Look for the "K86" mile marker, along with a battery box for grade crossing equipment.

12.9 miles: Reach the end of the trail in Bloomville, where you cross Route 10 at its intersection with Feed Store Road.

Endpoints: Cato, Fair Haven.

Location: Cayuga County.

Length: 14.1 miles.

Surface: Dirt and cinder with an occasional puddle.

Uses: All nonmotorized uses.

To get there: Ample parking can be found at the southern trailhead in Cato. Take I–90 to Weedsport, exit 40, turn left onto NY Route 34 north, and continue to Cato. At Route 370 turn left; the trail is 0.5 mile on your right. Look for the old Cato Milling Company. The trailhead is just next door.

Contact: Tom Higgins, County Planner, Cayuga County, 160 Genesee Street, Auburn, NY 13021; 315–253–1276.

Campground: Shon's Boat Basin & Campground, 14678 Lake Street, Fair Haven, NY 13064; 315–947–6635; 800–523–9878; fax 315–947–6343; shons@zlink.net; www.fairhavenny.com/shons.

The Lehigh Valley Railroad (LV) was one of the "Anthracite Roads." This was an informal group of railroads in the East that specialized in the transport of the black gold known as anthracite coal. The LV basically ran from Buffalo to Jersey City, New Jersey. There were extensive port and coal transloading facilities on Lake Ontario at Fair Haven and on Lake Erie in Buffalo to complement their connections to the anthracite fields of eastern Pennsylvania.

This branch of the LV originated in Sayre, Pennsylvania and ran past Dryden and Freeville on its way to Auburn, Cato, and points north. It was originally part of the Southern Central Railroad, which was completed in the fall of 1871.

An interesting incident took place on the day of the "golden spike" ceremony. Near Cato, a farmer whose land was traversed by the railroad felt that he was unfairly compensated for the use of his land. On the day the first official train came out of Sayre carrying company executives for the ceremony, he and his son took apart one rail. As the train approached, the engineer saw the damage and was able to stop without incident. After the farmer was arrested and repairs made, the rest of the day went without problems. Regular passenger service was inaugurated the next year.

The LV bought up the Southern Central (SC) formally in 1895, though it had really been part of the LV for many years prior. The LV wanted to upgrade the lightly constructed line to the lake so it could greatly increase the coal traffic to be shipped at Fair Haven. The SC built many wooden trestles that were upgraded to gravel fills to raise the weight limits, allowing heavier coal cars.

The LV as well as other railroads of the era owned steamship companies that plied the waters of the Great Lakes. This conflict of interest was noted by the federal government's watchdog agency, the Interstate Commerce Commission. The Panama Canal Act of 1912 declared railroad ownership or interest in waterborne common carriers illegal, including the LV's lines on the Great Lakes.

Being tied to "King Coal," the LV had to weather the decline in traffic of that commodity as oil and gas became more popular among the consumers of the Northeast. The line past Fair Haven to the coal docks at North Fair Haven was dismantled in the 1930s when the coal facilities there were discontinued. The site of that operation is now known as Fair Haven State Park.

The LV struggled through numerous reorganizations and bankruptcies until in 1976 it was joined with other bankrupt eastern railroads to become Conrail.

• •

MILE BY MILE

0.0 mile: An interesting shelter at the beginning of the trail features a large sign listing all the allowed uses. As you get under way, you'll be on a bit of a fill about 5 feet tall.

0.7 mile: Grade crossing of Veley Road, which is a quiet residential street with a few houses. Just after this crossing a swampy area will appear on your left as the trail becomes more cinder.

1.2–1.4 miles: The trail is wet here due to beaver activity that has flooded the forest on your right. Some farm fields are visible off to your left.

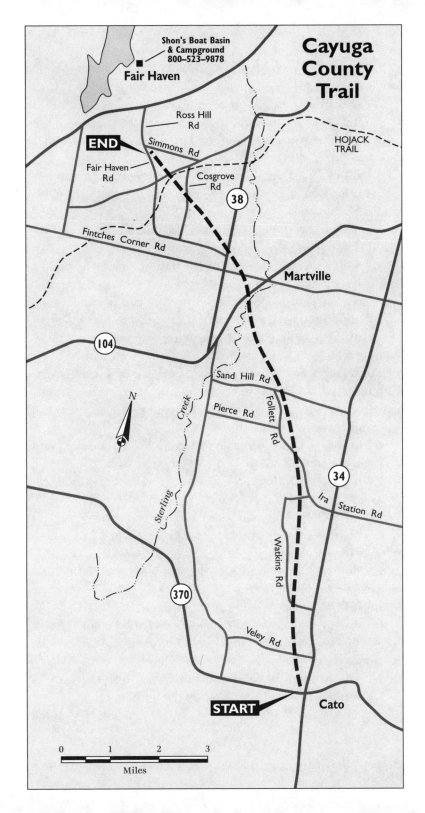

1.7 miles: Grade crossing of Watkins Road, a lightly populated residential street.

2.1–2.5 miles: Reach an eerie green lagoon of scummy, stagnant water. This is a result of more beaver activity. Many birds are here, though. Seasonally the rail-trail may be a little wet, though not too bad.

3.1 miles: Signs here point out the underground fiber-optic cable. This is another use for a rail-trail: a right-of-way for telecommunications.

3.3 miles: Another marsh on your right has some distinctive tall elephant grass.

3.9 miles: Grade crossing of Ira Station Road. The open area here has some remaining ties in the ground, evidence that this site was a small switching yard at one time. Multitracks and an old industrial building, probably a milk transfer warehouse, show that some traffic originated here. The spacing between the doors on the building is 36 feet. This was the span between the doors on old-style milk or reefer cars. On the north side of Ira Station Road is another old rail-served freight storage building with an interesting multicolored green roof. An eclectic mix of old and new silos can be seen in this neighborhood as well.

4.2 miles: A pond is on your left with a few birdhouses on poles to attract residents.

4.4 miles: An agricultural grade crossing to access the fields on either side.

5.0 miles: Make a grade crossing of Follett Road and Ira Station Road, which snakes along next to the trail. This area is listed on some maps as Ira Corners.

5.3 miles: A small wooden bridge with a gravel deck crosses a small stream.

5.4 miles: Grade crossing at Pierce Road.

5.6 miles: An access road appears and allows work trucks on the right-of-way. Some antique farm equipment is rusting away in the woods nearby also.

5.7 miles: You're traveling on a fill about 10 feet high.

5.8 miles: The trail goes sharply downhill to the right, over a culvert, and then uphill back to the trail. If you stop here and look to your left, you'll see the abutments to a former bridge.

5.9 miles: Head into a bit of a cut as the trail becomes a glass-smooth dirt highway with a canopy of trees overhead.

6.3 miles: Grade crossing of Sand Hill Road, and then into a bit of a cut with a 25-foot fill right after.

6.6 miles: Travel on a 25- to 30-foot-tall fill as you make a crossing of Ira Station Road once again. Some older farm outbuildings and silos are seen here, along with a concrete pad just next to the trail. It seems to have had some kind of railroad-related purpose.

7.1 miles: An agricultural grade crossing to access the field on your left.

7.3 miles: Enter a dense canopy of foliage that will both shade and cool you in the summer.

7.7 miles: A pond is off to your right. The trail has had some culverts installed to allow water to pass underneath in times of high water.

8.1–8.2 miles: Travel on a fill about 10 feet high that grows to about 25 feet. The trail crosses over Sterling Creek via a mesh-deck bridge. Just after the bridge you'll cross NY Route 104, a busy highway (be careful).

There are numerous agricultural buildings along The Cayuga County Trail.

A rural section of trail near Fair Haven.

8.3 miles: Just after the highway the trail runs parallel to Queens Farms Road. This is the village of Martsville; some railroad heritage is visible along the trail in the form of freight transfer buildings. Fintches Corner Road is just ahead.

8.8 miles: On a small fill again.

9.1 miles: Travel on an isthmus between two ponds and then into a small cut just before the grade crossing of NY Route 38. Look for the beautiful garden on your left.

9.5 miles: A pond has appeared on your left, along with an agricultural grade crossing and some residential houses.

10.7 miles: Visible from the trail is a quarry operation that has scarred the hillside.

10.8 miles: Head into a cut again and then steeply up to a crossing—Cosgrove Road—which must have gone over the railroad in years past by way of a bridge. Today it has been filled in, making for a bit of a challenging climb.

10.9 miles: Here stands a genuine Lehigh Valley telltale signal. It's made of poured concrete and stands about 20 feet tall with an iron bracing and cross arm. Some of the "strands" remain. These hung down to warn anyone on top of the train of approaching height obstructions, such as low highway bridges. Today the signal serves only as a reminder of the bridge that is no longer there.

11.3 miles: Cross the Hojack Trail (see Trail 30) just south of Sterling Station Road. The Hojack Trail runs east-to-west from Oswego to Rochester.

11.5 miles: Head into a bit of a cut that may be wet and muddy.

11.9 miles: Onto a small fill. A farm is off to your left.

12.1 miles: Simmons Road appears on your right. It gets closer and crosses over the trail, along with Ross Hill Road and Fair Haven Road, by way of a three-way intersection.

12.4 miles: On a small fill.

12.8 miles: The trail opens up; tall grass is on both sides. This wide-open area is a possible site for a nice picnic.

14.1 miles: End of the line here at NY Route 104 in the community of Fair Haven. The trailhead here has a few restaurants and stores to allow you to "refuel." An interesting side trip is the nearby Fair Haven Beach State Park on the shore of Lake Ontario.

Endpoints: Kingston, Port Jervis; the trail continues to Scranton, Pennsylvania. (Only Westbrookville to Summitville and High Falls to Kingston shown here.)

Location: Sullivan, Olster, and Orange Counties in New York.

Length: 90 miles (23 miles open).

Surface: Crushed stone.

Uses: Walking, cross-country skiing, fishing, biking, horseback riding.

To get there: Most of the corridor in New York runs along scenic U.S. Route 209, except for the section north along the Delaware River (NY Route 97) from Port Jervis, New York to the Roebling Bridge. Route 209 is accessed via I–84, which runs east to west through Port Jervis, and via I–17 crossing Wurtsboro. Access to Kingston is easy via the New York Turnpike, I–87. Several parking options are noted on the accompanying maps.

Contact: For information on the entire corridor, contact Andrew Helgesen, D&H Canal Heritage Corridor Alliance, 1 Pine Street, Ellenville, NY 12428; 914–647–5292. For more details on the Basher Kill, contact Patricia Vissering, DEC Region 3, 21 South Putt Corners Road, New Paltz, NY 12561; 914–256–3090.

Accommodations: Baker's Bed & Breakfast, 24 Old Kings Highway, Stone Ridge, NY 12484-5713; 845–687–9795; fax 845–687–4153; dbakersbandb@aol.com; www.bakersbandb.com. Captain Schoonmaker's Bed & Breakfast, 913 State Route 213, High Falls, NY 12440-5717; 845–687–7946; info@captainschoonmakers.com; www.captainschoonmakers.com. Inn at Lake Joseph, 400 St. Josephs Road, Forestburgh, NY 12777-6240; 845–791–9506.

Bike repair/rentals: TABLE Rock Tour & Bicycles, 292 Main Street, Rosendale, NY 12472; 845–658–7832; fax 845–658–7391; TABLERockToursandBicycles@yahoo.com; www.TABLERockTours.com.

Campgrounds: So Hi Campground, 425 Woodland Road, Accord, NY 12404-5232; 845–687–7377; fax 845–687–7723; sohicamp ground@aol.com; www.sohicampground.com. Catskill Mountain Ranch, 538 Mount Vernon Road, Wurtsboro, NY 12790; 845–888–0675; fax 845–888–0216; info@catskillmountainranch.com; www.catskillmountainranch.com.

Food: Depuy Canal House, Route 213, High Falls, NY 12440; 845–687–7700; fax 845–687–7073; lfraser@ulster.net; depuycanal house.net.

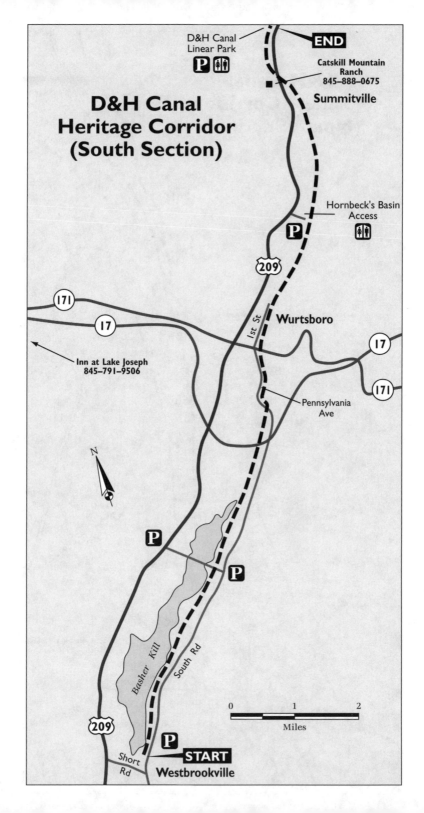

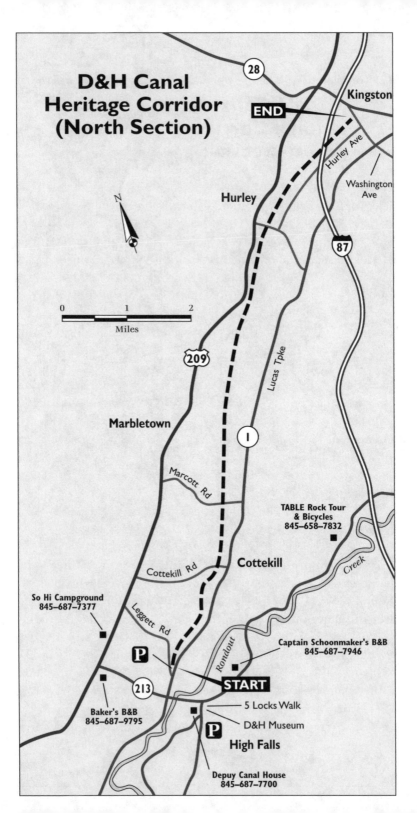

C ompleted in 1828, the Delaware & Hudson Canal was the first million-dollar private enterprise in America. During its seventy years of active duty, it was the main economic artery for the Northeast. It was built to transport anthracite coal from Pennsylvania mines in the Scranton/Wilkes-Barre area to eastern markets.

Not all the 90 miles of off-road travel in the corridor in New York State is open to the public, but some significant sections are accessible. For the experienced rider on a hybrid bike, the entire corridor could be traveled by linking together a variety of canal, towpath, rail-trail, and significant road sections with wide shoulders.

The preservation of the corridor is alive and well due to several historical societies and museums. The D&H Canal Heritage Alliance, an all-volunteer organization, is spearheading the conversion of many segments along the corridor in New York State.

This corridor includes not just canals, but also later modes such as the Ontario & Western Railroad, which parallels the corridor from Port Jervis to Kingston. Interpretive signage at the D&H Canal Linear Park in Summitville tells much of the story: "The D&H Canal was first visualized by Maurice and William Wurts and financed through the influence of Philip Hone, Mayor of New York City. . . . It contained 108 locks, 22 viaducts, 136 bridges, 22 reservoirs, and 16 dams, and the canal was originally only 4 feet deep and 20 feet wide at the bottom, but was later enlarged to a depth of 6 feet and the bottom to 32 feet."

In Pennsylvania the canal could not extend the whole way to Scranton because of the Moosic Mountain Range, but coal was transported by a gravity railroad to the canal at Honesdale, Pennsylvania.

A remnant of the D&H and a fascinating piece of architecture spanning the Delaware River in Lackawaxen, Pennsylvania, is the Roebling Bridge. It was built in 1848 by John Roebling, who constructed many other engineering marvels, such as the Brooklyn Bridge. Built to carry the D&H Canal over the Delaware River, the bridge is an aqueduct also designed to avoid impeding the flow of timber logs downriver to Philadelphia. The aqueduct was abandoned in 1898 but thankfully was restored; it's now managed by the National Park Service. This structure is the oldest existing wire suspension bridge in the Western Hemisphere and now carries

The trailhead at D&H Linear Park offers services and canal heritage interpretation.

automobile traffic! For more information, contact the Upper Delaware Scenic and Recreation River, National Park Service; 570–685–4871; www.nps.gov/upde.

If your travels carry you as far as the unfinished portion of the corridor in Pennsylvania, the Wayne County Historic Society and Museum in Honesdale, Pennsylvania, is a must-visit; 570–253–3240; www.waynehistorypa.us. There you can also see a replica of the famous Stourbridge Lion, the first steam locomotive run on rails in the United States, and the original 1829 passenger coach—the Eclipse. For real rail buffs, it's worth the trip to Scranton to visit Steamtown National Historic Site; 570–340–5200; www.nps.gov/stea/.

Basically, two large sections of the 90-mile corridor are formally open. The first extends from Westbrookville north 12 miles through Wurtsboro to Summitville. This includes sections of the O&W Railroad and the Delaware & Lehigh Canal Towpath. A few miles south of Westbrookville is the Neversink Valley Area Museum and D&H Canal Park in Cuddebackville, New York; 914–754–8870; www.neversinkmuseum.org.

HIGH FALLS

This charming hamlet was first settled in 1676 by settlers eager to harness their grist- and woolen mills to the powerful falls that have existed since the ice ages. With the advent of the Delaware & Hudson Canal in 1828—and the discovery of natural cement during the canal's construction—High Falls became a thriving village. In the nineteenth century cement mills clustered along the creek and kilns were built into the hillside. During the canal's enlargement in 1850, the canal company acquired most of High Falls and subdivided it into streets and lots that today still form the heart of the village and are part of a National Historic District. John Augustus Roebling, designer of the Brooklyn Bridge, built one of his first five "wire rope" suspension bridges over Rondout Creek below the falls. The bridge was a water-filled aqueduct that carried canal boats and their teams of mules or horses over the Rondout.

Though the canal was supplanted here in 1898 by the Ontario & Western Railroad (the "Old & Weary"), many of the canal and mill ruins are still visible today along the Five Locks Walk, a National Historic Landmark. The walk and D&H Canal Museum are approximately 1 mile from the O&W Rail Trail in High Falls. The museum is located on Mohonk Road (County Route 6A) in an 1883 former Victorian Gothic chapel and parish hall and features artifacts, enlarged photographs, sophisticated dioramas, and working models of a lock and gravity railroad car. The museum tells the story of the D&H Canal, America's first million-dollar enterprise, and is open weekends in May, September, and October, Saturday 11:00 A.M.–5:00 P.M. and Sunday 1:00–5:00 P.M. From Memorial Day through Labor Day, open Thursday through Monday 11:00 A.M.–5:00 P.M.; Sunday 1:00–5:00 P.M. Admission is $3.00 adults, $1.00 children, $7.00 family. The entrance foyer is open twenty-four hours a day year-round and provides brochures for local attractions, including self-guided walking tour maps of the village, canal, and nearby pottery stores, antiques shops, and B&Bs. A fabulous assortment of restaurants can be found within walking distance, including the Deputy Canal House, a 1787 stone tavern that earned its four-star distinction in 1971.

The 5.5-mile section north from Westbrookville to Wurtsboro on the O&W Railroad is part of the larger Basher Kill State Wildlife Management Area. This 3,000-acre stretch of wetlands and uplands is managed by the New York State Department of Environmental Conservation and offers additional trails looping around the 2.5-mile-long lake. There are wonderful opportunities for canoeing, bird-watching, and fishing, with a chance to catch largemouth bass, chain pickerel, and bowfin. In Westbrookville the southern trailhead of the O&W is located at the junction of Short and South Roads, just 0.5 mile east of Route 209. The trail ends at Pennsylvania Avenue near Wurtsboro. Take Pennsylvania Avenue north 0.5 mile, cross Sullivan Street to the immediate right, and continue to Linton Lane and Pine Grove Drive, where the D&H Canal Towpath becomes visible. The D&H Canal continues 6 miles north to Summitville and links with the D&H Canal Linear Park on the opposite side of Route 209. Exercise caution when crossing Route 209.

The next major section of open rail-trail begins 25 miles north at High Falls. This large section is also on the O&W Railroad line and extends north from NY Route 213 in High Falls for 11 miles to Hurley and Washington Avenues in Kingston. High Falls is not to be missed: It has five restored locks that lower the canal 70 feet. Don't forget to visit the D&H Canal Historical Society and Museum in High Falls. Afterward take part in the walking tour; for information, call 914–687–9311 or visit www.canalmuseum.org. If you have time, you might also visit the Hudson River Maritime Museum in Kingston; 914–338–0071; www.olsternet/~hrmm.

Endpoints: Scottsville, Cuylerville; Letchworth State Park, Nunda.

Location: Livingston County.

Length: 4.8 miles for the northern stretch, 23.7 miles for the main segment; 6.7 miles for the section within Letchworth State Park.

Surface: Dirt, cinder, gravel.

Uses: All nonmotorized uses; snowmobiling in winter.

To get there: To reach the main segment of the trail, take exit 46 off I-90, the New York Thruway, and then take I-390 South to exit 11. Turn west onto NY Route 251, following this west and then north to the village of Scottsville in the town of Wheatland. The trailhead is in Canawaugus Park, which is on your right as you come into the village.

For the Letchworth State Park segment, take exit 46 off I-490, the New York Thruway, and then take I-390 south to exit 7 (Mount Morris). Turn left at the end of the ramp and take NY Route 408 for 1.8 miles to the traffic light in the center of Mount Morris. Stay on Route 408 by turning left at the light. Continue one block, turn right at the next light, and proceed south on Route 408 for 11 miles to the center of the village of Nunda. At the traffic light, turn right and proceed west on NY Route 436 for 4.5 miles to the parade grounds entrance of Letchworth State Park. Continue on the park road for 0.5 mile to reach the parking area.

Contact: Friends of the Genesee Valley Greenway, P.O. Box 42, Mount Morris, NY 14510; 716-658-2569; fogvg@aol.com.

Accommodations: Country Inn and Suites by Carlson, 130 North Main Street, Mount Morris, NY 14510; 585-658-4080; fax 585-658-4020; cx_mtmo@countryinns.com; www.countryinns.com/mountmorris.ny. Glen Iris Inn, 7 Letchworth State Park, Castile, NY 14427; 585-493-2622; fax 585-493-5803; mltnwt@aol.com; www.glenirisinn.com.

Bike repair/rentals: Massasauga Bike Rentals and Tours, 2139 Mill Street, Nunda, NY 14517; 716-468-5964; massasaugabikes@aol.com; www.massasaugabikes.com.

Campground: Woodstream Campsite, 5440 School Road, Gainesville, NY 14066; 585-493-5643; fax 585-493-5643; camp@woodstream campsite.com; www.woodstreamcampsite.com.

Food: Broman's Genesee Falls Inn, P.O. Box 238, Portageville, NY 14536; 585-493-2484; fax 585-468-5654; lynneygirl@juno.com; www.10kvacationrentals.com.

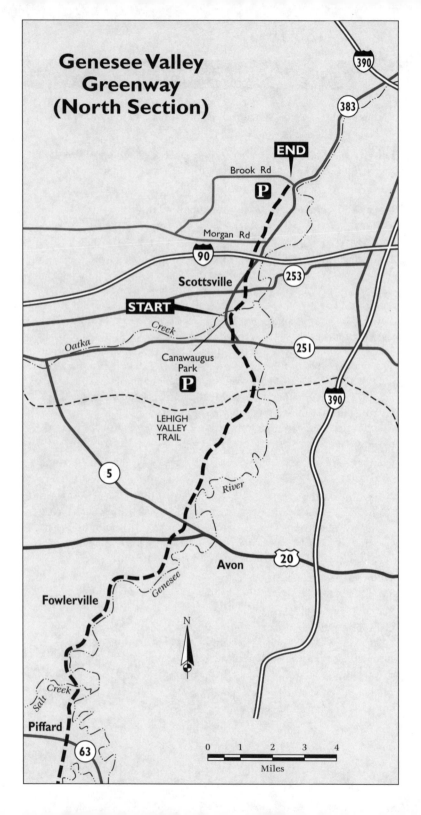

Genesee Valley Greenway (North Section)

390

383

END

Brook Rd

P

Morgan Rd

90

253

Scottsville

START

251

Oatka Creek

Canawaugus Park

P

390

LEHIGH VALLEY TRAIL

5

River

20

Avon

Genesee

Fowlerville

Salt Creek

Piffard

63

N

| 0 | 1 | 2 | 3 | 4 |

Miles

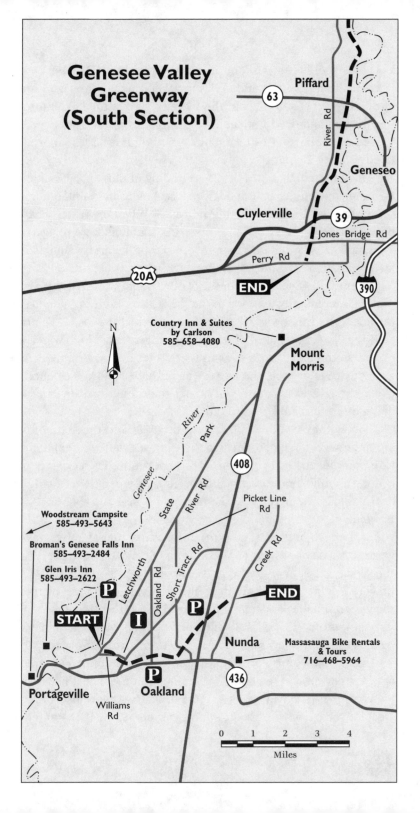

This trail is reminiscent of many found in the Midwest, especially in its rural and agricultural setting, and in the number of other defunct rail lines in the vicinity. The number of railroads in this area is indeed unusually high; a lot of rail use was once required to support both the inbound and outbound transportation needs of area farmers.

An additional factor in the overbuilding of railroads was that the farming community had enough political clout to maintain competition for their business among railroads. When big trucks became prevalent and began to replace railroads, the lines were relegated to a secondary position, and many went out of business. Thus today's large number of abandoned rail lines are in beautiful rural landscapes.

Opened in 1840, the Genesee Valley Canal was an engineering marvel, second only in scope to the Erie Canal. Built from Rochester to Olean, the canal was 113 miles long and had 104 locks. The river could really only be used efficiently during times of high water, and of course the canal froze over in the winter or was drained. Unbeknownst to everyone, the canal was obsolete before it opened because the railroads, coming on-line at the same time the canal was being built, operated year-round.

The canal went out of business in 1878, and the state of New York conveyed all its property to the Genesee Valley Canal Railroad Company for the princely sum of $100 per mile. The company proceeded to build a railroad line on the canal towpath. Eventually this entity became a part of the Pennsylvania Railroad—its Rochester Branch.

At the turn of the last century, the Pennsy operated two passenger trains a day between Rochester and Olean. By the depression of the 1930s, passenger traffic only warranted a "doodlebug"—a gas-powered, self-propelled rail-bus, which carried both passengers and the very profitable U.S. mail. After World War II the post office moved its business onto trucks, and the Pennsy abandoned all passenger service. There were a few rail-fan trips, however, up until the early 1950s.

In 1961 the Pennsy applied to the Interstate Commerce Commission for permission to abandon the line, arguing that it had lost fifteen shippers in eleven years, and the branch was now losing money. Despite vociferous protests from local shippers, the ICC granted the

Biking along the Genesee Valley Greenway's northern segment is both a scenic and rural experience.

abandonment in 1963; the H. E. Salzburg Company was commissioned to scrap the rail and pull out the ties. In that same year the majority of the line was then sold to Rochester Gas and Electric Company, which proceeded to install transmission lines on part of the right-of-way.

In the mid-1980s the state of New York acquired full-fee title to 10 miles of the corridor south of Rochester. In 2000 it acquired from Rochester Gas and Electric the remaining 80 miles of the former lands of the Genesee Valley Canal and the Pennsylvania Railroad's Rochester Branch.

Trail development activities began in 1991 under the direction of the New York Parks and Conservation Association. Development since 1994 has continued through the efforts of the Friends of the Genesee Valley Greenway, working in partnership with the New York State Office of Parks, Recreation, and Historic Preservation and the New York State Department of Environmental Conservation. Much of the information in this chapter has been provided by Fran Gotcsik of the Friends of the Genesee Valley Greenway.

MILE BY MILE

Main Trail Segment

0.0 mile: From the access point, the main segment of the trail goes 4.8 miles north and 23.7 miles south. You can go either way. We'll first describe the section to the north of the access, and then the longer stretch southward.

Heading north, you'll immediately encounter a throughplate girder bridge over Oatka Creek. This is the only remaining railroad-era bridge on the trail. The canal was carried over the creek by means of an aqueduct. Remnants of the stone foundation are still visible to the west. Just across the bridge on the west is the approximate location of Lock 3 and the house of a canal toll collector. Nothing visible remains of these structures.

The trail enters a heavily treed, wide area to the west that was once a center of commerce. Warehouses, lumber- and coalyards, and a planer mill were located here in the days of the canal. In the time of the railroads, warehouses, a slaughterhouse, and a sawmill, feed mill, and cider mill operated here. On the west, look for evidence of the island formed by the intersection of the Genesee Valley Canal, Oatka Creek, and the Scottsville Canal. When initially built, the Scottsville Canal extended from Oatka Creek to the Genesee River. With the opening of the Genesee Valley Canal in 1840, the Scottsville Canal became obsolete, but a small section, still visible today, was used to feed water from Oatka Creek into the Genesee Valley Canal. The cut-stone guard locks for the feeder canal are located on the north bank of Oatka Creek to the west.

0.3 mile: To the west on the hill is a nineteenth-century home built of cobblestones, a construction technique unique to this area.

0.7 mile: Good view of the original dimensions of the canal prism to the west. The trail forms the eastern boundary of the village of Scottsville.

0.8 mile: NY Route 253.

1.3 miles: White fences on the east surround the pastures of a thoroughbred horse farm. The canal prism continues on the west, though the water and a ditch to the east may appear to be the prism.

1.7 miles: NY Route 383, Scottsville Road. The railroad went under the road, but after the railroad was abandoned, the underpass was removed. Newly installed ramps help you climb to the road.

2.2 miles: The trail goes under the New York Thruway. The railroad was still operating when the Thruway was built in the 1950s, helping preserve the route for the Greenway today.

2.3 miles: Private driveway crossing of the trail. On the west the canal prism retains its original dimensions. The trail is very open, providing expansive views of the neighboring farm fields.

2.7 miles: Morgan Road.

2.9 miles: Water in the old canal prism to the west.

3.1 miles: On the east is the original location of Severance, a former flag stop on the railroad, used to take on passengers and agricultural products. High-tension utility wires pass over the trail.

3.2 miles: There's a big dip in the trail; the black railbed cinders are gone. The railbed may have been washed out here at some time. More telegraph poles are visible on the east.

3.4 miles: Enter a tunnel of green.

3.5 miles: The trail opens up again. To the east are many of the farms that have made this an important agricultural area for more than a century.

4.0 miles: Coates Road. At one time this was a paved road that accessed a house to the west. It functions only as a farm lane now.

4.1 miles: Lock 2—the best-preserved cut-stone lock remaining from the Genesee Valley Canal. It was finished in 1839 and cost $18,230 to build. Locks measured 15 feet wide and 90 feet long. A lock tender's house was located adjacent to this lock, but has long since disappeared.

4.4 miles: Several old telegraph poles from the railroad era, still with a few glass insulators, remain on the east.

4.5 miles: A clearing with views to farm fields to the left and right.

4.6 miles: To the east are white fences bordering the many pastures of another large thoroughbred horse breeding farm. Looking north along the trail, tall trees form a canopy over the path. The railbed is very straight along this section. The canal prism can be seen very clearly in the west. Note the flatness on the berm side of

Gates ahead denote the crossing for Brook Road near the northern end of the trail.

the canal prism. In 1896 volunteer bicycle enthusiasts worked to develop the top of the berm as the Scottsville Bicycle Path, which extended from Rochester's Genesee Valley Park to Scottsville. After the
advent of the automobile, bicycling faded from popularity and the
path became overgrown. The greenway uses the other side of the
canal prism where the railroad operated from 1882 to the 1960s.

4.8 miles: Brook Road. A parking lot for vehicles and horse trail-
ers is located along a short, wood-chip path to the west. Part of the
wood-chip path uses the berm side of the canal.

*Turn around now and go back to the bridge over Oatka Creek to be-
gin your trek to the south. Back at the bridge, reset your odometer to 0.0.*

0.0 mile: Head south on the trail. First up is a 60-foot through-
girder bridge crossing Oatka Creek; it's known locally as the "George
Bridge." When the trail was scheduled to be dedicated by Governor
George Pataki in 1996, everyone thought that it was fitting, because
the bridge had already been long ago labeled GEORGE in graffiti. The
New York State Office of Parks, Recreation and Historic Preservation
(OPRHP) saw things differently, however, and made sure the bridge

was sporting a fresh coat of black paint for the visit by the important guest. After the dedication ceremony, the mysterious GEORGE reappeared once again on the bridge.

Canawaugus Park was developed as a community park in 1966. In this initial area, look for the evidence of the old railyard. The remains of a guard lock for a feeder canal are located on the north bank of the creek.

0.2 mile: The ditch on the west side of the trail is actually the canal—now dry. The towpath is actually the treadway for the railroad—now trail. Along the way you'll find that portions of the canal have been filled in to accommodate a straighter alignment for the railroad.

0.7 mile: Travel on a bit of a fill with farmlands beyond the tree line to the east; the canal is still to the west, with more farmlands beyond that. An agricultural grade crossing is seen here as well.

1.0 mile: Grade crossing of Route 251. The gate system is designed so that, even when closed, there's enough room for snowmobiles and horses—and certainly enough for bikes.

1.3 miles: Large vistas to the east with an agricultural grade crossing.

2.4 miles: The railroad's right-of-way encroached on the canal path through here to straighten out a curve.

2.5 miles: This locale was once called Wadsworth Junction. Large abutments here on each side of the trail carried the old Lehigh Valley Railroad overhead as it headed east over the nearby Genesee River. Years ago this general area hosted four different railroad corridors. There were two east-to-west-running corridors, the LV mainline (as noted before) and the New York Central's Peanut Line. The two north-to-south-oriented corridors were the old Erie line to Rochester (still active as the Livonia, Avon & Lakeville Railroad) and, of course, the old Pennsy line you're traveling today. Head east for a short distance to the river here for a little side trip. Check out the old Lehigh Valley Railroad's deck-truss bridge over the Genesee River and, to the west, the long sweeping fill that swings around to meet the Pennsy line. To get across the Erie line on the west side of the river, the river itself, and the Pennsy line, the Lehigh did not want to go to the expense of an elaborate interlocking tower and all the mechanisms that went with it. Instead the company opted for a sophisticated viaduct, 3,000 feet long. The capping monument to that decision is this bridge—slated to once again be used as part of the Lehigh Valley Trail, a trail that is being developed to the communities of Rush and Mendon.

2.7 miles: Joseph Spezio, owner of a former quarry located to the west, donated the land to the east along the river as a conservation area. A fine thing indeed.

3.3 miles: Here you'll find a 150-foot-long concrete pad with a rail on the west side. It looks to be a scale for weighing railcars.

3.4 miles: The New York Central's Peanut Line crossed overhead here.

3.8 miles: This is beaver country, with some creative countermeasures enacted by the trail managers to prevent trail washouts. There's also a double-arched canal culvert.

4.4 miles: The canal prism is still largely visible in this area.

5.9 miles: Grade crossing of a driveway that used to cross the railroad by an overhead bridge—which has long since been filled in.

7.4 miles: The abutments here once carried the Erie Railroad's long-abandoned double-tracked east-to-west-running line into Avon, which is just east of here.

7.6 miles: Ramps have been installed to take the trail up the slopes on the north and south sides of NY Route 5. Obviously another bridge was filled in by the New York Department of Transportation.

7.7 miles: Inspect the concrete huts on the west side of the trail. They must have been used by section crews of the railroad.

8.5 miles: Grade crossing of U.S. Route 20.

8.8 miles: Travel on a cinder fill here; a relatively wide area suggests a passing siding.

9.1 miles: A turning basin for the canal was in this area.

10.1 miles: The canal bed was dug out in this area to a much deeper depth. It probably wasn't done for the canal purposes, but for a long-forgotten project that needed dirt.

10.4 miles: The remains of Lock 5 and the foundation of the lock tender's house are visible here. Local Boy Scouts cleared much

In winter the trail is excellent for cross-country skiing.

of the vegetation to uncover this old infrastructure. The restoration of the old park bench was an Eagle Scout project.

10.7 miles: Travel close to the Genesee River.

11.8 miles: Right past the gates controlling access to the trail, the railroad right-of-way is shared by a driveway that leads to three neighborhood houses.

11.9 miles: Cross Fowlerville Road (County Route 5) at a grade. The Fowlerville railroad station was on the south side of the road by the current grassy area.

12.1 miles: A large pile of ties here is slowly rotting into the earth.

14.3 miles: Reach York Landing. Before the canal was built, this area was the head of navigation for the Genesee River. Only during times of high water could boats go beyond this point to Geneseo and Mount Morris. After the canal was built, this area served as a turning basin for canal boats and a busy center of activity where gristmills processed farmers wheat into flour for transport and warehouses stored goods to be shipped. After the canal closed, the York rail station was located here, but the area was never again as active. Eventually, the school closed and other buildings were torn down, burned, or moved. When the river is low, you can still see the remnants of the dam and the river lock.

14.6 miles: Cross York Landing Road.

15.3 miles: The large farm fields here are owned by the Abbey of the Genesee, a group of cloistered monks.

15.6 miles: Salt Creek is below you here about 40 to 50 feet down. It flows through a massive stone culvert, some of which has collapsed on the west end.

16.5 miles: A good view of the Abbey is afforded here.

17.0 miles: A fence line on the east side here marks the perimeter of a company called Atofina Chemicals, which has adopted this section of trail. The canal is filled with cattails.

17.5 miles: The Yard of Ale restaurant is located here on NY Route 63 in the hamlet of Piffard. Be sure to check out the plaque commemorating the Genesee Valley Canal, erected by the town of York's historical society and placed in the nearby garden. It says in part, "Rochester to Olean. Operated from 1836–1878. This section of the Canal open as far as Mt. Morris on September 1, 1840. The canal provided a way to transport both goods and people making Piffard an active commercial center."

18.2 miles: Evidence of a stump fence. Many years ago it was a standard practice to build fences out of tree stumps.

18.3 miles: Grade crossing at Chandler Road. You'll see a smattering of houses nearby, along with some agricultural outbuildings.

19.4 miles: It's apparent that the railroad switched back and forth over the canal here in an attempt to gain a straighter alignment.

19.8 miles: Electric wires come onto the right-of-way here; in the distance you can see the State University of New York at Geneseo and the 1941 Historical Aircraft Group Museum at the Geneseo Airport. In 1972 Hurricane Agnes severely damaged the right-of-way here. You'll probably notice some changes in the grades here and just ahead.

20.5 miles: Big meadows on the west side of the trail are remainders of salt mining operations. The ponds on the east are great for birding.

21.5 miles: Route 39/20A in the hamlet of Cuylerville in the town of Leicester.

21.6 miles: On the west is the former location of the Cuylerville railroad station and, before that, Cuyler's Basin on the canal. No evidence of the station or the basin remains here now. The trail is lined with hedgerows and, on the east, utility poles belonging to Rochester Gas and Electric Corporation. The utility sold the canal and railroad corridor to New York State in 2000, but has retained utility rights.

21.7 miles: The weathering steel bridge was erected in 2001 on the cut-stone abutments remaining from the half through-plate girder bridge removed in 1963. The deck-plate girder railroad bridge was removed in 1963. The gravel lane beyond the bridge to the west was originally part of the street, now paved, that links Route 39/20A and River Road farther west. It led to a saltworks located in this area around the turn of the twentieth century. The lane extends to the east to the Sink Hole, a pond created when Beard's Creek filled a depression resulting from subsidence due to the collapse of the Akzo Nobel Salt Mine in 1994. Salt mine cavities were located under the trail in this area. Because of the collapse, the mine, once the size of Manhattan, filled with water and is now closed. American Rock Salt has developed a new mine farther east. Its towers and conveyors are visible in the distance.

22.2 miles: This weathering steel bridge over Beard's Creek was installed in 2001 on existing railroad-era abutments. To the west the stones and timbers in the creek below are remnants of the foundation of the aqueduct that carried the canal over the creek. The canal locks, aqueducts, and culverts were constructed upon wooden foundations. Remains of the curved stone walls of the aqueduct are visible to the west on the north bank of the creek.

22.3 miles: Jones Bridge Road. The canal prism continues on the west. The utility poles have switched from the east to the west side of the trail. The canal and railroad followed a very straight course between Cuylerville and Mount Morris.

22.4 miles: The trail crosses Somps Creek on a concrete slab built by the railroad. The utility poles on both sides of the trail may explain why the trail lacks the tree canopy found elsewhere. The canal prism is still located on the west, directly adjacent to River Road.

23.0 miles: Perry Road hedgerows continue to define the limits of the trail.

23.4 miles: To the west across River Road and within the canal prism is a large area of wetland.

23.7 miles: The driveway to the east is the treatment plant for Seneca Foods. The trail is closed beyond this point, awaiting development of a safe crossing of the tracks of the Genesee & Wyoming Railroad.

Letchworth State Park Segment

To reach the trail: Leave the parade grounds parking lot and turn left onto the park road. Go 0.2 mile down the hill. The trail entrance is on your right. In this location the Genesee Valley Greenway is also Trail 7 of Letchworth State Park, and it forms a part of the Letchworth Branch of the Finger Lakes Trail. The yellow blazes on the trees mark the Finger Lakes Trail.

0.0 mile: The trail is heavily wooded in this area. For the first 0.2 mile, the canal prism is on your right. The land drops off steeply to your left.

0.2 mile: Probably due to the steepness of the terrain, the narrowness of the corridor along the hillside, and the railroad's interest in eliminating major curves in the track, the railbed switches its orientation with respect to the canal prism for the next 1.5 miles. At times the prism is on your left, sometimes the trail is within the old prism, and at other times the prism is on your right.

0.8 mile: The original dimensions of the canal prism (42 feet across at the top, 26 feet wide at the bottom, and 4 feet deep) are clearly visible on the right-hand side.

1.8 miles: River Road. Although unpaved and very remote today, River Road was an important thoroughfare for early settlers. During the time of the railroad, this area was known as Lewis Switch.

2.2 miles: Williams Road. The trail detours left onto the unpaved road and continues east along it to Short Tract Road. Beaver dams caused water to overflow the old canal prism and flood the trail between here and Short Tract Road. Because the beavers have left, the trail will soon be restored to its original towpath/railbed location.

2.7 miles: Short Tract Road. After crossing the road, gaze east into the deep, totally man-made valley to your right. The area on either side of the road is known as the Deep Cut. More than half a million cubic yards of dirt and rock were removed from here by the canal builders in the 1840s. The Deep Cut allowed the canal to pass

Friends of the Genesee Valley Greenway member Joan Schumaker enjoys a winter stroll along the trail.

through this area on its way to the Genesee River at Portageville without additional locks. The trail, however, does not have the same luxury of level passage through this area. The timber-trestle road bridge over the railbed was eliminated in the 1970s, and the area was filled in. As a result, the trail must descend 0.1 mile to the former railbed.

2.7 miles: Reach the first of a series of six interpretive signs along the trail between here and Oakland Road. The signs were produced by the New York State Office of Parks, Recreation, and Historic Preservation Historic Sites Bureau interpretive staff. This one provides information about the Deep Cut.

2.9 miles: The canal prism is now located to your left.

3.0 miles: The stone on the left represents the remains of Lock 60, the last of a series of seventeen locks between here and Nunda to the east.

3.1 miles: Lock 59 is located to the right. It is a relatively well-preserved composite lock. Composite locks featured rough cut-stone walls lined with wood. Wooden timbers were anchored in the vertical indentations visible in the stone walls, and horizontal planks were nailed to these timbers. As canal construction progressed, a lack of funds required that this less expensive form of lock be used rather than the fully cut, dressed-stone locks found farther north.

3.2 miles: There's a fork in the trail here. The canal towpath and locks continue to your right, down a short slope. Straight ahead is the route of the railroad. An interpretive sign pertaining to the Genesee Valley Canal Railroad is located here.

Canal Trail Fork

3.2 miles: Lock 58 is located at the bottom of the short descent. Note the massive curved-wing walls at the lower gates of the lock and the size of the stones used in the lock's construction.

3.3 miles: Lock 57. Another interpretive sign describes the construction and operation of composite locks.

3.4 miles: Lock 56. A few of the vertical timbers that lined the stone walls still survive at the far end of the lock. Note also the metal rods used to hold the timbers in place.

3.5 miles: Lock 55. Another interpretive sign describes some of the engineering challenges that the canal builders faced.

3.6 miles: Two interpretive signs are located within 0.2 mile. The first describes the wide-open area at the head of Lock 54, which functioned as a water reservoir. Directly in front of the sign, across the open area, are the remains of a stone waste weir that was used to control the level of water in the canal. Note the massive, curved stone walls at the lower gate of Lock 54. The second interpretive sign provides a brief history of the building of the Genesee Valley Canal and its relationship to the Erie Canal.

3.7 miles: Oakland Road. During the time of the canal, the hamlet of Oakland, to the south, consisted of a number of mills, factories, churches, and homes. The trail leaves Letchworth State Park at Oakland Road. Follow the Greenway logo signs, turn left, and continue along Oakland Road up a slight incline for about 0.2 mile to join the railbed section of the trail. The canal continued straight ahead, on the north side of Route 436, but when the railroad purchased the canal in 1880, it did not buy the section of canal between here and Nunda because of the steep grade.

Rail-Trail Fork

3.2 miles: From here 7 miles northeast to Tuscarora, the railroad selected a different route that did not involve the steep grades the canal encountered. The railbed is built on a plateau with heavily wooded terrain on both sides.

3.5 miles: On your right is one of only a few remaining railroad mile markers. The wooden post is covered with metal on two sides. Any evidence of its number has long since disappeared.

3.8 miles: Oakland Road, east side. There's a steep incline up to the trail. The railroad crossed Oakland Road on a concrete-slab overhead bridge, which has been removed. There is no canal prism visible here because the canal was located down the hill, close to Route 436. This corridor was developed by the railroad in the early 1880s. The trail passes through a wooded area. The trail surface is primarily grass, but the railbed cinders are still underneath.

4.5 miles: The trail opens up with views to the southeast across farm fields to the village of Nunda and the hills above the Keshequa Creek Valley.

4.9 miles: Picket Line Road.

5.0 miles: Reach the site of the West Nunda passenger station on your right. The trail is lined by hedgerows and very straight in this area.

5.5 miles: Hay Road. To the east are magnificent views across the farm fields and to the hills of surrounding the Keshequa Creek Valley.

6.0 miles: Route 408. Limited trailhead parking is available here on the grassy area. Across Route 408, the trail also becomes the cart path for the Triple Creek Golf Course. On your left is the fourth hole. Farther on through the tunnel of trees are entrances to two other holes.

6.3 miles: The trail enters a clearing with the golf clubhouse up the slope to your left. Directly in front is the putting green, so follow the Greenway logo signs to detour to the left and loop around the putting green. The row of trees to the east at the edge of the course marks the location of the canal and the Nunda Branch of the Greenway trail that extends from Pentagass Road to the village of Nunda. Lock 38 is located along the eleventh tee of the golf course.

6.7 miles: Pentagass Road. The trail is closed between here and Creek Road. Beyond Creek Road, the Greenway is open for approximately 2 miles until it dead-ends at Keshequa Creek. The creek has caused significant bank and railbed erosion and bridge abutment deterioration, preventing development of the trail in the Tuscarora and Sonyea State Forest area.

Endpoints: Glens Falls, Fort Edward.

Location: Warren County.

Length: 9 miles.

Surface: Crushed stone.

Uses: All nonmotorized uses.

To get there: Take I–87 to exit 18, then head east on Corinth Road for 0.6 mile. Turn right (south) onto Richardson Street. Go about 0.5 mile; the road bends to the left. Look for the parking area on your right just after the turn.

Contact: John Dimura, Project Manager, NY Thruway Authority, 200 Southern Boulevard, Albany, NY 12209; 518–436–3034. Glens Falls Feeder Canal Alliance, P.O. Box 2414, Glens Falls, NY 12801; 518–792–5363.

Accommodations: The Glens Falls Inn, 25 Sherman Avenue, Glens Falls, NY 12801; 518–743–9365; fax 518–743–0696; info@glensfallsinn.com; www.glensfallsinn.com.

Glens Falls is a community that ties into the memories of many people who lived through World War II. In 1944 *Life* magazine sent a team of photographers to this community for a multimonth series titled "Hometown USA" illustrating the effects of the war on the city, and detailing how residents coped with life after it. The following is excerpted from those articles:

> Glens Falls contains, in microcosm, every aspect of the American Idea, every potential for achievement of the American Ideal. . . By working together now, the people of Glens Falls are striving to build a better place. Just as their success or failure will affect the future of hometowns all over America, so too will it affect the future of hometowns all over the world.

Such fitting words. Though written nearly sixty years ago, they still apply today to this clean, well-run community, which is undergoing yet another transformation. This is a community that had its roots on the river; after later adopting the canal for business and transport, it has seen the value of reinventing the canal and its towpath for recreation and alternative transportation. Another linear corridor exists in town: A long-dormant industrial spur to businesses on the north side of town (and passenger route to Lake George) has been resurrected as an extension of the Warren County Bikeway (see Trail 22). Both projects bode well for Glens Falls's future as not only a tourist destination but also a place where residents can enjoy a good family experience on a local trail—whether the rail-trail or, in this case, the canal towpath trail.

The canal was dug in 1824 to carry needed water from the Hudson River to the Champlain Canal 7 miles to the east. The locks were built by 1830 so canal boats towed by mules could carry timber and other local products to markets in Albany and New York City. For almost one hundred years, the canal was busy with commercial traffic. A change to railroads and trucks brought about a decline in the last half of the twentieth century.

• •

MILE BY MILE

0.0 mile: The Van Dusen Sawmill once operated at this area between the Hudson River and Lock 14. Boats, rafts, and logs made their way into the canal at this point. The guard lock, still standing, still controls the amount of water entering the canal and on into the Champlain Canal. This is Feeder Canal Lock in Warren County—part of New York State's plan to use the canal system for recreation. Look for the two park benches nearby as you head out to the east.

0.23 mile: Grade crossing of a neighborhood street—Bush Street—which also crosses over the canal.

0.87 mile: Note the old abutments that at one time carried a road over the canal. You're also near a massive wood-pulp log yard for Finch-Pruyen & Company. These trees are brought to the nearby mill to be made into fine papers.

1.0 mile: Note mile marker on the trail, which points out the miles from Lock 14, where you started.

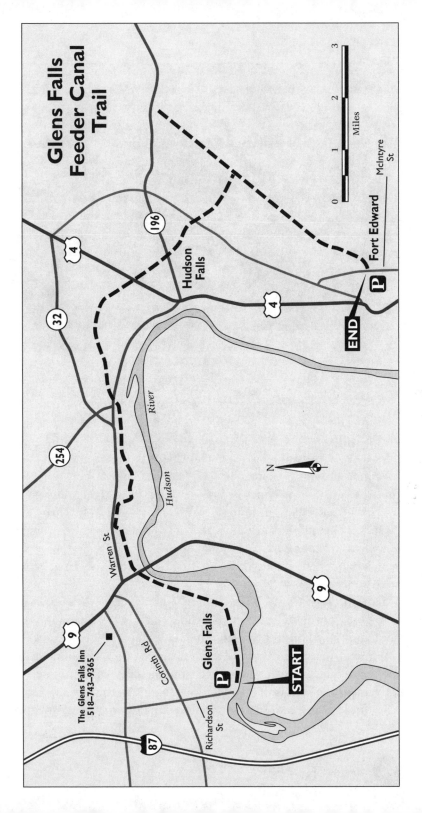

The start of the Feeder Canal Trail near Lock 14 includes a relatively new bike-ped bridge.

1.35–1.5 miles: You're passing by a local Coca-Cola distributorship and a metalworking facility called Riverside Fab. The nearby road is called Murray Street.

1.6–1.75 miles: Here's a good vista of the river, the dam, and the Finch-Pruyen Company in the distance. This is the area of the Hudson River where James Fenimore Cooper placed the well-known Cooper's Cave. There used to be stairs to take you to this area, but these were abandoned for safety reasons. The cave still exists, but it was never quite the cave that Cooper made it out to be. There has been some recent activity trying to make this area accessible to the public once again.

1.8 miles: Although the founding fathers laid out Glens Falls 0.5 mile to the north, their new village flourished at the foot of the hill. Abraham Wing built the first commercial enterprise in 1765: a combination tavern, inn, and store on the corner of the present Warren and Ridge Streets. Power generated from the falls was harnessed on both sides of the Hudson River. By 1830 the Glens Falls Feeder Canal offered economical shipping; industries prospered. The sawmill,

gristmill, kilns, and black marble quarry on this spot were consolidated as the Glens Falls Company, later purchased by Samuel Pruyn
and Jeremiah and Daniel Finch. Today Finch-Pruyn manufactures
fine printing papers. All these and other bulky items were transported by the canal boats. The old sawmill washed away in the flood
of 1869. Later a dam spanning the entire Hudson River was built. A
modern replacement of that original dam was completed in 1935.
The power canal between the Hudson River and the Feeder Canal
was the forebear of Finch-Pruyn.

Today the area is a parking lot for administrative personnel of
the paper company. Look for the tracks buried in the pavement here
as well. Then come out onto the street, take a quick left, go north
over the bridge, take a right at the Glens Falls Civic Center, and head
east onto Oakland Avenue. This avenue runs parallel to the paper
mill, but you're now on the north side of the canal.

2.06 miles: Still on Oakland Avenue, bear left, slightly uphill, to
a traffic light. Take a right and head east on NY Route 32, Warren Street.

2.35 miles: Look at the National Guard Armory on your right
with its castellated turret. Just beyond is the celebrated Hyde Collection Art Museum.

2.65 miles: Check out the interesting Victorian-era houses here.

2.77 miles: Take a right and head south onto Shermantown Road.

2.89 miles: Go past a cement plant on your left; you'll see a gate
for the Feeder Canal
Trail. Head left into
the park at 2.94 miles.

2.94 miles: This
interesting segment
grows much more
industrial than the
largely rural early
segment of the trail.
Look for the railroad
tracks to come in
close by on your
right; you'll shortly
be in the midst of

The trail passes through industrial neighborhoods as
well as more rural areas.

one of the region's larger cement producers, Iron Clad Cement. Look to your left for its large storage silos.

3.3 miles: Go past the Iron Clad Cement Company's Glens Falls office.

3.37 miles: Travel beneath the CP/D&H Railroad bridge over the canal and trail. This makes a very photogenic scene.

3.58 miles: Note the large brownfield, where a manufacturer (originally the Imperial Wall Paper Company in 1915) made various pigments for paints. It went on to become the largest American producer of pigments. Unfortunately, as in most areas of the country, old industries did not treat their grounds with careful stewardship, and the site became highly contaminated. In summer 2001 it was being remediated for redevelopment.

3.7 miles: Head past an old abutment that apparently carried a road into the old paint manufacturing facility.

3.77 miles: The parallel Route 32 is getting closer with some commercial development and services nearby. Note the concrete retaining wall on the canal.

4.04 miles: The trail crosses NY Route 254 here. This is busy road with relatively fast traffic, so be careful.

4.09 miles: Note the old industrial buildings beyond the canal, which is on your left here.

4.34 miles: More abutments over the canal. They once carried a road over the canal.

4.40 miles: Return to a more rural ambience as you get farther from both the busy road and industry.

4.61 miles: Reach a grade crossing at Warren Street—which also is the boundary with the community of Hudson Falls.

5.0 miles: Look for the wooden mile marker here. The concrete wall lining the canal has disappeared.

5.47 miles: The canal is again concrete-lined as you come into a town park area and intersecting U.S. Route 4. Look for the replica of a lock tender's shanty at this location. The tender's duties included collection of tolls, opening and closing of gates, and controlling the flow of water into and out of the locks. These structures were built strictly for utilitarian purposes and contained a woodstove for the cold springs and falls in upstate New York. (The canal closed in the

At 3.37 miles the trail follows the canal underneath the CP/D&H Railroad bridge.

winter due to freezing). There's an ice cream store here as well as other services nearby. Go across Route 4, take a left across the bridge over the canal, then take an immediate right onto the small, aptly named Lower Feeder Street. The trail is paved for the next 0.5 mile or so—from Route 4 to NY Route 196.

5.6 miles: This area is known as Boat Basin Park. The sign here states, "Today's Boat Basin Park was once the turn around basin for boats operating out of Hudson Falls. In its hey-day, the Feeder Canal was home to over 80 canal boats. The basin was stone lined and 200 feet deep. It could hold 6 boats—90 feet long and 14 feet wide. They docked here, unloaded cargo etc. When the Highbridge on Martindale Avenue was lowered, to ease modern traffic, its huge supporting blocks of limestone were pushed into the abandoned basin. The stones were recently rediscovered and they now form the 3-tiered retaining wall."

5.7–5.83 miles: At a grade crossing of Route 196, where the trail turns back to stone dust again, look for the west end of the Griffin Lumber Company on your right. Huge old coal towers are seen here. Farther along this section you'll reach the Pleasant Street grade crossing. Go down the next cross street, Pleasant Street, and check out the old lumber company—formed in 1848 and still in business today. It has a smattering of interesting old buildings, including the office, which was built in 1913 and sports a tile roof. Across the street are some old Griffin Lumber buildings that have been sold off to other users. For example, the American Legion Post is actually an old lumber shed. The whole village is a step back in time.

The Five Combines can be seen at the 6.3-mile mark of the trail.

6.1 miles: Lock 12.

6.2 miles: Lock 11. Then cross over Burgoyne Avenue and enter the Combine Park area.

6.3 miles: Here are the five locks that make up the Five Combines. A sign here notes that the Feeder Canal is 40 feet wide in most places, allowing two boats to pass through these well-trafficked locks. Often disputes and fights would occur among impatient boatmen. The lock tender was supposed to keep order, but sometimes the boat with the toughest crew managed to get to the head of the line. It took fifteen minutes to go through one lock, or an hour and a quarter to get through the Five Combines. By 1845 the original wooden locks were replaced with cut-stone versions. Each of the Five Combines is 100 feet long and has a change in elevation of 11 feet, making for a combined drop of 55 feet. Lock tenders were on duty twenty-four hours a day to assist operating the gates and locking boats through. In 1985 the area was placed on the National Register of Historic Places. In 1991 the New York Department of Transportation stabilized the lock walls.

6.4 miles: The Feeder Canal seems to divert away and come back to you as you travel down an access road that parallels it.

7.0 miles: Lock 3.

7.1 miles: Lock 1.

7.2 miles: At the T intersection that ends the Feeder Canal, go right (southwest) along the Champlain Canal Trailway. (You can also head left for about 1 mile until the trail dead-ends. The Feeder Canal Alliance is hoping to create a loop that would add 5 to 7 miles on this end of the trail.) The trail heads southwest to a nice pond and some ball fields.

7.85 miles: This is a very rural stretch, with farms on your left and the remains of the old Champlain Canal on your right, along with more farms.

8.0 miles: Mile marker 8.

8.3 miles: A large farm with abandoned outbuildings is found here, along with more rural vistas. The trail becomes the access road to this farm and a few houses nearby.

8.6 miles: The trail diverts off the road and once again becomes a side path as you pass a couple of industries that specialize in recycling.

9.0 miles: Reach the end of the trail at McIntyre Street, where some ball fields and a small pond are found. Work commenced during the summer of 2001 to continue the trail to Lock 8 of the Champlain Barge Canal, adding another 3 or 4 miles.

Endpoints: Amenia, Millerton; Copake Falls, Boston Corners.

Location: Dutchess and Columbia Counties.

Length: 7.68 miles and 3.68 miles in two separate sections as of 2001. This project will eventually link together about 46 miles of corridor between Wassaic and Chatham.

Surface: Asphalt.

Uses: All nonmotorized uses.

To get there: *Amenia to Millerton segment:* From NY Route 22 in downtown Amenia, take NY Route 343 east one block to Mechanic Street. Follow this a short distance to just past the fire station. The trailhead parking is on your left. Another option for starting in Amenia is to take the train from New York City to Metro-North's newly opened Wassaic Station. To access the unused/abandoned section of right-of-way, pedal out onto Route 22 and head north. A short distance beyond the end of the active rail, you'll find the cinder-surfaced, primitive, but not officially open rail-trail. If you'd rather stick with a paved surface, then continue on Route 22 about 2.5 miles to a right turn onto Lavelle Street. Follow this for 0.3 mile, then turn east-northeast onto Railroad Avenue. At its intersection with Mechanic Street, you'll find the trailhead. *Copake Falls to Boston Corners segment:* From the Taconic State Parkway, take NY Route 23 east to Hillsdale, then Route 22 south. Go 4.2 miles to the intersection with NY Route 344. Turn left and continue 0.4 mile. Park in Taconic State Park or wherever safe and appropriate. The trail crosses Route 344 at the Depot Deli, which used to be the old Copake Falls passenger station.

Contact: Harlem Valley Rail Trail Association, Box 356, Millerton, NY 12546; 518-789-3733.

Campgrounds: Camp Waubeeka Family Campground, 133 Farm Road, Copake, NY 12516-1601; 518-329-4681; fax 518-329-5781; waubeeka @taconic.net; www.campwaubeeka.com. Oleana Family Campground, 2236 County Route 7, Copake, NY 12516-1433; 518-329-2811; fax 518-329-0703; ole@taconic.net; www.oleanacampground.com.

I
n its final days, the Harlem Division had a tumultuous life under the thumb of the infamous Penn Central, but things started out in the early 1800s with optimism and hope. Originally chartered in 1831, the New York & Harlem Railroad opened in Manhattan in 1832.

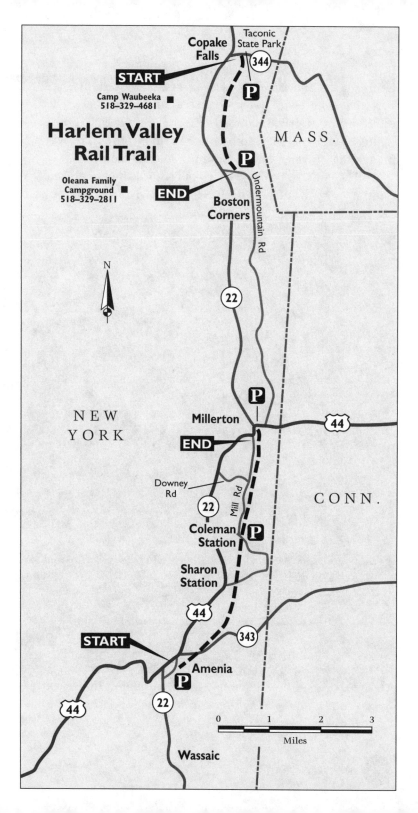

By 1852 it was extended 131 miles to the village of Chatham, where it intersected and joined up with three different railroads. The first was what would later be known as the Boston & Albany Division of the New York Central Railroad (NYC); the second was the Rutland Railroad, which came south out of Vermont; the third was a NYC branch that traveled to the community of Hudson Falls.

In 1873 the New York & Harlem was acquired by the New York Central Railroad and became its Harlem Division. From the point of

Locals take advantage of the paved path at the Millerton trailhead.

view of the local residents, the line was one of NYC's most well-respected divisions, and it ran pretty uneventfully (excepting a couple of major derailments, described later) until the changeover to Penn Central in 1968.

In 1969 the Penn Central was in dire financial straits and searching for ways to stem the flow of red ink on various light-density lines. Of course the line traversing the bucolic Harlem Valley fell into its line of sight, and Penn lobbied to shut down passenger service to Chatham almost immediately. Interestingly, though, since 1961 the Harlem Valley Transportation Association had been waging a grassroots campaign (under the leadership of Lettie Gay Carson) to keep rail service alive in the Millerton to Chatham section. This group was successful while the New York Central Railroad was in charge of things, but when Penn Central came to town it was a different story.

After long and protracted court battles, Penn Central was finally given permission to abandon passenger service on March 20, 1972. This effectively limited passenger service to as far north as only Brewster.

When Conrail came into being in April 1976, it ran only freight operations, but that too came to an end when the line was abandoned between Wassaic and Millerton in March 1980. This was a year after the segment from Millerton to Ghent near Chatham was abandoned.

In the ensuing years, some parts of the right-of-way were sold to private landowners, particularly in Columbia County, but the majority stayed in public hands. Elinor Mettler, editor and publisher of the *Roe Jam Independent,* a Columbia County newspaper, first proposed a rail-trail in the early 1980s, and she was instrumental in building the organization known today as the Harlem Valley Rail-Trail Association. The first segment of trail, from Amenia to Coleman Station, opened on September 21, 1996, with an emphasis on activities for local children. These included bicycle decorating and a scavenger hunt under the direction of Bridget Barclay of the Dutchess County Planning Department.

In the summer of 2000, a segment opened in Millerton all the way to the downtown area; yet another segment opened in November of that year. Most recently a 3.78-mile segment was opened in

Columbia County to bring the trail to the old railroad junction hamlet of Boston Corners.

In the summer of 2001, Dutchess County executive Bill Steinhaus announced that $2 million had been obtained to acquire and build the section from Millerton north to the Columbia County line, and $846,000 to build the section between Metro-North's Wassaic Railroad Station to Amenia in the spring of 2002.

Steinhaus noted, "In addition to the enjoyment of local residents, the rail-trail has truly become a recreational resource of regional importance, and an economic resource on which the surrounding communities can build. . . . The significance of this link and the trail's ability to produce economic spin-offs for the surrounding communities cannot be overestimated."

This book, written in the summer of 2001, describes the trail's Amenia to Millerton section from south to north, and the Copake Falls to Boston Corners segment north to south. Check with the Harlem Valley Rail Trail Association to see if new sections have been opened by the time you read this.

. . . .

MILE BY MILE

Amenia to Millerton

0.0 mile: You'll be starting at the kiosk at the Mechanic Street parking lot, which is also the area where the old Amenia Station once stood. In the language of the old Harlem Division, this is 84.59 miles from Grand Central Station in New York City.

The town's name, Amenia, is from the word *amenable,* or "pleasing," and it's evident that the views of the beautiful valley are the reason for this name. The village itself had a couple of railroad-era hotels that are no longer around. One was near the present trucking company's location. The village still has some very interesting architecture worth checking out. In some early advertising, Amenia billed itself as the "Gateway to the Berkshires."

0.15 mile: As you head more east than north, you come upon a fill with a couple of houses on each side of the trail; a driveway is directly adjacent to you.

0.34 mile: Now you're into a bit of a cut. The trail tends to travel a bit more to the east of north.

0.55 mile: On your right, you'll come upon a genuine concrete "ring post." When the train came upon the obelisk, the engineer was obliged to ring the bell, because a grade crossing was imminent.

0.6 mile: Grade crossing at Sheffield Road, which features an old Sheffield Farms Creamery building still standing. It's now a sculptor's residence. Such buildings had extremely thick masonry walls that acted as insulation in the days before refrigeration. The milk from railroad's "milk-run," which picked up milk cans put out by farmers along the route, was cooled by ice cut from local ponds. Once the train was made up, these precious perishable cargoes of milk and other dairy products were shipped out daily to New York City at the high speed of 60 miles per hour.

1.1 miles: Grade crossing at Route 343. On the right you'll find an agricultural supply house called Crop Production Services. Note the area closest to the trail and you'll discern the faint remnants of rail service. On the other side of the road, you'll see some sheep on the hillside above the trail. The trail actually bisects the farm in this area; the farmer and trail managers have installed a chicken-wire fence to keep the farm animals from wandering onto the pathway. The trail begins a gentle curve to the north in this area.

1.63 miles: You are now onto a fairly large fill that tops 40 feet in height. A wooden fence protects folks from inadvertently biking off the embankment.

2.12 miles: Cross over a small stream by a culvert. This unnamed stream runs for about 2.5 miles from a small pond on your left to the Webatuck Creek on the east side of the trail. Note the old ties and riprap in the area which seem to tell a story of a onetime flood. They were actually installed together during the reconstruction after the flooding caused by Hurricane Diane in 1955. New ties were dumped in with the riprap in an attempt to expedite the roadbed's reconstruction. The ties are still there, and looking none the worse for wear.

2.3 miles: Grade crossing of Lower Sharon Station Road. You 're heading almost fully north now. There's parking here for a few cars as well.

3.1 miles: Grade crossing at Sharon Station Road. Here you'll find the passenger station, exquisitely restored in summer 2000 by a family from New York City. This station was a little bit different from most country stations in that it had a second floor where the agent and his family lived. If you stop just adjacent to the station and look to the west, you'll see the faint remains of the spur that led to the old Manhattan Mining Company, about 300 yards west of the station—under the wetlands today.

3.62 miles: You'll see some old railroad ties here pushed off to the side in small piles as you enter a forest with another lush wetland on the west side of the trail. Be on the lookout for derelict ancient telegraph poles with arms still attached.

4.2 miles: Grade crossing at Sheffield Hill Road. This is the site of the old Coleman Station. Look for the remains of an agricultural building on the east side of the corridor that used to transfer goods to railcars on a siding. There's trailhead parking here for fifteen cars. Note the signage on the far side of the road: "This area was once part of colonial Connecticut, an area known as 'Oblong.' A strip of land 2.75 miles long by 20 rods wide. In 1731, New York and Connecticut swapped parcels, with Connecticut gaining a small piece that is now part of Fairfield County Connecticut."

4.53 miles: You're now going over the first of a number of nicely rebuilt deck-girder bridges. The county has constructed this component of the trail in a very unusual fashion—with 1.5-inch-square, extruded aluminum pickets capped by treated lumber. These make for a very distinctive, almost signature effect.

4.63 miles: Look to the footing on the west side of the trail for a "home-signal." This was a signal tower that protected a switch.

4.77 miles: Pass over a twin culvert. This is late railroad construction—perhaps from the 1950s—and obviously necessary, because the little stream near the trail at one time flooded and washed out the corridor. These culverts are somewhat unusual in that they are about 8 feet in diameter and made of corrugated metal.

4.96 miles: Cross a bridge over Indian Lake Road. The approaches to this bridge are new. When the railroad operated here, the clearance was very low, and trucks couldn't pass under the right-of-way. When the county upgraded the corridor as a trail, the bridge was raised to meet modern clearances, but the downside is that the approaches require a slight uphill trek to the bridge deck. The bridge itself is much like the previous one, with aluminum pickets.

5.0–5.11 miles: Right after the bridge, you find a cut through limestone and other rock. This cut, 100 feet high and deep, is the deepest on the line and was the scene of two major train wrecks. The first during the infamous blizzard of 1888, when a plow train with five locomotives came north from Coleman Station and hit a wall of snow and ice at 45 miles per hour. The wall was as tall as the cut was high.

Because of the narrowness of the cut, the plow couldn't throw the snow to the side; it all wedged up until it was solid ice and would give no farther. The plow then broke apart, and the locomotives crashed through it and into the wall of ice, derailing and killing five of the crewmen. Twenty-four years later, in 1912, another similar incident took place in the cut, but without loss of life. It's hard to imagine while going through this area that snow could fill the entire crevasse, but it has done so a number of times.

5.24 miles: Here's another bridge much like the others, but with a twist: This one crosses over Mill Road and the little stream at the same time with the steam channelized in a concrete box under the bridge. It's very unusual to say the least.

5.49 miles: If you're out here on a hot summer day, you'll look forward to this section: a 35-foot-tall, hand-hewn, moss-covered rock cut that drops the temperature by a good eight or ten degrees.

5.87 miles: Another of the now-ubiquitous girder bridges. This one spans Downey Road and offers grand vistas of the valley.

6.42 miles: A girder bridge over a small stream.

6.73 miles: You are now passing by a farmhouse (look for the llamas); the river is on the other side of the house. There are also some pretty exotic-looking hens and they'll let you know who's the boss as you pass on by. On the north side of this house, the driveway parallels your path for a bit, then intersects with it.

6.96 miles: The grade crossing of the driveway and Mill Road comes very close to the trail. In fact, the county has placed a fence between you and the country road to define each space. Look for the nice plantings along the road.

7.13 miles: Look for the remnants of a railroad signal on the river side of the trail. Constructed on a little outcropping built of ties on the riverbank, it's very substantial and New York Central–like.

7.17 miles: Pass over another deck-girder bridge, this one across Webatuck Creek with a few houses in a village setting nearby. Then you're into a cut right away.

7.30 miles: Another bridge over Webatuck Creek, then a crossing over Mill Street; then you emerge into a village setting again.

7.51 miles: Cross a bridge again, with a signal relay box nearby in the woods to the east, along with a battery box. Look for the telegraph signal poles with the insulator arms still on them. The Eugene L. Brooks Rail-Trail Station is on your right. This building is the headquarters of the Harlem Valley Rail-Trail Association; you'll find some outdoor seating here as well.

7.68 miles: The trail ends here at the grade crossing with Route 22. There were three tracks here crossing the road as late as 1960. Looking north, across the street you'll see the "new" (in 1911) Millerton Station, which was located at mile marker 92.67. This station was also considered to be a union station in that the old Central New England Railroad, running east to west, crossed the Harlem at a grade about 0.25 mile farther north.

The Millerton passenger station today houses a real estate company, but look across the right-of-way and you'll see the "old" or original Millerton Station, a much more modest wooden structure that today hosts a crafts shop.

Downtown Millerton looks like everyone's ideal of just what a downtown is supposed to be. With lots of interesting places to visit, Millerton is becoming a destination for folks from all over the state. Look for the various lunch and dining choices as well as shopping in the fascinating stores. The Oblong Book Store is a special experience in itself.

Copake Falls to Boston Corners

0.0 mile: At this trailhead is a nice deli that serves great sandwiches. The building is actually the old Copake Falls Station. While standing at the trailhead sign, you'll notice that the entrance to the Taconic State Park is just across the street, as is Bash Bish Bicycle

A split-rail fence provides an interesting study in vanishing-point perspectives as seen on the Harlem Valley Rail Trail.

Shop. The road also leads to Bash Bish Falls State Park in Massachusetts. As you head south on the trail, note the sign on the fence to your right: The Rails-to-Trails Conservancy, it tells you, highlighted the Harlem Valley Rail Trail as one of the nation's first 500 rail-trails. As you get past the station, look into the woods to your left to see the remains of an old spur that once led to the iron mine.

0.1 mile: Come upon a double-track bridge over Bash Bish Brook. It's an interesting structure in that it's really two different kinds of bridges, side by side, with a newly constructed decking across both for trail users. The east structure is a deck-girder type, while the west is a deck-truss bridge. As far as we know, this is the only example of such a bridge on a rail-trail in the Northeast. The west structure is used today as a separate sitting and viewing area. Built with pressure-treated benches, timbers, and railings, and sporting a brown chain-link fence, its ambience lends itself to quiet contemplation of the natural surroundings.

0.2 mile: The trail begins to swing around to the south-southwest as you get into a cut; there's about 40 feet of hill above you on the west side. Also seen here is the first of many farm fields.

0.51 mile: Farm fields now line both sides of the trail. Head into a small cut, then pass signage telling you of an agricultural grade crossing. Quickly arriving are some spectacular vistas of the Taconic Valley.

0.63–0.99 mile: You're now on the low-traffic and appropriately named Valley View Road. The railroad came through here and actually used an alignment just to the right (west) of the dirt road. Parts of the right-of-way in this area were bought by adjoining landowners and bulldozed out, however, so the trail instead uses the road. Look for the old New York Central Railroad battery box between the road and the old right-of-way at 0.84 mile.

0.99 mile: The trail continues once again. Note the sign: WARNING TO HIKERS! HUNTING IS PROHIBITED ON THIS TRAIL. HOWEVER, BEWARE OF CROSS-FIRE FROM ADJOINING AREAS. This area also has some parking for trail users. Note the bollard here as well. A bollard is a post inserted into the trail's right-of-way at a grade crossing. It serves three purposes: to slow bikers along the trail so that a safe crossing of the road can be made; to prevent cars and other unauthorized vehicles from accessing the trail; and (when designed with a locking mechanism) to allow access to the trail by police or other emergency personnel.

This bollard is a bit different from the norm in that it has a much-enhanced brace built onto its back side. The intent is to ensure that no one can drive *through* the bollard to access the trail.

1.24 miles: Look for the farm fields up to your left and descending to your right. Be on the lookout for more agricultural grade crossings, with supplementary signage asking you not to trespass onto the farmer's land.

1.33 miles: Travel on a fill that's about 50 feet above the farm fields to your right. It then slopes down away from the trail even farther, to well over 70 feet. There are grand vistas; you're protected from going down the slope by a split-rail fence.

1.49 miles: A park bench for resting is found here. It looks out over farm fields and meadows on each side of the trail with a great view of the Catskills to the west. Be on the lookout for a railroad-era culvert here as well. It's a box culvert with concrete capping of stones.

1.76 miles: Here you'll find another culvert much like the earlier one. Still, the real prize here is a genuine concrete mile marker that says "NY103" on each side. It's 103 miles to Grand Central Station in New York City.

2.59 miles: Look for a small wooden culvert here, as well as a series of unusually large-diameter trees along the right-of-way; they may have been around in even the Penn Central days. They serve as a permanent reminder of the days of "deferred maintenance."

2.72 miles: Another mile marker, with "NY102" on each side. Also here is another concrete culvert, then a small cut. Look for the old telegraph pole lying on the east side of the trail; it features a single telegraph arm without insulators. The usual pole line on this corridor had five cross arms.

3.65 miles: A split-rail fence protects a large fill (35 feet high) through this section. Look for the concrete box culvert that carries Preechey Hollow Brook under the corridor. Just ahead is another mile marker: "NYC101."

3.78 miles: Reach the trailhead for the south terminus at Undermountain Road in the hamlet of Boston Corners. A lot with twelve parking spaces is found here. This terminus is located about 2,000 feet east of the north-to-south-running Route 22. Plans are under way for the trail to continue south and link up with the already open section at Millerton.

Endpoints: *South section (isolated):* Eastview, Graham. *North section:* Baldwin Place, Graham.

Location: Westchester County.

Length: 19.82 miles.

Surface: Asphalt.

Uses: All nonmotorized uses.

To get there: *North section:* Start at the Baldwin Place trailhead, which is located on NY Route 118 just north of its intersection with U.S. Route 6. Additional parking for this trailhead was being built in the summer of 2001. Head south on the trail. *Note:* Some parts of this trail travel on roadways. These sections might be busy, depending upon when you go, but the terrain isn't very hilly. *South section:* Take the Saw Mill River Parkway to exit 23 and then head west on Old Saw Mill River Road for about 100 yards to a park 'n' ride parking lot. The trail is on the northwest side of the parkway starting at the overpass for Old Saw Mill River Road.

Contact: David DeLucia, Director of Park Facilities, Westchester County Department of Parks, Recreation and Conservation, 25 Moore Avenue, Mount Kisco, NY 10549; 914–864–7070.

Bike repair/rentals: Bicycle World, 7 East Main Street, Mount Kisco, NY 10549-2203; 914–666–4044; fax 914–666–4049; IMARCOS@ ALTAVISTA.COM. The New Yorktown Cycling Center, 1899 Commerce Street, Yorktown Heights, NY 10598-4409; 914–245–5504; fax 914–245–5263; tom@yorktowncycle.com; www.yorktowncycle.com.

T his trail features a number of innovative etched-metal signs placed in strategic areas that point out interesting historical features and anecdotes.

After the Civil War, the nation saw a boom in the planning and construction of railroads. Financiers in New York City saw the Saw Mill River Valley and the counties of Westchester and Putnam as having great passenger and freight potential. There was even a fairly big iron-ore mine near Brewster, New York, run by the Tilly Foster Iron Mine Company. To provide service to the area, the New York & Boston Railroad Company was formed in 1869. The railroad surveyed and

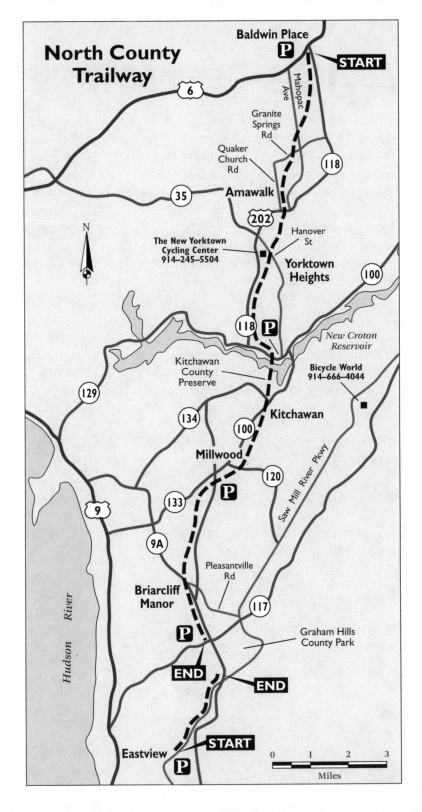

North County Trailway

Baldwin Place P

START

Mahopac Ave

6

Granite Springs Rd

Quaker Church Rd

118

35 **Amawalk**

202

N

Hanover St

The New Yorktown Cycling Center 914–245–5504

Yorktown Heights

100

118 P

New Croton Reservoir

Kitchawan County Preserve

Bicycle World 914–666–4044

129

134 100 **Kitchawan**

Millwood

9 133 P 120

Saw Mill River Pkwy

9A

Pleasantville Rd

Briarcliff Manor

117

P Graham Hills County Park

END **END**

Hudson River

Eastview **START**
P

0 1 2 3

Miles

laid out the grade, but politics and underfinancing conspired to doom the project; the company ended up bankrupt.

A more modest enterprise was formed in the wake of the Panic of 1873. The new New York City & Northern finished the job in 1881. One of the last impediments to completion was the towering trestle that spanned the valley at Eastview. This spindly structure rose 80 feet above the valley floor; it was taken out of service in 1883 when a loop around it was finished. No sign of this structure is visible today.

The iron mines near the line's northern end—Tilly Foster and Mahopac—were closed following cave-ins in 1893. It was said that in one case, the miners knew that a collapse was imminent because they saw rats running out of the mine. The men wisely followed their lead; not a life was lost that time.

After one last financial reorganization as the New York & Putnam Railroad, the line was taken over by the New York Central (NYC) in 1894. It was commonly known as the Putnam Division of the New York Central Systems and affectionately known to the locals as "the Put."

In purchasing this line, the NYC wanted to make sure that the road did not fall into competing hands, especially those of the hated New Haven Railroad. The company succeeded in that regard, but the new acquisition sat between two existing NYC routes that were strong and viable. The first was the Harlem Division, which ran out of the city, following the Harlem River Valley north to Millerton, and eventually Chatham, where it connected with the Boston & Albany Division. The second was the Hudson Division, which ran on the east bank of the Hudson River. Both lines are still in operation today. The Harlem is now known as Metro-North Harlem Division and is in service as far as Wassaic, New York. North of this community it has been converted into the Harlem Valley Rail Trail (see Trail 11). The Hudson Division is now known as Metro-North Hudson Division and still offers daily commuter and Amtrack service all the way to the Albany area.

In 1929 the New York Central ran the first diesel-powered passenger train in the country on the Put. Shortly afterward, it tried out a diesel-powered freight train; this was less successful, because the heavy engine tore up a section of rail. The death knell of steam power had been sounded, however, and the line was fully dieselized as quickly as technically possible. By 1951 steam was no longer seen on the Putnam Division.

The line experienced a decline in passenger ridership with the changing commuting patterns caused by highway construction. The last commuter run took place in 1958. By this time the line's freight business consisted mostly of just a local switcher to service the small shippers. Still, one important through-train kept things interesting: "High and wide" (extra-sized) cargoes heading to New York City came by way of the Put. This was because of the tunnels and other clearance-restrict-

A bicyclist on one of the more rural segments of the North County Trailway.

ing objects found on the sister routes. Even this advantage ended with the single-tracking of the West Shore Division of the New York Central in the early 1960s, which allowed that line to carry larger loads.

This shut the door on the Put's chances for survival as a viable through-route. The stretch from Eastview to Mahopac was abandoned in 1962, and the section from Mahopac to Carmel was abandoned in 1969. With the arrival of Conrail in 1976, a study concluded that the line should be cut back to Chauncey.

Aside from the signage, one other thing that makes this rail-trail unique is the quaint, almost doll-house-like stations that still sit along the right-of-way. At the height of its operations, the Put had twenty-two passenger stations. Most had a residential flavor to reflect the surrounding communities. In southern Westchester they were primarily constructed of stone; those to the north were made of wood.

One of the more interesting stations is at Briarcliff Manor, located just west of the trail on the north side of Pleasant Street. This Tudor-style station was originally a lodge built by Walter Law. In 1909 he donated it to the town to be used as a passenger station. In 1910 the original station was moved by flatcar 3.5 miles up the line to Millwood, where today it serves as the town library. The entire neighborhood here still has a turn-of-the-twentieth-century feel to it.

* *

MILE BY MILE

South Section

0.0 mile: This peaceful section ends only 0.5 mile from the current southern terminus of the North County Trailway. Because of its isolation, there won't be a lot of folks around; keep your eyes open for bluebirds and other interesting things. Begin by heading steeply uphill to get to the right-of-way, then continue north on the trail. (In the future the trail will be built out to the south, connecting directly with the South County Trailway; see Trail 20.)

The first thing you'll notice on the trail is a fairly lengthy section of track. This isn't actually sitting on ties, but merely on the ground; it's the section of rail that was once installed on the bridge over the parkway. When the county rebuilt the bridge for trail use, it removed the rail.

You can cross the bridge, by the way. On the other side, a path runs down to Saw Mill River Road and the neighborhoods there.

0.14 mile: Note the 1930s-era New York Central concrete cribbing retaining wall on the west side of the trail. It rises up about 35 feet above the right-of-way.

0.28 mile: Pass into a fairly big cut. It stands about 40 feet up on the west and 20 feet on the east.

1.0–1.4 miles: An uphill grade becomes noticeable as the trail swings a bit to the west side to pass under a set of transmission lines and return to canopied forest. A genuine New York Central concrete mile marker is here: "NYC22." Look for another concrete cribbing retaining wall as well.

1.65 miles: Emergency call box.

2.5 miles: Another emergency call box. The trail continues to turn a bit to the west-northwest.

2.72 miles: Reach the end of the trail. You're about 0.25 mile from the Route 117 trailhead that connects to the northern section. This tantalizingly short section may be open sometime in 2002.

North Section

0.0 mile: Start at the trail's northernmost point in the Baldwin Place neighborhood of Somers.

0.1 mile: Travel on a fill that's 12 to 15 feet high; there's a school off to your right, as well as the Muscoot River. A timber bridge is found here also. The trail is fairly wide and nicely paved in this section.

0.2 mile: A high-pressure gas line is found here, along with a residential neighborhood off to the left. A man-made pond is nearby.

0.4 mile: Travel in a cut about 15 feet high.

0.6 mile: A series of telegraph poles is evident now. These have two cross arms and are extremely wide, with about twelve spots for insulators. No glass insulators are intact in this area.

0.8 mile: Pass over a stone culvert that's part of the fill.

1.0 mile: Another culvert with a stream passing through.

1.1 miles: An overlook on your right allows you to pull off and view the wooded valley.

1.2 miles: Stone walls on both sides mark what was once a farmer's field. Remnants of railroad ties are visible here also.

1.4 miles: This interesting cut is about 15 feet high on either side. You'll come out onto a big (25 to 40 feet) cinder fill; it's about 0.2 mile long and has a split-rail wooden fence to complement the trail.

1.8 miles: Agricultural grade crossing. There are some nice meadows.

2.2 miles: Grade crossing of Mahopac Avenue, which basically parallels most of the northern reaches of this rail-trail.

2.3 miles: Grade crossing of Granite Springs Road. This was the site of the old depot at Granite Springs, the first stop after Baldwin Place. The hamlet was once known as West Somers. A hotel and two stores were built near the depot, and the police station was moved to be near the "action." A bottling plant was the main employer. Located north of the depot area, the Granite Springs Water Company's complex is now used by the Chase Manhattan Bank as a records storage facility.

2.6 miles: Apple orchards in this area are owned by the Stuart family. In business for six generations, they're a local landmark.

4.5 miles: Grade crossing of Quaker Church Road and Route 202/35/118. *Note: A blind reverse curve on the highway makes for a dangerous crossing. Be careful!*

This was also the site of the Amawalk Station. The usual ancillary businesses sprang up nearby: a general store, coalyard, carriage maker, blacksmith, and small milk bottling plant. The convenient railroad connection here meant that Amawalk Mountain was host to some of the county's earliest residential developments.

On Quaker Church Road, a Mr. Hallock built a water-powered mill complex that was a big local employer for about 115 years starting in the late 1780s. His wife was the local postmistress. It then became Amawalk Nursery, the largest grower of Christmas trees in the county.

4.7 miles: A pressure-treated timber bridge crosses over Hallocks Mill Stream. The bridge abutments are of concrete. It looks as if this area was double-tracked at one time, no doubt to provide a runaround past the nearby Amawalk Station.

5.5 miles: A genuine New York Central concrete mile marker reads "NY37": 37 miles to New York City. A telltale signal is found here also. This device was used to warn trainmen who might have been on top of the cars to duck, because a low-clearance area lies ahead. It's of typical construction; hanging wires are the distinctive feature.

5.6 miles: Grade crossing at Hanover Street. A Rexall drug store is found here, and a condo development sits pretty much adjacent to the railroad right-of-way in the old Yorktown Heights yard.

Yorktown Heights was known as the hamlet of Underhill through most of the nineteenth century, but the center of the activity was in the town of Crompond, 3.5 miles to the northwest. With the coming of the railroad in 1881, the activity center shifted to Yorktown Heights Station. Farmers began shipping produce to New York City, and the residents of New York City used the railroad to get to vacation destinations in Westchester County. Today you'll find myriad services and restaurants, as well as an interesting park dedicated to the railroad's coming into Yorktown Heights. The highlight here is the newly restored railroad station.

6.6 miles: Cross under Old County Way by way of a newly built concrete box culvert/tunnel under the road. You're heading downhill here as well getting closer to the reservoir.

7.0 miles: Cross under Revere Drive by way of a similar tunnel.

8.4 miles: Grade crossing at Birdsall Drive.

9.0 miles: Grade crossing at Route 118, where you'll also find a convenient and well-used trailhead parking area.

9.1 miles: Here is one of the major highlights of the trail: a spectacular bridge over the New Croton Reservoir. Built with concrete arches on the approaches at each end and of the through-truss variety, this twin-span bridge is simply a magnet for bird-watchers, strollers, bikers, and other outdoor enthusiasts. This segment was opened in 1999 after being "the missing link" for many years.

9.2 miles: A fill about 50 feet tall has caused the canopy of vegetation to close in on you.

9.4 miles: In this area are several huge concrete blocks measuring 30 feet by 30 feet. These must have been the footings for a signal tower or signal bridge in this area. Look also for the ancient ties that are still here under the canopy of trees.

9.5 miles: Power lines are the reason the landscape has opened up around here. A small stream may be flowing in the right-of-way.

9.7 miles: Head into a cut that's about 85 feet high.

10.0 miles: The bench here was donated by Club Fit, a local health club. Right after comes a modern tunnel/culvert under NY Route 134. Look for the original granite abutments; they're still in place to support the bridge, which was taken out a few years ago. The New Croton Reservoir is visible now. Kitchawan Station was located here at one time.

10.2 miles: Travel into the Kitchawan County Preserve, still going downhill. It's mountainous up to the west and slopes downhill 50 to 60 feet to the east.

10.6 miles: A typical New York Central 70-foot through-girder bridge over Route 100.

11.0 miles: Head into a cut, still going downhill.

11.1 miles: Look for the NYC-style telephone box on your right as you continue downhill.

This outstanding truss bridge at New Croton Reservoir is a highlight of the North County Trailway.

11.3 miles: You're generally in the woods now. Look for the man-made swimming area as you travel on a 25-foot fill.

11.9 miles: Approach Millwood Station. This semirestored, genuine "Old Put" station is gaily painted bright red and sits among some housing of the same era to give a definite railroad village feel to the area. Millwood Supply Company, just east of the trail, used to be a rail-served customer, with freight doors on the trail. Look in the grass next to the building and you'll see a section of eighty-pound rail. Just before the station area comes NY Route 120, and just before that—on the north side of the road—is an old oil transloading area. This company is now out of business, and the area has been converted to light industrial/commercial uses. A bench is provided to allow for shaded viewing of the parade of trail users passing by.

12.2 miles: Another small parking area is here for the use of trail patrons.

12.4 miles: A paved bridge is here with pressure-treated railings. The original railroad abutments were used, but everything else is of new construction. Just ahead is a path to Station Road (Route 133), which has an A&P food store if you need something to drink. A drugstore and pizza restaurant are other choices.

12.7 miles: Reach a junction for the Taconic State Parkway, which will pass overhead momentarily. Shortly after this the state Department of Public Works yard will appear on your left. The trail diverges again from the road to travel alone on the Putnam Division right-of-way.

13.5 miles: Pass Echo Lake on your left.

13.6 miles: There's a jog in the path here as you crest the hill. Nearby appears the footing and slab for a station; then you're back out on the road again.

13.7 miles: Head onto NY Route 100—but you're protected by a guardrail. You're on the east side of the highway.

14.2 miles: A short concrete bridge with pressure-treated guardrails crosses the Pocantico.

14.3 miles: Make a grade crossing of Old Chappaqua Road, which leads to Route 100 off to the west. A small fill here is close to a marsh on the west side of the trail.

14.7 miles: The trail now diverges from the road and gets on the right-of-way of the railroad.

15.2 miles: The Pocantico River is crossed once again.

15.3 miles: Pleasantville Road passes overhead.

15.6 miles: Pass over the meandering Pocantico River. You'll also cross here to the east side of the highway by way of a clearly marked crosswalk. A 10- to 12-foot-wide shoulder bikeway is now your path.

15.7 miles: This access road will take you to a park complex within the Briarcliff College complex. The restored Briarcliff Manor Passenger Station is located here.

The freight doors on the side of the Millwood Supply Company building are a carry-over from the company's days as a rail customer.

15.8 miles: The bridge over the highway and trail is of railroad-era heritage.

15.9 miles: You're out of the woods now and adjacent to NY Route 9A/100, where you share the road—but the bikeway is separated by a guardrail and plenty wide.

16.1 miles: Pass through some wetlands fed by the Pocantico River on a 6-foot fill above it all.

16.6 miles: Reach an access point to a small neighborhood road on the west as you come down to the same level as the highway.

16.9 miles: Travel on a small fill as you enter the woods along the Briarcliff-Peekskill Parkway, also known as Route 9A/100.

17.1 miles: Head uphill, around a bend, and up to the level of Route 117, where you'll find trailhead parking and the end of the trail. Though the trail ends here as of this writing, there are plans to continue it southward to the Eastview area and eventually to Elmsford and other points beyond.

Endpoints: From New Croton Reservoir Dam in Cortlandt, New York, to Van Cortlandt Park Golf Course in the Bronx.

Location: Westchester County.

Length: 26.30 miles.

Surface: Dirt, grass, cinder, and gravel.

Uses: All nonmotorized uses.

To get there: The northern trailhead is at the dam at New Croton Reservoir. This is best accessed from NY Route 129, which runs northeast to southwest between U.S. Route 9 and the Taconic Parkway; it's just northeast of the small community of Croton-on-Hudson.

Contact: Brian Goodman, Old Croton Trail State Park, 15 Walnut Street, Dobbs Ferry, NY 10522; 914–693–5259.

Accommodations: Alexander Hamilton House, 49 Van Wyck Street, Croton-on-Hudson, NY 10520; 914–271–6737; fax 914–271–3927; alexhous@bestweb.net; www.alexanderhamiltonhouse.com.

Bike repair/rentals: E/T Cycle Center, 75 South Riverside Avenue, Croton-on-Hudson, NY 10520-2648; 914–271–6661; fax 914–271–6803; etcycle@verizon.net; www.etcyclecenter.com. Tarrytown Cycles, 11 North Broadway, Tarrytown, NY 10591-3201; 914–631–1850; fax 914–631–1853; bikemaniac@aol.com.

O f course many trails (and not just rail-trails) provide a connection between communities. But when you come upon a trail that has been in the ground for more than 150 years of continuous use—well, that's something special. And this trail discreetly passes through all sorts of neighborhoods, is scenic as well as historic, and has plenty of services nearby. It's definitely a trail worth visiting.

In the late 1820s New York City's population growth was outstripping its ability to supply water for residents and industry. Water for sanitation and fire-fighting apparatus was critically needed. In response to these needs, the government embarked on a project to build an aqueduct—a tunnel from the reservoirs at the northern end of Westchester County straight to the heart of the city.

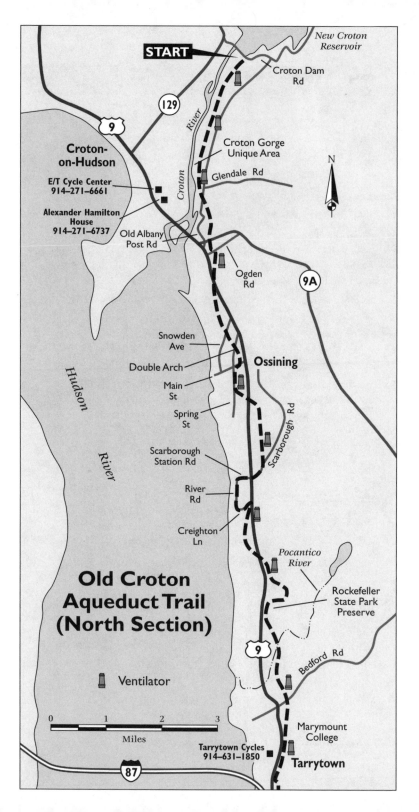

START

New Croton
Reservoir

Croton Dam
Rd

129

9

Croton-
on-Hudson

Croton Gorge
Unique Area

E/T Cycle Center
914–271–6661

Glendale Rd

Alexander Hamilton
House
914–271–6737

Old Albany
Post Rd

Ogden
Rd

9A

N

Snowden
Ave

Double Arch

Ossining

Main
St

Spring
St

Scarborough
Station Rd

Scarborough Rd

River
Rd

Creighton
Ln

*Pocantico
River*

**Old Croton
Aqueduct Trail
(North Section)**

Rockefeller
State Park
Preserve

9

Bedford Rd

🏛 Ventilator

0   1   2   3
Miles

Marymount
College

Tarrytown Cycles
914–631–1850

Tarrytown

87

Hudson

River

Croton

River

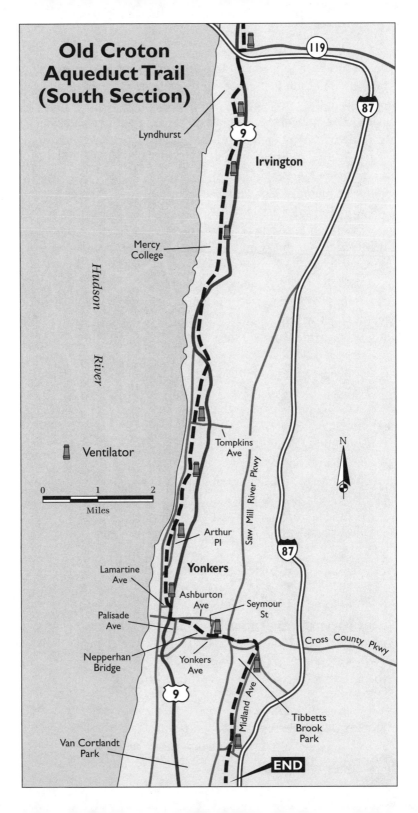

The tunnel was a wonder of engineering. Built with an elliptical shape (8.5 feet tall by 7.5 feet wide), this brick-lined stone tunnel was built in the late 1830s by strong-backed Irish immigrants. The design and engineering were largely done by Major David Douglass, a U.S. Army engineer. Toward the end of the project, he was succeeded by John Jervis, who had extensive experience in both canal and railroad engineering.

One of the most amazing facts about this aqueduct is that it was built to maintain a grade of 13 inches of descent for its entire 41 miles, to the end in the heart of New York City. This feat was accomplished without dynamite or power equipment—only rudimentary surveying equipment and lots of picks and shovels.

In 1968 New York State purchased from the city of New York the land, right-of-way, and accoutrements that made up the sections of the aqueduct within Westchester County. What a forward-thinking and visionary idea—and certainly one ahead of its time.

This trail has a set of twenty-one mile markers similar to the mile marker obelisks found on dead railroad corridors. Built of stone and standing usually about 10 feet tall, they provided a way for air to get into the aqueduct, ensuring that the water remained fresh and also keeping the pressure in the aqueduct in check. Some are numbered, but most are not. They were generally built about a mile apart.

And finally, one of the best features of this trail is that you are never far from civilization. For most of the way, you merely have to head west away from the trail and toward the Hudson River to find a series of villages that have all the services you could hope for. And the Metro-North commuter train parallels the trail.

Note: Parts of this trail feature on-road connections that are not for the faint of heart. Busy roads, jogs that don't seem to make sense, and the absence of a clearly marked pathway in some areas combine to make this trail a relatively poor choice for families. The 22 miles from the dam to Lamartine Avenue in Yonkers are part of the Hudson River Greenway. South of there the route is extremely congested, with numerous crossings where cars aren't looking for bikes or pedestrians. The route is also difficult to follow.

0.0 mile: At the very beginning of the trail, head south down the white gravel road away from the dam and into the forest.

0.49 mile: Now out of the forest, you come to a beautiful over-look of the dam. The first of the many ventilators is found near here as well. They seem to be reminiscent of a rook on a chessboard.

0.9 mile: This cut seems very narrow; it's for the underground aqueduct, whose right-of-way is actually much narrower than a rail-road would need.

1.03 miles: Grade crossing at Quaker Bridge Road.

1.34 miles: Ventilator tower 2.

1.78 miles: Croton Gorge Unique Area.

2.39 miles: Cross Glendale Road as you pass the third ventilator tower.

2.41 miles: This is a bit tricky. The GE facility here at the grade crossing at Fowler Avenue forces you to make a detour. Take a right at Fowler Avenue and then a left onto Old Albany Post Road. Go

The Old Croton Aqueduct Trail starts at the picturesque reservoir dam.

across NY Route 9A then left onto Ogden Road, which is uphill. Then turn right again onto the trail.

3.46 miles: Reach the fourth ventilator tower. You're also passing a condo complex on your right. Note the informal connector the residents have cut into the trail.

3.65 miles: You are now making a grade crossing of Route 9, otherwise known as North Highland Avenue.

4.31 miles: Come to the first of the drain weirs—masonry structures built to regulate the flow of water through the tunnel. They could even shut off the water entirely, which was sometimes needed for maintenance purposes.

4.37 miles: Grade crossing at Snowden Avenue.

4.54 miles: You're now going past a grade crossing at North Mountain and Matilda Streets; the trail crosses right between both streets. It becomes paved as you head through a landscaped park here. It's a steep uphill; you might want to walk.

4.67 miles: Reach the top of the hill. The park's steep stairs descend down on the other side; just before you cross the river, you'll see another drain weir at Ann Street. (If you call for an appointment, you can get a tour and descend into the tunnel below; 914–693–5259). You'll come to the famed double-arched bridge area of Ossining as you approach the downtown area. The double arch is actually formed by the aqueduct bridge spanning another bridge, which carries the street called Broadway. Both spans cross the Sing Sing Kill gorge. This double bridge is considered to be the highlight of this trail's engineering; it was a marvel when built in 1839.

4.73 miles: It's worth a little detour here. After the bridge take a right and head down the short path to the overlook underneath the bridge.

5.0 miles: Continuing south, you now come to Main Street, Ossining. The famed Crescent and Barlow Block was the premier place to do business in this town for many years.

5.5 miles: Main Street becomes Spring Street. Follow this on-street route for about four blocks, and then take a left into the park at the corner of Everett Avenue. You'll find the fifth ventilator here. This section gets a little bit confusing as you go through the urban parks; just remember to head basically southwest through the second park. If you follow the path, it meanders around the ball field and, at the far side, kind of veers to the right to get to Route 9. Cross Route 9; just to the right of the apartment complex, directly across the street, you'll find a little path through the woods to a parking lot. At the far side of the lot, pick up the formal trail again.

6.6 miles: Here you'll find the sixth ventilator; right after that, the trail is on a fill.

6.8 miles: Scarborough Road crossing. Here is another diversion. Turn right onto Scarborough Road; shortly ahead you'll come to the intersection with Route 9. Turn right here and then make a quick left onto Scarborough Station Road. Follow this for two blocks and, at the T intersection, turn left onto River Road. Follow this for one block and turn left onto Creighton Lane. This will curve gently to the right. At 2nd Street turn sharply left onto River Road, which has curved around to meet you. At the next intersection (Route 9 again), turn right and look closely for the trail; it's on your right and heading south-southwest. This diversion is mostly intended to avoid the Sleepy Hollow Country Club.

8.0 miles: Seventh ventilator tower.

8.37 miles: Archville Bridge. A stone tablet says the Archville Bridge was constructed in 1998 by the DOT and the Rockefeller family. This restored the crossing for the first time in seventy-four years. The first bridge, an arch bridge built in 1839, was removed in 1924 to build the road.

9.01 miles: The eighth ventilator is here. Shortly ahead, the trail diverts to the right along the road that leads into the Rockefeller State Park Preserve.

9.47 miles: Here's a light-duty bridge, but it's safe enough for cars. As soon as you cross over, take a right; do not bring bikes into the Rockefeller State Park Preserve. There is a 20-mile hiking-only trail system within this special place donated to the state by the Rockefeller family.

10.15 miles: This is the tallest fill yet, at 90 feet. Reach a drain weir, then cross over the Pocantico River.

11.2 miles: Ninth ventilator tower.

11.32 miles: Here's another slight diversion. Across Bedford Road is the Sleepy Hollow High School. Follow the driveway into the campus. When you come to the school building, take a left and continue around the school to your right as far as you can go. Go down the staircase to reach the courtyard. Here the trail begins again, heading west for a short distance before turning south.

12.3 miles: Tenth ventilator tower. Marymount College is two blocks to the east, along with a direct connection to the North County Trailway.

12.5 miles: Continue along Broadway (Route 9); lots of stores and services are available in Tarrytown. In about three or four blocks, take a left onto Leroy Avenue. In less than 50 yards, you'll see a parking lot on your right. Just after that is the trail heading south again.

13.0 miles: Eleventh ventilator tower.

13.09 miles: Here's the grade crossing of NY Route 119—a busy road on the approach to the Tappan Zee Bridge. Take a right here and head back onto Route 9 for approximately 0.5 mile.

13.61 miles: You're now going past the Food Technical Center on South Broadway. At the next light, cross to the west side of the road.

The Old Croton Aqueduct Trail is unique in that it has been here since the early 1800s—before many of the neighborhoods that have grown up around it.

13.69 miles: There's a break in the stone wall along the road. The trail begins to become usable once again.

13.81 miles: You're now traversing the Lyndhurst property of the National Trust for Historic Preservation.

14.05 miles: Twelfth ventilator tower.

15.1 miles: Main Street, Irvington. More shops and schools can be seen; you'll then go past the thirteenth ventilator.

15.28 miles: Cross a huge fill—probably 100 feet tall—that spans a small stream known as Wickers Creek. Indian artifacts dating back 5,000 years have been found there.

16.1 miles: Pass by the fourteenth ventilator. Mercy College is here as well. Numerous college students use the trail for getting to school and around town.

17.0 miles: Here is the park office headquarters—a doublewide trailer (at least at the time of this writing). The "Overseers" house, the brick Italianate on Walnut Street across the way, is being rehabbed into a visitor area as well as offices for the aqueduct trail managers. This is the last building standing that housed aqueduct field personnel. It closed the day the water stopped flowing to New York City in 1955.

18.34 miles: Cross Route 9 and another short street next to it; the trail continues right across the street. Signage here notes this as the Old Croton Aqueduct Trailway State Park.

19.17 miles: Grade crossing at Tompkins Avenue past the fifteenth ventilator tower. (It's numbered 18.)

20.2 miles: The sixteenth ventilator is at Odell Avenue, about two blocks from the Greystone Station on the Metro-North line.

21.1 miles: The seventeenth ventilator tower is adjacent to Arthur Place.

21.3 miles: You're now in densely urban Yonkers, about two blocks south of Glenwood Station; you'll see the eighteenth ventilator tower. You may want to head back north from here because the route gets tricky. Take a left onto Lamartine Avenue and after three blocks take a right onto Route 9, Broadway. Go about two blocks and turn left uphill at Ashburton Avenue. In one block, at the intersection with Palisade Avenue, ease right onto the trail. It's on a fill as it approaches the Nepperhan Avenue Bridge, which carries the aqueduct over Nepperhan Avenue.

22.4 miles: Here's the nineteenth ventilator at the crossing at Seymour Street. You're back on the street—this time Yonkers Avenue—and continuing to head east.

22.5 miles: Cross over the Saw Mill River Parkway. This area is extremely busy, with large numbers of speeding cars entering and exiting the highway. *Be careful: Drivers are not generally on the lookout for pedestrians or bicyclists.*

22.91 miles: The railroad bridge overhead carries the old Putnam Division of the New York Central Railroad. This entire line is dormant, but it's open as a trail from the north side of Yonkers essentially all the way to the Putnam County border. It will be a few years longer before this segment is complete. To learn more about other segments of this line that are open, see the North County Trailway (Chapter 12) and the South County Trailway (Chapter 20).

23.2 miles: Another tricky area. On the approach to the Cross County Parkway, Yonkers Avenue starts to curve to the south and then under the parkway.

23.5 miles: Just on the other side of the highway overpass you'll see both a weir and the twentieth ventilator tower. These mark the boundary of the off-road path once again. You're within Tibbetts Brook Park, with Midland Avenue on your left for company.

24.6 miles: Reach the twenty-first and last of the ventilator towers at the southern end of Tibbetts Brook Park.

25.1 miles: The last weir is found here. You're now in the confines of Van Cortlandt Park and the borough of the Bronx within the city of New York. Shortly into this area, you'll travel another section on the sidewalk adjacent to a limited-access highway and then descend a flight of stairs to the park itself.

26.3 miles: Follow the path that leads to the golf cart path. You're now at the golf course within the park and at the management building.

Endpoints: Ontario Street in downtown Canandaigua to Route 96 in Phelps.

Location: Ontario County.

Length: 19 miles (23.1 miles when complete).

Surface: Grass, cinder, gravel.

Uses: All nonmotorized uses.

To get there: The trail begins in downtown Canandaigua on the north side at 200 Ontario Street between NY Route 332 (Main Street) and East Street. The trailhead has a kiosk, gravel parking lot, and split-rail fence.

Contact: Ontario Pathways, P.O. Box 996, Canandaigua, NY 14424; 716–394–7968; www.ontariopathways.org.

Accommodations: Sutherland House Bed & Breakfast, 3179 State Route 21 S, Canandaigua, NY 14424; 585–396–0375; fax 585–396–9281; goodnite@frontiernet.net; www.sutherlandhouse.com.

The east-to-west oriented segment of this rail-trail—from Canandaigua-to-Stanley—was originally constructed in 1851. Hard times struck soon after; like many early, independently built shortlines, it was plagued by cost overruns, low revenues, and bankruptcy. The federal government stepped in in 1862, when President Abe Lincoln authorized the expenditure of $50,000 to revive the line so men and supplies could be moved southward. The line was primarily built to carry coal to the lake and make connections with the freighters based at the Sodus Point Coal facility. More than 5 million tons of coal was shipped north to the lake every year. By 1913, the Northern Central Railroad became part of the Elmira Branch of the giant Pennsylvania Railroad.

The south-to-north segment—between Stanley and Phelps—was originally known as the Sodus Point & Southern Railroad when it was built in 1873. After the usual round of bankruptcies and mergers, it was eyed by Edward Harriman, father of famed New York governor Averill Harriman. He bought the line in 1881, largely because the family summered at Sodus Point on Lake Ontario and loved the area. However, Mr. Harriman, a shrewd businessman, sold it just two years later to a new company, the Northern Central Railroad, for twice what he had paid for it.

Much of the southbound traffic carried local agricultural products, and these trains largely ended up in Newark, New York, where many canneries were located. Another local shipper was C. R. Zornow Company, in Seneca Castle, which shipped twenty cars a day of various grains.

The community of Stanley, where the two components of the Ontario Pathways project will eventually join, was a major interchange point for trains and had among its residents more than 200 railroad employees. The railroad declined, however; the last passenger train ran in 1935. The line was converted from steam to diesel locomotives in 1957, and Stanley's days as a rail hub were virtually gone.

The Stanley-to-Phelps segment was a major interchange for three different rail lines: the Northern Central (encompassing the Stanley–Canandaigua branch), the Lehigh Valley (Geneva–Naples), and the Sodus Point & Southern, which ran 34 miles from Stanley to Sodus. Much of the Pennsylvania coal being shipped to the Great Lakes and then on to Canada traveled this route.

Passengers also traveled to Sodus Point beach for a swim or a shopping trip to Penn Yan, Geneva, or Canandaigua. The long-distance traveler could board a Pullman berth at 9:00 P.M. from Stanley and arrive well rested in Washington, D.C., at 7:00 A.M.

Ontario Pathways (OP) purchased two line segments within Ontario County from the Penn Central Corporation in May 1994 for $100,000. (Penn Central by then was essentially a real estate company, peddling off the unwanted segments that did not go into Conrail.)

Ontario Pathways, Inc., was formed at that time as a nonprofit corporation to build the trail, manage it, and make sure it became a part of the community. OP is a unique organization. Even with well over 1,000 rail-trails open around the country these days, only a small handful are owned by private entities like OP; most are owned by government agencies of some sort. This sort of nongovernment-owned trail is so unusual that the Rails-to-Trails Conservancy loaned

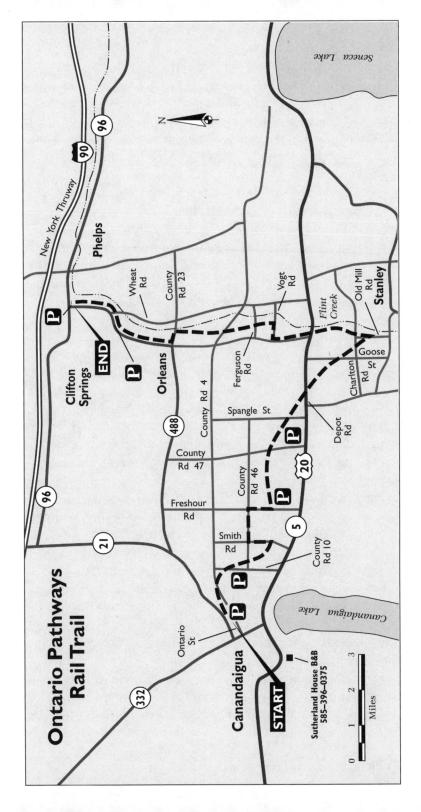

the money needed to seal the deal and give OP some working capital to start up operations. This land conservancy project was the first that RTC took on and thus it was the one that gave the *conservancy* part of its name special meaning. Thus OP and RTC have been partners and growing together. For more information on this conservancy program within RTC, please contact the Florida RTC office at 850–942–2379.

The Herculean task of owning and managing a linear corridor that passes through eight communities is one that calls out the can-do spirit of small-town America. Even the local community college is involved: The recreational construction classes of Dr. Martin Dodge were responsible for the design, engineering, and actual construction of one of the bridges on the trail system. A local engineer, Gary DelDuca, donated hundreds of hours designing other bridges and organizing the rehab projects. Other sections have been cleared and maintained by various scouting organizations, including six Eagle Scout projects. Kudos to everyone involved.

Ontario Pathways is very much a community-based, family organization with a wide range of monthly outdoor activities geared toward learning about the flora and fauna found along the trail. Each month a different theme is highlighted, and each month more and more folks are learning about the project, and their neighborhoods.

The trail is approximately 10 feet wide, with a worn single track of cinders running between grass sides. Eighty percent was open as of this writing; call before coming to check on newly opened sections.

For the most part the trail is protected on both sides by trees, shrubs, and, in some places, dense undergrowth; you'll pass through an occasional woodlot as well. There's a lovely view from the trestle crossing over Canandaigua Outlet and a spectacular view of Flint Creek from a trestle nearly 40 feet high and 300 feet across just north of Stanley. From Stanley north to Phelps, the scenery becomes more interesting and varied. Much of this branch of the trail is wooded and follows the approximate route of Flint Creek northward. In several sections you are high above the creek, watching it unwind below you. You'll pass high shale cliffs, an old wooded railroad water tower in Orleans, and a small waterfall as you continue toward Phelps. There are several bridges or trestles on both branches of the trail.

MILE BY MILE

0.0 mile: Starting out at the downtown Canandaigua trailhead, you'll notice that the track next to the trail is still active. The Finger Lakes Railroad currently operates here on a triweekly basis to serve one customer to the south. This dual-use corridor is fairly unusual—there are only about seventy in the country.

0.7 mile: The trail now begins to curve away from the active line and head more toward the east.

1.0 mile: Grade crossing at County Route 4. You might have to walk your bike down the hill to the highway and back up on the other side. The old railroad bridge through here was taken down in the 1970s to facilitate trucks.

1.05 miles: Cross over the outlet of Canandaigua Lake by way of a nicely redone bridge. Ontario Pathways creatively built an ornate metal gate on the approach to the bridge. This gate covers half of the opening, preventing unauthorized motorized vehicles from going onto the bridge. It's much nicer looking than many others you'll see on a trail.

1.2 miles: You're passing by the Ontario County Fairgrounds. This is also a good place to access the trail, with ample parking. Most of the adjacent landscape is farmland, meadows, and small orchards, with apple trees flowering in the spring.

1.4 miles: Grade crossing of County Route 10.

2.11 miles: Cross over a small stream.

2.15 miles: Grade crossing of County Route 46.

3.14 miles: Grade crossing at Smith Road. Turn left (north) onto this low-volume road for 0.72 mile to avoid a short, privately owned section.

3.86 miles: At the intersection of Smith Road and County Route 46, turn right (east) and travel 1 mile to Freshour Road.

4.86 miles: Turn right (south) onto Freshour and continue .8 mile where you'll see the trail once again.

5.65 miles: The trail continues to the east.

7.15 miles: Grade crossing at County Route 47 in the old hamlet of Ennerdale. The trail begins a gentle curve to the southeast here.

8.26 miles: Grade crossing at Spangle Street.

8.85 miles: Coming in from the south is Depot Road.

9.13 miles: Cross over the small stream known as Rocky Run and then over busy Route 5/20 by way of a through-girder bridge.

10.6 miles: Cross over Goose Street.

11.1 miles: Cross at Charlton Road.

11.41 miles: Cross over Flint Creek by way of the signature bridge of the Ontario Pathways. This structure is 300 feet long and more than 40 feet high above the stream below. It was redecked entirely by volunteers.

11.81 miles: Grade crossing at Old Mill Road. The trail in the stretch ahead is not open as of this writing; you must turn left and head north on this low-volume road for 3 miles. The trail may be open by the time you read this.

12.26 miles: Intersection with Charlton Road. Go straight and continue north.

13.75 miles: Intersection with Route 5/20. Use caution and continue north.

14.82 miles: Intersection with Vogt Road. Turn right here and head east.

15.22 miles: Turn left and head north on the trail again.

15.84 miles: Grade crossing at Ferguson Road. Memorable vistas of the adjacent farms are seen here.

16.62 miles: Grade crossing of County Route 4. Just before the highway you'll see that C. R. Zornow Company, a big grain agricultural processing plant, has adopted this section of the trail. This is an intact, circa-1920s rail-served grain facility. Such facilities once dotted rural America but are largely gone today. This one remains prosperous, however. The trail goes right through the facility; please stay on the driveway, and don't wander around the plant. This facility is about 0.3 mile long.

17.46 miles: A large fill here (more than 75 feet tall) crosses over a small stream. A view of an impressive cut-stone arch bridge awaits if you descend to the stream.

17.8 miles: A petroleum pipeline owned by the Buckeye Pipeline Company is crossed here. All the foliage has been trimmed back to accommodate an aerial view of the pipeline corridor.

Most trails have barriers of some sort to prevent access by unauthorized vehicles. The OP's barriers are designed to be aesthetically pleasing as well as functional.

18.1 miles: A large gully on the west side of the trail leads 70 feet down to Flint Creek, which will follow you for much of the way.

18.29 miles: Grade crossing of County Road.

18.31 miles: You are now looking at virtually the only steam-locomotive-era, 40,000-gallon water tank on a rail-trail in New York; it's listed on the National Historic Register. Parts of this structure have been restored, and more reconstruction is in the works. This is the village of Orleans. In addition to the water tower, some abandoned commercial buildings are waiting to be redeveloped for trail users.

Here's a rarity—a genuine, 40,000-gallon water tower. Towers like this one were originally located every 20 miles to service steam locomotives, but as diesels (which don't need a lot of water) took over in the 1950s, only a handful of old towers escaped the wrecker's ball.

 136 RAILS-TO-TRAILS

18.33 miles: Head west off the trail here just north of the water tower and get onto NY Route 488. Follow this north for 2.2 miles. As of this writing, the trail in this section is closed, but plans to open it are in the works.

20.5 miles: Grade crossing of Wheat Road. Head east for 700 feet, then turn north onto the trail once again. This 0.5-mile segment was cleared by Eagle Scout Aaron Gil of Clifton Springs. It is still maintained by his family.

21.1 miles: Here you will see an official OP 1.50 mile marker installed by Ontario Pathways. In addition, a high-pressure natural gas pipeline crosses the trail.

21.21 miles: A series of two-armed telegraph signals is found here, minus insulators.

22.0 miles: A small, 25-foot modern bridge spans a smaller stream here as wetlands appear on the west side of the trail.

22.3 miles: A through-girder bridge here spans the meandering river, with a three-step waterfall just east of it—very impressive and serene.

22.5 miles: The very large granite and concrete abutments here guard what once was where the double-track Lehigh Valley mainline crossed both the river and the Pennsy line/OP Trail. This is one of a only a couple of double-track abandonments in New York. It is both impressive and eerie in its own way, carrying a bridge no more, but instead huge electric transmission towers. This area is sort of a study in forgotten industrial infrastructure. The Lehigh Valley right-of-way is badly overgrown and not open to the public.

22.8 miles: Here's a 100-foot, deck-girder bridge crossing Flint Creek. The bridge has its original timbers still in place, but is nicely upgraded with both pressure-treated decking and railings as well as a sign noting that it was restored in 1997 with generous support from the G. W. Lisk Company, Clifton Springs. Look below on the northern end of the bridge and you'll see that in the distant past, a flood scoured the riverbank past the northern abutment. Large amount of riprap have been placed in the river to prevent this from happening again.

23.1 miles: The trail turns grassy and ends at NY Route 96 with a parking lot for a dozen cars and trail kiosk similar to the one in downtown Canandaigua.

Endpoints: Goshen, Monroe.

Location: Orange County.

Length: 10.5 miles.

Surface: Asphalt.

Uses: All nonmotorized uses.

To get there: Take NY Route 17 to exit 124 (Goshen), and follow NY Route 207 for about 1 mile into Goshen. The mileage guide provided by the county markers on the trail and in this book are both based upon placing the Erie Railroad Passenger Station in downtown Goshen at the 0.0-mile mark. This is where you should start. This passenger station has been rehabbed as the village of Goshen Police Department. It is located on West Main Street, which runs parallel to Route 207 but one block to the northwest. When coming into Goshen and passing the Buick dealership on your right, look for Railroad Street on your left. Take this left; the station and police department are just ahead, and there's plenty of parking in the back. An alternative parking lot can be found by taking South Church Street southeast (right) out of the central square for two blocks and then right onto St. James Place. Parking is ahead as noted by signs.

Contact: Graham Skea, Commissioner, Orange County Department of Parks Recreation & Conservation, 211 Route 416, Montgomery, NY 12549; 845–417–4900; ocgparks@warwick.net; www.ocgovernment1home.htm. Orange Pathways, 182 Greenwich Avenue, Goshen, NY 10924; 845–294–8886.

Accommodations: Caren House Bed & Breakfast, 1371 Orange Turnpike, Monroe, NY 10950; 845–782–0377; fax 845–782–7449; carenbb@warwick.net; www.carenhousebb.com.

Chartered in 1832, the Erie Railroad was one of the earlier railroads in the country. It originated at Piermont on the Hudson River, close to the spot where the present-day Tappan Zee Bridge lands on the west shore. The section to Goshen was finished by late summer 1841, and the segment to Middletown opened two years after that. The goal of the Erie was to reach Dunkirk on Lake Erie.

One of the area's biggest events was the Hambletonian, a harness race. This was held at the Good Time Track in Goshen and was

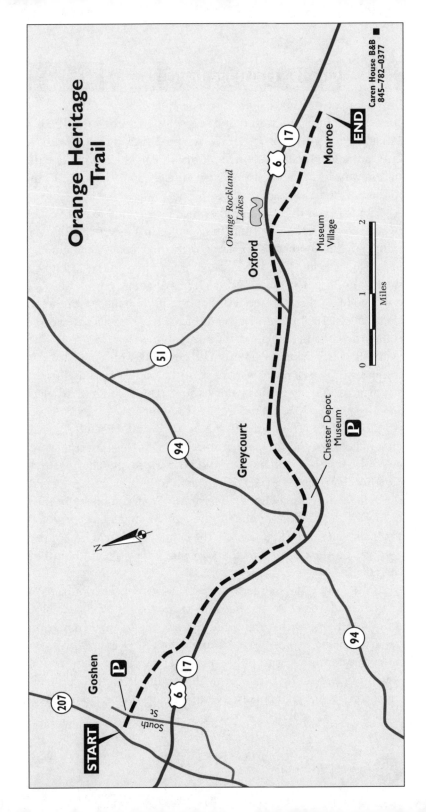

Orange Heritage Trail

N

Goshen
207
START
P
South St
6
17
94
94
Greycourt
Chester Depot Museum
P
51
94
Oxford
Orange Rockland Lakes
Museum Village
6
17
Monroe
END

Caren House B&B
845-782-0377

0 1 2
Miles

one of the country's most prestigious harness track events. The Erie Railroad and the competing Lehigh & New England Railroad brought droves of patrons to Goshen for these equestrian events.

Another unusual train that came through here in the 1920s and 1930s was a "Ski-Train." This traversed the Erie's north-to-south Newburg Branch, which junctioned off this line at Greycourt. The destination was the ski area at Salisbury Mills, New York, about 15 miles to the northeast.

The Erie was built as a broad-gauge line, with 6 feet of space between the rail—standard track has a gauge of 4 feet, 8.5 inches. A reminder of this anomaly is apparent on the trail today: The right-of-way is unusually wide. The broad-gauge track enabled the Erie to carry wider and larger items than its standard-gauge competitors. The downside was that it made it difficult to interchange with the other railroads. In 1880 the entire mainline of the Erie was converted to standard gauge in a single day—a stupendous feat.

In the early days, presidents' and governors' messages were very important news. The newspapers of the country used all sorts of strategems to deliver these stories first. The Erie Railroad back in 1842 helped the *New York Sun* get a scoop on New York governor Seward's message. The competing *New York Herald* used the standard channels to get the message from Albany to New York: It went by courier down the east bank of the Hudson River. The resourceful *Sun,* however, took it to Goshen by courier. From Goshen it sped on the Erie to Piermont, where it boarded an Erie steamboat for the trip to the big city. Planning ahead, the *Sun* editor had a typesetter on the boat who set the story before the boat docked in Manhattan. The *Sun* was on the street with the governor's message an hour before the *Herald.*

In 1960, after the merger with the Delaware, Lackawanna & Western Railroad, the company became known as the Erie-Lackawanna Railroad. It was at this time that the crack passenger name trains (such as Pacific Express, Erie Limited, and Lake Cities Express) were being discontinued, and only commuter service to New York City was provided. By this time even the mainline freight service had moved to the better-engineered Graham Line; the line in the Goshen,

Chester, and Monroe area was downgraded and relegated to local freight service.

In 1983 even the commuter service was moved to the Graham Line. The line through Goshen was abandoned in 1985, with the rails gone by 1986. In 1988 Orange County bought the right-of-way. In April 1990 Orange Pathways, Inc., was organized as a local nonprofit agency to advocate for the trail. Trail construction began in 1991, and every couple of years another segment is opened to trail users.

In the late fall of 2000, it was announced that the Orange Heritage Trail had received a federal enhancement grant of $304,000 to extend the trail from Museum Village to the Harriman Train Depot— a 3.1-mile extension. A 2-mile, packed limestone trail had been installed by Orange Pathways, Inc., and the county from Goshen to Hartely Road. The enhancement grant covers 80 percent of the $380,000 estimated project cost. Orange County has approved a contribution of $50,000, while Orange Pathways has pledged up to $26,000. When complete, it's envisioned that the entire trail will be open from Middletown to Harriman. A recent thoughtful amenity is the inclusion of emergency call boxes at points along the way.

MILE BY MILE

0.0 mile: Starting at the train station, follow the railroad's path to the east, toward Monroe, by crossing West Main Street, going north for three blocks, then taking a right onto Market Street. This is a very narrow alley-type street; Howell's Breakfast Deli is on the corner. Once you're past the deli, take a right and then a quick left into a parking lot next to a large gray, formerly rail-served building. It's marked as the VILLAGE PARKING LOT. It's actually the railroad right-of-way.

0.25 mile: Past the alternative parking lot, cross Green Street at a grade. The county has a mile marker pointing out that this is the officially designated starting point, which is 0.25 mile from the station. You'll notice that the right-of-way is actually double wide. This is partially because there are two tracks in the area (given its former mainline status) and partially because the railroad was built to accommodate the 6-foot broad-gauge track. You'll travel slightly upgrade for the first sections of this trail.

0.77 mile: Grade crossing at South Street and Butler Road. Here you'll find a nice sign: WELCOME TO THE HERITAGE TRAIL, FUNDED BY ISTEA GRANTS FROM NY DEPARTMENT OF TRANSPORTATION—NO RACING, 20MPH SPEED LIMIT. Nearby, you'll see an Erie mile marker saying "JC58" (Jersey City, 58 miles).

1.83 miles: Grade crossing at Duck Farm Road. U.S. Route 6 is very close off to your right; just beyond that is Route 17. Chester is noted as being 3.2 miles ahead of you, while South Street is 1 mile behind.

2.49 miles: A trailside business here called the Private Pie specializes in pizza and lunches. There is also a bike rack for your convenience. Look for a grade crossing at Duck Cedar Road; to cross it, the trail will go steeply uphill, then immediately downhill on the far side. In years past there was a bridge here that carried the road over the railroad. It has since been filled in. Park benches on the trail here allow trail users to watch the duffers on the nearby golf driving range.

2.75 miles: You're now on a shelf. This leads steeply down on your left to a small meandering river known as the Otter Kill. Then you're quickly on a fill on both sides.

4.1 miles: The adjacent Route 6 now diverges by turning more to the south as you bend left and head more to the east. A whistle marker here provided protection to nearby crossing at Old Chester Road. Nick Lagai from Newington, Connecticut, recounted a story from the 1950s that brings this area to life. It seems that trains coming from Jersey City often needed to make up time, and this is the stretch of track where they'd do so. In fact, it was common to see cars on adjacent Route 6 racing with trains at speeds of more than 60 miles an hour until the engineer had to slow down for the South Street crossing in Goshen.

4.49 miles: You have now crested a hill and are on a downhill stretch as you pass under NY Route 94. This tall bridge was built in 1949; the shady surroundings provide a cool respite if the day is hot. Note the large mortarless stone-block-constructed retaining wall. It stands 8 feet tall here but slowly descends in height until you reach the station.

4.63 miles: Here's the lovely old Chester Station. Restored in the past few years by a federal grant and hundreds of hours of work by volunteers, this station offers a place to stop, check out local history, and rest for a bit. Other businesses in the village of Chester here are geared toward trail users as well, so explore and be pleasantly surprised. The contact person for the group that undertook the restoration of the station is Cliff Patrick, Chester Historical Society, 845–496–7669.

4.65 miles: Pass over a deck-girder bridge over Ward Road. Just ahead are some very large farms that specialize in onions. Note the rich black soil, very reminiscent of Iowa.

5.38–5.75 miles: You're now at the village of Greycourt. The New York Susquehanna & Western Railroad, better known as the "Susie Q," provided interchange here with the Erie. Its mainline

The old railroad station at Chester has been lovingly restored by the Chester Historical Society. Trail users can stop in and learn about the town and the railroad's history here.

This old, derelict Penn-Central flatcar is now used as a loading platform for a public freight transfer dock.

passes overhead on a girder bridge, but you'll also find a team track and small yard still operational here. In fact, this area of the trail is something of a rarity: It's a rail-with-trail, or a dual-use corridor. Though not a mainline track, what's adjacent to you is a storage track for track maintenance vehicles and a siding for agricultural transfer from boxcars to trucks. It's still a live railroad, so be careful and stay aware. Note two rare Penn Central flatcars used as a platform for operating forklifts during the transloading process. The yard ends at the 5.75-mile mark, but the existing railroad right-of-way is slightly above you as it ends at a bridge over Seely Creek. There you'll find another old double-track deck-girder bridge that carries the stub end of the existing track from the yard. The trail is carried by a modern bridge constructed on the abutments of the original third span. Just before this area, look to your left; you'll see the alignment of the old Newburg Branch, which carried ski trains to Salisbury Mills. This branch is clearly visible from Seely Creek, because both lines crossed this waterway.

6.0 miles: Note that the soil in these adjacent farm fields is a conventional brown in color.

6.1 miles: Here is a small white brick building with a concrete patio and an iron fence. This is the recreational center for a homeless shelter operated by the city of New York. The large, off-trail complex was built in the 1930s and still houses almost 1,300 people. A large railroad-era signal cabinet is on the north side of the trail near here.

6.38 miles: Another rail-era infrastructure building of concrete and stucco lies on your left.

6.83–7.11 miles: Travel on a big fill as you carve to your right. There's a concrete culvert tunnel underneath the right-of-way.

7.15 miles: Cross a small bridge with concrete abutments that passes over a seasonal stream. The modern bridge for the trail has pressure-treated timbering; the old railroad bridge still has its original timbers.

7.55 miles: You're looking at the footing for the old William's Dairy Company creamery on your left. Once rail-served, it was torn down in 2000.

7.66 miles: Reach a small hamlet within Oxford. A little farther on, the restored stucco building on your left is called "It's Curtains for You," a drapery dealer. At one time it was probably a railroad-era hotel.

7.72 miles: Enter Oxford proper on a pretty big fill. The railroad right-of-way was protected by some interesting old fencing in this area, which passes over the streets of Oxford. Made of concrete posts with iron pipes as crosspieces, it's evidence that people were assumed to be walking through here. Oxford Station was here at one time. Double-track, mainline, pressure-treated timber crosses over County Route 51. On the east side of town, there's a rare bit of railroad infrastructure: a little platform built out on the side of the fill. Constructed of ties and timbers, it provided track maintenance workers a place to "hide" when two trains were passing by.

7.8 miles: An ancient cemetery is seen to your left, with stones dating back to the early 1800s. Its access is almost exclusively via the rail-trail right-of-way.

7.89 miles: Pass under high-tension electric transmission lines, which create an open air to the right-of-way.

8.1 miles: Head slightly uphill as you pass under Route 17.

8.5 miles: The newly reconstructed bridge over the trail is the access road for the Museum Village. Long an Orange County landmark, this replica of an early American village helps students and families understand life in the nineteenth century. By exploring the re-created village and its twenty-five exhibition and demonstration

1842 First to ship milk into New York City (from Orange County).

1842 First to use a conductor bell cord to signal the engineer.

1847 First to use iron rails rolled in America.

1850 First to construct a telegraph line along the right-of-way.

1851 First railroad to use a telegraph for its operations (from Goshen).

1851 First railroad in United States of 400 miles or more in length.

1851 First through-railroad to connect the Atlantic Ocean and Great Lakes.

1851 First to use broad 6-foot gauge—the widest on the American continent.

1861 First to provide tank cars for moving oil.

1867 First to bring fresh California produce into New York City.

In addition, the Erie provided the widest and highest clearances between New York and Chicago, carried the most perishables from the West Coast to New York, and had the most complete radio-telephone communications system among trunk-line railroads.

buildings—many staffed with costumed interpreters and craftspeople—folks learn what it meant to be a pioneer. Exhibits of early machines, crafts, farming techniques, and other nineteenth-century activities give exciting insights into the daily lives of our forebears. Phone 845–782–8247 for more information.

9.18 miles: As you now pass the park 'n' ride lot in Monroe, look for mile marker "JC50" and Orange Rockland Lakes. The trail ends here as of this writing, but construction is planned soon to carry the trail closer to its eventual terminus in Harriman.

Endpoints: Cleveland, Fulton. The trail passes through the towns of Constantia, West Monroe, Central Square, Pennellville, and Volney along the way.

Location: Oswego County.

Length: 24.9 miles.

Surface: Cinder, gravel, dirt.

Uses: All nonmotorized uses.

To get there: Take NY Route 49 to just east of the town of Cleveland at the Oswego–Oneida county line. Look for Hallenbeck Road, which runs north off Route 49. There's not much in the way of parking, but this is a quiet rural area, and it's safe to park here. Note that the trail stops in the center where I–81 crosses. No provision yet has been made for a safe crossing here. The description that follows will thus end just east of the highway and start again on the west side.

Contact: Oswego County Promotion & Tourist Department, 46 East Bridge Street, Oswego, NY 13126-2123; 1–800–596–3200.

Campground: Lazy K-RV Ranch Camping, 965 Stone Barn Road, Cleveland, NY 13042-3203; 315–675–8100; 888–381–6415; fax 315–675–8860; www.lazykrvranch.com.

This trail is part of the old New York Ontario & Western Railroad (O&W), which was a rambling rural operation noted for having three main sources of revenue: coal, milk, and people. One look at a system map will tell you why milk was a factor—the trains ran through many rural miles of upstate New York. They continued to Weehawken, New Jersey, which provided an indirect connection into the New York City market.

You'll also see that coal was a factor because of the line's connections into eastern Pennsylvania coal fields. But it's harder to reason out the connection with people. You have to go back to the days before the interstate highways, before today's myriad choices of recreational activities.

At the turn of the twentieth century, the O&W was not only one way but in fact the only way to get to the major resorts in the Catskill

Mountains. Through the 1920s and later into the depression years of the 1930s, the O&W ran many passenger and excursion trains into the Monticello, New York, area. Some of the later name trains, such as the Mountaineer, were upgraded with hardwood-trimmed seats; the train logo was embossed onto the seat backs of custom parlor cars. These cars were painted maroon and black with orange trim. As a finishing touch, the train was fitted with streamlined engines. First class all the way to the Catskills! After the war, with the paving of highways into the Catkills, the passenger service was scaled back to one train a day, in summer only.

The management of the O&W recognized that the line was not blessed with a lot of origin traffic. And having no large cities on-line meant that the rail was relegated to being a bridge route—a route that originates most of its traffic off-line, and whose destinations are also located mostly off-line. The major bridge route traffic here was coal from the Scranton area delivering to the New Haven Railroad connection at Campbell Hall, New York. The other major coal connection was at Oswego, New York, on Lake Ontario, where connections were made transferring the black diamonds to lake freighters for points west. Major cost-saving efforts took place in the late 1930s to try to salvage the bottom line. One of the most innovative was the conversion to diesel power very early. In 1941 General Motors' Electro Motive Division brought in matched sets of FT diesels, and the steamers soon were history.

Looking at this event in retrospect, it seems almost ironic—the O&W derived a major portion of its revenue from coal, the power source for its steam locomotives. It was almost as if it assisted in its own demise by converting to diesel.

The lack of traffic in the rural stretches of upstate New York proved too costly, however, and the railroad was given permission by the federal government to abandon operations on March 29, 1957. Everything was either sold or scrapped, and only one stretch of the O&W still is a railroad—the section from north of Fulton to Oswego. At least two parts are rail-trails: the Sullivan County Rail Trail, and this one.

There are several interesting small bridges on this trail with steel-mesh decks. The county hopes to put wood decking over the mesh.

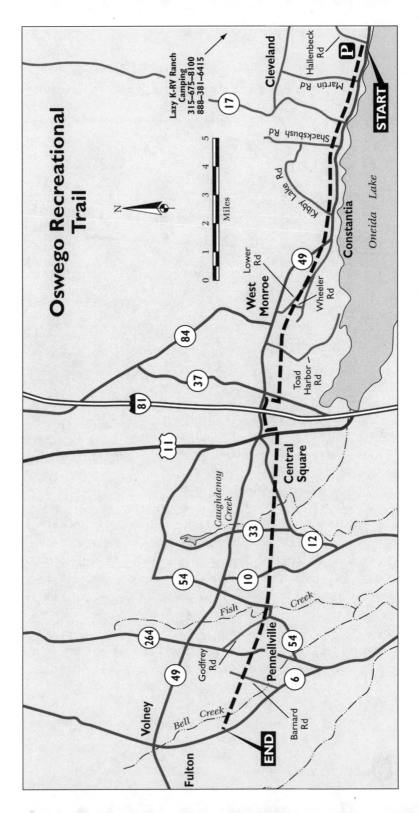

MILE BY MILE

Eastern Section

0.0 mile: Head west from Hallenbeck Road.

0.5 mile: The cinder-based path is nice and wide at first. In some places the ties remain in place. Pass over Cold Spring Brook by way of a small bridge as you get closer to the town of Cleveland.

0.7 mile: Grade crossing of North Street in the town of Cleveland. The access road to the town garage known as Sand Street shares the trail.

0.9 mile: Grade crossing of Center Street. At the same time you'll cross over Black Creek via a small bridge and then head back into the woods again. It might be wet in this area.

1.1 miles: Grade crossing of West Street. A community water tower is found here, as well as some genuine O&W ties, some of which might have date nails in them. Date nails have a broad head, almost like roofing nails. The last two numbers of the year are also stamped in raised letters on the head; 22, for example, indicates 1922. They were driven into the center area of every tenth tie so the maintenance crews would know the age of a particular section. The practice was discontinued in the 1960s. Today date nails are collector's items.

1.3 miles: A school is on your left, as well as a ball field. On your right is a marsh with some interesting birds.

1.5 miles: Grade crossing of Martin Road.

1.6 miles: Travel on a bit of a fill about 6 feet above the surrounding area. Cinders and clinkers are visible here as you navigate a washboardlike surface. Clinkers, by the way, are pieces of coal that only partially burn. Clinkers, if allowed to build up, would clog the firebox of a steam locomotive. They were considered waste, and thus made an excellent material for filling in the right-of-way in problem areas.

1.8 miles: Travel between two farm fields. Deer are very plentiful here, so be on the lookout. More O&W ties are here also.

2.2 miles: Part of the trail may be washed out here. It's only a minor inconvenience to trail users.

2.5 miles: An 18-inch-diameter culvert of modern construction.

2.8 miles: Another culvert with beaver-dam construction nearby to flood the fields here.

3.1 miles: Grade crossing of a dirt road known locally as Crandall Road. You'll also find some residential houses and barns. In about 100 yards you'll come upon County Road 17, which is paved. You can take this road south to Oneida Lake and Route 49. Good views of the lake and the Bernhard Bay area are the high point here.

3.2 miles: Travel on a fill about 25 feet high as a stream known as Crandall Creek flows below you to the lake.

3.3 miles: There's a cemetery here, then another ball field.

3.5 miles: Go over another fill, this one about 25 feet tall.

3.6 miles: Grade crossing of Railroad Street. Look on your right for the concrete dock/slab. This certainly had some railroad heritage; most likely it was a team track, a place where a side track was laid and a public area for loading and unloading cars was maintained. Sometimes such areas were nothing more than open spots to park trucks. In other places a wooden or (in this case) concrete dock was constructed to allow for easier freight transfer.

The trail soon grows bumpy; some potato-sized rocks are a recent addition to the pathway.

3.9 miles: A drainage ditch on each side is filled with water. A steel culvert is visible.

4.0 miles: Grade crossing of Shacksbush Road.

4.3 miles: Farm fields line the trail, with an agricultural grade crossing between them.

4.5 miles: Reach an access point with some mobile homes abutting the trail.

4.8 miles: Agricultural grade crossing.

5.0 miles: Grade crossing of Johnson Road.

5.2 miles: Grade crossing of Le Veille Road. Look for the impressive beaver dam in this area.

5.3 miles: Cross over Dankins Brook by way of a recently constructed 35-foot bridge that is horsesafe with its guardrail in place.

5.7 miles: The trail turns sandy and, with its washboard effect, you'll be hard-pressed to notice the lovely meadows on each side past the tree line.

5.9 miles: A red outbuilding marks the location of the Oneida

Lake Flyers, a radio-controlled aircraft club. Members maintain the grassy strip that lies just beyond the building. Notice the picnic tables and wind-sock at the clubhouse.

6.5 miles: An access point here is marked by a sign that introduces the snowmobile rider to the Lakeside Inn.

6.6 miles: A mobile home park is nearby as you approach the grade crossing for Kibby Lake Road in the town of Constantia.

7.0 miles: Cross over another bridge built with cut-block stone abutments. This is over the Scriba Creek. The eastern approach is about 20 feet high; you then head steeply downhill to the grade crossing below at Hatchery Road. In years gone by there used to be a bridge over the road at this location, but not anymore.

7.1 miles: Wander Inn is located here at Mill Street and Railroad Street. It is in this location that a small yard and servicing facility for locomotives was sited. Today there are some residential houses nearby.

7.4 miles: Grade crossing of Redfield Street. The trail opens up again after you pass through town.

7.8 miles: You're coming into another residential neighborhood. Notice the walkway through the marsh to the left.

7.9 miles: Grade crossing of Route 49. Be careful of the traffic.

8.1 miles: Into a canopied forest. You may encounter some trail wetness, blowdowns of weak trees, and the dreaded washboard effect.

8.2 miles: The access points here are for entry into a nature preserve/trail on the north side of the trail.

8.4 miles: A wooden boardwalk bridge traverses the surrounding marshland. Cinder fill gets you above the surrounding marshes.

9.1 miles: Someone has cut an access point to the trail from their backyard. Scenic large meadows are found just past the tree line.

9.4 miles: Return to canopied forest with meadows on each side.

9.5 miles: Reach an agricultural grade crossing with a companion culvert. Both are more than fifty years old.

9.7 miles: Lower Road runs parallel to the trail on your left, along with a few residential houses.

9.9 miles: Grade crossing of Lower Road. Shortly after this, the trail will become washboard for a while.

10.2 miles: A wildlife management area is here with some bird-houses installed.

10.3 miles: Grade crossing of Wheeler Road.

10.7 miles: The trail opens up in this area to reveal a murky green wetland on both sides.

11.2 miles: Grade crossing of Depot Drive. Given the name of this street, a rail siding was likely once located in this area. This is also evidenced by the wide-open terrain and the agricultural buildings nearby. Perhaps a milk transfer team track was here. Nearby there is an unusual concrete pole. Standing about 9 feet high and triangular in shape, it certainly is of railroad construction but for what purpose we do not know. Look for the wildflowers in this area.

11.5 miles: Look for wide-open fields here with trimmed grass just beyond the tree line. There's also another concrete culvert.

11.9 miles: Grade crossing of Toad Harbor Road. The trail soon grows very open and scenic in a large wetland with many cattails.

12.5 miles: Cross over Big Bay Creek by way of an open mesh-deck bridge. Built with the typical (for this trail) guardrail sides, it's sufficient for braver horses.

12.6 miles: A snowmobile trail intersects the rail-trail at this point. It's marked by a sign advertising sled repairs.

13.3 miles: Agricultural grade crossing.

13.6 miles: Grade crossing of NY Route 37. This is where you should divert and take the roads for a while. Ahead lies a missing bridge over Little Bay Creek as well as I–81. A provision is in the works to allow passage through these obstructions.

Take a right onto Route 37 and head north, then turn left onto Route 49 and head west for about 2 miles until you come to U.S. Route 11. Take a left and head south to the town of Central Square. These roads offer some stores and restaurants for you to refuel and recharge your batteries. The trail starts up again at the Village Pharmacy Plaza, about 0.5 mile south of the intersection of Route 11.

Central Square was at one time the site of a junction of the New York Central's (predecessor to Conrail) branch to Watertown and the O&W's mainline. A union station was erected by both railroads in 1903, replacing one destroyed by fire. A union station is a passenger station where two railroads joined together—in this case the NYC and the O&W. It still stands today, restored and open to the public on the weekends. The Central New York Chapter of the National Railroad Historical Society owns the building and was responsible for the remarkable turnaround. This station ranks as one of the best in the country in terms of thoroughness in restoration, friendly staff, and historical research records on hand. It's simply a must-see for anyone visiting the Central Square area. Call 315–676–7582 for information.

This was a busy place in the early years of the century with twelve through-trains and an equal or greater number of local freight trains. Central Square was one of the largest cities served by the O&W so there was a lot of local coal and milk traffic, particularly creameries receiving raw milk. One still stands next to the station.

Reset your odometer at 0.0 for the western section.

Once jointly owned by the New York, Ontario & Western Railroad (O&W) and the New York Central Railroad (NYC), the Central Square railroad station is now the home of the local chapter of the National Railroad Historical Society.

Western Section

0.0 mile: NYC 298 and O&W 226.33—these numbers represented the miles to New York City on the respective lines. This information is listed on the sign at the Central Square Station and faces no passenger trains anymore. Instead it faces the Conrail trains that pass each day going to and from Watertown, New York. For us it makes a convenient point at which to start counting trail mileage and begin the journey to the Fulton area.

Next door and up the line from the station lies a creamery complex that has been converted to become part of the Bob Smith Building Supply Company. The basic creamery building still stands and nicely represents the kind of structure that was once popular on the O&W. The trail continues west across Route 11, between the Ford dealer and the Village Pharmacy.

0.1 mile: A school is on your right, a residential neighborhood on your left. This area can be wet at times.

0.4 mile: Travel on a fill that's cinder-based and upward of 35 to 40 feet high. Shortly after this comes a high school, and then a cut that's notable mostly for its ability to hold water. It will be very muddy here. A trail has been blazed to the right and up the slope to avoid the water.

0.8 mile: Return to dry and level ground as you pass a pond. You're approaching the crossing of Elderberry Lane, where a few residential houses can be found. Another small, wet cut lies ahead; it's not as challenging as the last one.

1.5 miles: Head out into the open. Expansive vistas of beautiful farm fields are seen on each side.

2.0 miles: Pass County Route 12 on a grade. A small cut is seen, then you're back into the open and level ground.

2.4 miles: Back into the woods and onto a fill about 30 feet tall.

2.6 miles: Grade crossing at Fuller Road. Caughdenoy Creek comes right after the street, along with an interesting gorge that's part of the streambed.

3.5 miles: Grade crossing at Route 33 where a formerly rail-served grain dealer stands. Today known J&J Feeds, it still seems to be prosperous and serves the local dairy industry. Note the freight door that used to face the siding off the mainline. After this you'll be passing some large farm fields that are visible through the tree line insulating the trail.

3.7 miles: Travel on a fill about 15 feet tall.

3.9 miles: Take a small detour into the field on your left to avoid a wet area caused by poor drainage in the cut.

4.0 miles: Grade crossing at Chesbro Road: Head steeply up and then steeply down again on the other side. In years past a bridge used to span the railroad right-of-way. Recently this obsolete structure was demolished and the fill instituted. This is the primary reason why the trail drains so badly in this area now.

4.2 miles: Mesh-deck bridge with the usual iron railings. This one spans Buxton Creek. A marsh with interesting birds is seen after the bridge.

4.4 miles: The pond on your left will eventually expand to both sides of the trail. This is a result of beaver activity.

5.1 miles: Grade crossing of Route 10. There was once a bridge here, but no longer.

5.4 miles: Grade crossing at Bell Road. High-tension lines make a sizzling sound. The area is very open and scenic, with large farm fields being the primary vista.

5.6 miles: The trail is fairly wide around here, with a canopy of hardwoods to shade you.

5.9 miles: Travel on a small fill with some marshes and forests around.

6.1 miles: Reach a bridge over Fish Creek. It was damaged by vandals and recently refurbished by the county. For a photogenic scene, take a left onto NY Route 54 and follow this into Pennellville. Bear right onto Godfrey Road to return to the trail in about 0.6 mile. An old team track was in this area also. Check out the old grain dealer complex in town to see ghosts of the industrial past, and stop to view the "out" bridge from Route 54. It might be worth a picture from the body of water adjacent to the highway. You'll also pass by O&W mile marker 306 on Godfrey Road. The present owner has placed it in his front yard.

7.0 miles: Grade crossing of Godfrey Road. You're in a residential neighborhood; the trail is nicely wide here, with a cinder base.

7.7 miles: Travel on a 15-foot fill with a canopied forest for a roof. This fill is about 0.3 mile long.

8.0 miles: A 30-foot-long open-mesh bridge crosses Sixmile Creek.

8.2 miles: Grade crossing of NY Route 264.

8.7 miles: A high-pressure gas line intersects the trail here, and an agricultural grade crossing appears.

8.8 miles: Head into a nicely maintained dry cut, then into the open.

9.0 miles: Grade crossing of Barnard Road.

9.3 miles: Into the canopied forest again. Look for the antique farm planting equipment lying abandoned in the woods.

9.7 miles: A slight cut that can be wet with gooey mud turns into a slight fill with woods to the south and meadows to the north.

10.4 miles: Travel out of another short muddy area in a cut and onto a fill again, this one 10 to 15 feet high and dry. There seems to be some beaver activity in nearby marshes.

11.0 miles: The bridge over Bell Creek is a 30-foot, open-mesh steel deck type.

11.3 miles: Grade crossing at NY Route 6. This is a good area to park, with its grassy area and clearly denoted entrance to the trail. A large arch-type wooden sign announces the Oswego County Trail. This is the end for most visitors, though the trail does continue for about 1.8 miles, where it intersects with Maple Avenue. Take Maple west to the T intersection and turn left onto Fay Street. Places to eat, interesting industrial vistas, and a lovely river walk along the Oswego Canalway are among the things to do in Fulton.

A road crossing near Fulton.

Endpoints: Penn Yan, Dresden.

Location: Yates County.

Length: 7.5 miles.

Surface: Gravel, cinder, some asphalt.

Uses: All nonmotorized uses and snowmobiles.

To get there: Take exit 42 off the New York Thruway and head south on NY Route 14 for about 19 miles to NY Route 54. Head west on Route 54 for about 5 miles to its junction with NY Route 54A, where you will head southwest for 0.1 mile. Turn south onto Route 14A, continue 0.1 mile, then take a right onto Keuka Street. This leads into the trailhead parking lot at the town-owned Little League Baseball Park.

Contact: Philip Whitman, President, Friends of the Outlet Trail, Inc., 1939 Perry Point Road, Box 231, Dresden, NY 14441; 315–536–2701.

Accommodations: Wagener Estate Bed & Breakfast, 351 Elm Street, Penn Yan, NY 14527-1446; 315–536–4591; fax 315–531–8142; wagener-estate@wagenerestate.com; www.wagenerestate.com.

During the canal craze in the early 1830s, New York State built the Crooked Lake (original name of Keuka Lake) Canal, which ran 6 miles to Seneca Lake at a shallow 4-foot depth. Canal boats traversed the route in an amazingly slow six hours. This was primarily because of the twenty-eight wooden locks that brought the boats down 274 feet to the level of Seneca Lake. It was not surprising, then, to learn that the canal was never profitable and was taken over by a newer and better idea—the railroad.

In 1844, during the early years of the railroad craze, the Penn Yan & New York Railroad was built largely on the canal towpath. Nicknamed by the locals the "Corkscrew Railroad," because of the curvature built into the line, it ultimately became a part of the New York Central System. It, too, ran with declining success until Hurricane Agnes in 1972, which washed away many sections of the right-of-way. The railroad then abandoned it. The line was dormant until 1981, when the town of Penn Yan bought the corridor in the village

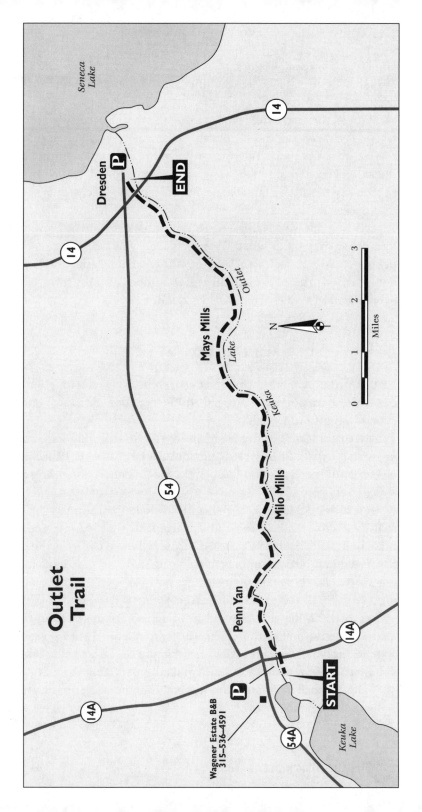

and the county bought the rest. It has since been sold to the Friends of the Outlet Trail, a local nonprofit organization that maintains the trail.

With all the grain mills (and, yes, distilleries also), this quaint village of Penn Yan has an interesting and storied past. Today residents realize just how lucky they are to have the rail-trail right in their midst. As you start along the trail, some boaters might be nearby; be sure to say hi as they launch their boats into the lake, which is just to the west.

You may be wondering where the unusual name of Penn Yan originated. Way back, when the community was being formed, the people could not decide on a name until someone suggested Penn Yan—because the place had an equal number of folks from Pennsylvania and Yankees from New England!

. . . .

MILE BY MILE

0.0 mile: A modern bike-pedestrian bridge gets you over the canal to the trail on the south side of the corridor. Head east on the paved trail toward Dresden.

0.1 mile: Cross under Main Street (Route 54) and past a parking area for the trail. A World Trail kiosk is here as well. World Trail is a series of exercise stations along the path. Each station represents a different exercise.

0.3 mile: Reach the remains of a wooden bent-timber bridge that once crossed the canal. This was a spur that led into the old mills on the north side of the canal. Carry's Rental Outlet is the current owner of the old complex, which originally belonged to a number of woodworking companies.

0.5 mile: A beautiful falls in the outlet is here, and just after comes Birkett Mills—another old grain mill complex. You then cross a curved bent-timber bridge that has been upgraded with pressure-treated timbers. This area also was the site of a boat basin where canal boats were turned on the Crooked Lake Canal from 1833 to 1877. Five tracks diverged from the mainline here to serve specific mills in the neighborhood.

0.6 mile: Into a decidedly more rural section of the trail, you'll find the third of the World Trail kiosks, this one for chin-ups. Look for beaver activity around here.

0.7 mile: You are now going under the active railroad deck-girder bridge, which is more than 70 feet above you. This was part of the Northern Central Division of the Pennsylvania Railroad (now Norfolk Southern Railroad). The original bridge here was wooden, but it was replaced by a steel span around 1890. The current bridge was installed around 1915. This north-to-south-oriented line is still active. On the trail and just west of the high bridge is the site of a turntable for the New York Central Railroad. There's not much left of the turntable—only a slight circular depression in the ground and a bit of concrete wall. You'll come upon more parking ahead, then cross Cherry Street. After this crossing the trail becomes gravel-surfaced. Signage here warns: "Natural areas possess hazards not normally encountered in your home surroundings. You are responsible for your own safety. Feel free to walk, run, ride your horse, bike, use a snowmobile, but don't litter, pick flowers, remove anything, or use a motor vehicle without authorization."

1.0 mile: The marker here identifies this area as St. John Mill, which was located across the outlet. Note that the outlet picks up speed here as you head toward Dresden. Look for occasional railroad ties.

1.2 miles: Travel on a bit of a fill. Some wetlands appear on your left, then some remnants of the Crooked Lake Canal.

1.4 miles: Grade crossing of Fox Mills Road, which of course is near Fox's Mills site. Note the rail still in the road's grade crossing. A welded metal strongbox here instructs trail users to please register and fill out a general questionnaire (where you came from, how you're traveling, how long you're staying, and so on). A nice sign tells you about the industrial history of the neighborhood. If you head south on Fox Mills Road and then take a quick right, you'll find the remains of the old mill, which apparently made paper.

1.7 miles: Go downhill and cross over a small bridge.

2.1 miles: Reach the site of Milo Mills, a paper mill that burned down in 1910 and then was rebuilt. This site had a dam with a regulating apparatus for the outlet. An old smokestack is still standing as a faint reminder of what was once here. Bits and pieces of machinery, including a huge flywheel and even a concrete floor from the factory are still visible. A sign warns you to keep away from these ghosts of an industrial past.

2.4 miles: A hillside on your left holds a treasure trove of old cans and bottles dumped long ago. Almost 0.1 mile long, it serves as a reminder of why we don't do this sort of thing anymore. (But it makes a great place for cultural scavengers to pick through.)

2.5 miles: A concrete whistle marker is seen here. It has an angled top with an etched-in *W*.

3.4 miles: Reach a falls—part of the outlet—while you travel in a cut. A huge volume of water pours through here, making for a lot of mist with rainbows as a bonus; it's a great place to sit and take in the sounds of roaring water. This was the site of the former Mays Mills.

3.7 miles: Come out alongside a paved road to the north. This is Outlet Road.

3.9 miles: A whistle marker is on your right, with the *W* facing you. A mile marker here says "D3"—Dresden, 3 miles. The outlet takes a series of sweeping turns, and you hear the falls ahead.

4.2 miles: Grade crossing for the Keuka Visitor's Center.

4.4 miles: Whistle marker on your right.

4.7 miles: Join up with a road that leads to the visitor center. Signs on the outlet itself warn canoeists of the impending falls.

4.8 miles: Reach the Alfred Jensen Visitor's Center on the trail; it's being restored by the Friends of the Outlet Trail. Here you'll find bathrooms and some signage about the trail and its sights. This structure used to be owned by a local tire dealer, who donated it to the Friends.

5.1 miles: Head back into the woods. You'll see lots of ties cast to the left side, but the most notable features here are the huge cliffs overlooking the outlet on your right. Some are more than 100 feet tall.

6.1 miles: Grade crossing of an access road to the other side of the trail, into the field between you and the river. Near here is the site of the old village of Hopeton, which once had a number of mills and residences—all gone today.

6.7 miles: Travel over a 15-foot deck-girder bridge with modern timbers for a good solid planking.

6.8 miles: Another 15-foot bridge, this one of the through-girder type. The original alignment of the railroad has been disrupted here by the reconstruction of Route 14, which is overhead. You'll travel deeper into the valley, then steeply down, and finally steeply up to the original alignment.

7.1 miles: End of the trail at the active Norfolk Southern Railroad line on the outskirts of Dresden. There's parking here at Seneca Street, where the Citgo station and the Crossroads Ice Cream Shop are located.

Endpoints: A loop beginning and ending at Pittsford.

Location: Monroe County

Length: 4 miles.

Surface: Stone dust, dirt, gravel.

Uses: Walking, cross-country skiing.

To get there: From New York State Thruway, take exit 45 and travel north on I–490. After 8 miles exit onto NY Route 31 and head west into the village of Pittsford. The trail can be located just off NY Route 96 (North Main Street), near the Depot Complex and old pickle factory. Route 31 divides the trail into two equal parts.

Contact: Doug Morganfield, Department of Parks & Recreation, 35 Lincoln Avenue, Pittsford, NY 14534; 716–248–6280.

H ere is one of the few opportunities to travel an abandoned railroad/canal and actually return to your car without seeing the same thing! This short trail is a pleasure for that reason and many more. A logical start is in Pittsford Village, settled in 1789; much of the central village area is a historic district. You'll find a number of restaurants and shops along Monroe Avenue in Pittsford Plaza as well as in the village itself.

From Depot Complex in the village, follow the Erie Canal Heritage Trail Towpath to the west. This is actually the "modern" Erie Canal, built from 1910 through 1912 for motorized canal traffic. At about 0.25 mile you cross Monroe Avenue (Route 31). Use Brook Road to skirt a maintenance facility; after a short distance, the trail connects with the towpath again. Continue on the towpath for a total of 1.1 miles from the beginning of your trip and see the "old" Erie Canal on your right. (If you hit Clover Street, NY Route 65, you've gone too far, although you may want to visit nearby modern Lock 32 and its park, located on the other side of Route 65.)

Turn right with the trail; you'll see the Long Meadow community on your right. In 0.5 mile you come to the site of the Odenbach Shipyard, which built landing craft for World War II. Immediately after that the trail crosses French Road; please use caution.

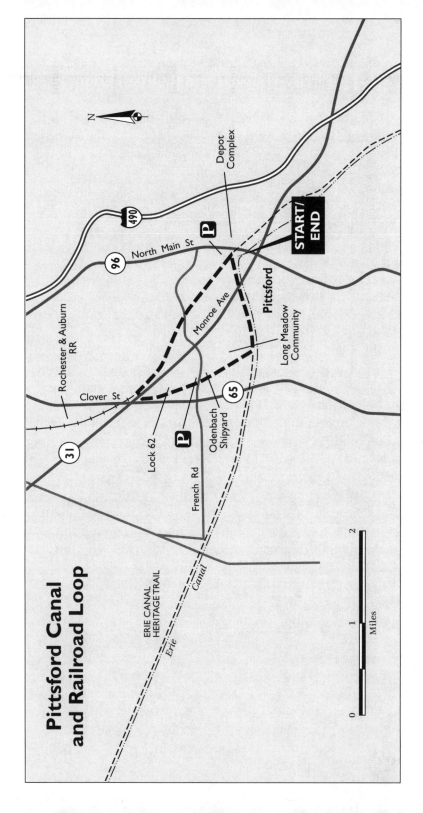

Pittsford Canal
and Railroad Loop

N

Depot
Complex

490

96

North Main St

P

START/
END

Pittsford

Monroe Ave

Long Meadow
Community

Rochester & Auburn
RR

Clover St

65

Lock 62

P

Odenbach
Shipyard

31

French Rd

ERIE CANAL
HERITAGE TRAIL

Erie

Canal

0   1   2

Miles

Shortly, historic Lock 62 will become visible. Lock 62 was built in 1857 and doubled in size to permit two-way traffic in 1873. After the second chamber was added, two boats could pass traveling up- or downstream in the same or opposite directions. The wooded gates have not survived, but the iron cleats that the lock master used for footing are still in place. When the original Erie Canal locks were being built, natural cement was not readily available, but a natural bedrock formation near the canal was used to make binding waterproof material that continues to hold the blocks together today. The canal that flowed through this site in 1857 was 70 feet wide and 7 feet deep. Lock 62 was one of seventy-two locks on the 350-mile route between Albany and Buffalo. Men and mules worked six hours at a time—traveling about 15 miles per shift, hence the song "Fifteen Miles on the Erie Canal." Old Lock 62 was abandoned in 1918 when the modern Erie Barge Canal was completed. The modern canal is 123 feet wide and 12 feet deep, with thirty-five locks.

After another 0.33 mile, you'll see the Spring House restaurant, built in the 1820s as an inn for the canal. Its "medicinal" springs unfortunately no longer function. Use the sidewalk and pedestrian signal here to cross over Monroe Avenue to your right.

The trail continues for 1.4 miles back to Pittsford Village on the abandoned Rochester & Auburn Railroad, which ceased to do business in 1960. The Oak Hill Golf Course on your left has been the site of numerous championships, including the U.S. Open, PGA, and Ryder Cup. Nazareth College appears before you cross French Road. The journey ends when you see the old pickle factory and the Depot Complex. The factory, built in 1914, was famous for its pickles, mustard, apple cider vinegar, and sauerkraut.

Endpoints: North-south segment, Philadelphia and Theresa. East-west segment, La Fargeville and Clayton.

Location: Jefferson County.

Length: North-south segment, 10.93 miles. East-west segment, 3.64 miles.

Surface: Dirt, cinder, grass, gravel.

Uses: All nonmotorized uses.

To get there: To reach the north-south segment, take I–81 to exit 49, then head southeast on NY Route 411/26 for about 11 miles into the town of Philadelphia. Just before the intersection of U.S. Route 11, turn right (southwest) onto Garden Street. This will bring you to the local water treatment plant, where parking is available. The old railroad grade is on your left as you head down Garden Street toward the water treatment plant.

For the east-west segment, take I–81 to exit 49, then head west on Route 411 for about 4.3 miles. In the village of La Fargeville, look for the Agway store on your left. The trailhead is on your right, across the street from Agway. There is no good parking area very close to the trailhead, but you'll find safer spots just down the street.

Contact: Sissy Danforth, Executive Director, Thousand Island Land Trust, P.O. Box 238, Clayton, NY 13624; 315–686–5345.

The Thousand Island region of New York is a special treat that belongs on everyone's must-visit list. The main community of this extraordinary area is Clayton. Located on the St. Lawrence River (the border between the United States and Canada), Clayton is unique in that it's the only community on the river that has kept intact nearly its entire core village of nineteenth- and early-twentieth-century buildings, both commercial and residential. A small, compact village with only thirteen principal streets, Clayton sits on a peninsula that protrudes into the St. Lawrence River.

Originally settled in 1822, Clayton first made its mark as a river transportation hub, with shipbuilding and other marine services offered here. With its proximity to the Adirondacks, lumbering also was prevalent in the area. But Clayton's main claim to fame was that it was major point of disembarkation for the railborne tourists going to the Thousand Islands, and indeed, it has remained prosperous for 150 years by serving tourists. This prosperity is evidenced by the intact and eclectic mix of stone, brick, and wood-frame architecture. Be sure to take a walk in the village and savor the sights. (Call the Thousand Island Land Trust for a map that lays out a walking tour of the village.)

Today Clayton boasts another claim to fame: It's the home of the Antique Boat Museum, the largest collection of wooden boats in the world. Here you'll find an astounding group of mahogany-finished speedboats, runabouts, and launches. Call 315–686–4104 and prepare to be amazed.

One of more interesting sights for those interested in industrial archaeology is the Frink Park on Riverside Drive (the northernmost street on the peninsula). The park is actually the site of the old railroad station, which was unfortunately torn down in the late 1970s. Across the street was the Frink Snow Plow Company, which went into business in 1920 and built quality plows for worldwide customers for many years.

The railroad line was built in the 1870s to connect Philadelphia to the St. Lawrence River at Clayton. At its peak more than ten passenger trains a day terminated at Clayton. The freight operations side of the railroad was less well known than the passenger side of things, but it too had a claim to fame. The line was used primarily to ship an especially fine grade of hay produced locally to horses in New York City. Eventually, however, the highway network became more reliable; New York Central stopped running trains up here in the 1950s. The successor company, Penn Central, sold 18 miles of corridor to Thousand Island Land Trust (TILT) in 1994 for $30,000. Most land trusts in the United States today focus on rectangular properties. It takes the truly visionary land trust to see the incredible value in linear properties. TILT has the vision.

A perfect example of just how well loved this trail is, and just how respected TILT and its vision are in the towns, is the aftermath of the 1998–99 ice storm. This freak storm coated the entire area with several inches of ice and caused hundreds of trees to snap like twigs

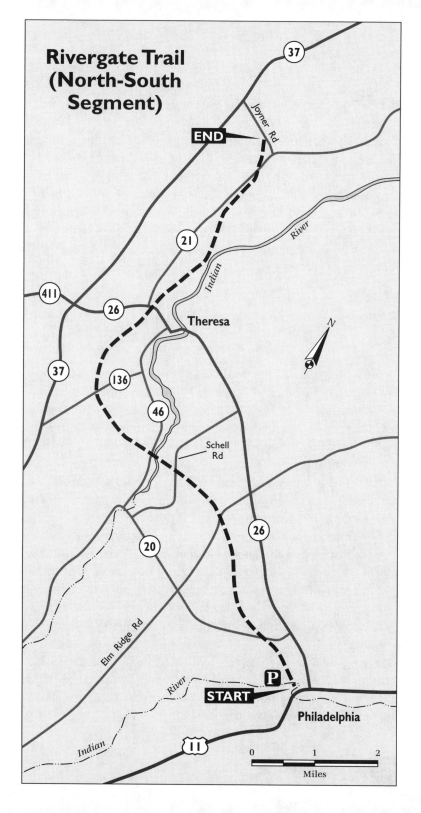

across the trail. To the rescue came the local ATV and snowmobile clubs. They spent thousand of man-hours cutting and removing trees that had toppled, opening the trail much sooner than anyone had expected.

In November 2000 TILT attended a property auction in Jefferson County and successfully bid on five additional parcels of the Penn Central right-of-way in the town of Alexandria. This new acquisition adds approximately 2.5 miles to the 18 miles of railroad bed now owned by TILT, and runs from Redwood to the St. Lawrence County line. It's hoped that eventually the entire railroad line—from Philadelphia to Morristown, with a leg to La Fargeville and Clayton—will be opened as a trail.

● ●

MILE BY MILE

North-South Segment

0.0 mile: Starting out on the trail and heading northwest, you'll first notice the 80-foot deck-girder bridge that spans the Indian River. In the early spring of 1999, TILT rebuilt this bridge, which has been upgraded and decked with pressure-treated timbers as well as boasting a good sturdy railing. Take in the interesting sights from this elevated vantage point.

0.19 mile: Here you'll see the first of many spectacular farmland vistas. In the spring you'll find not only a stunning array of flowering trees, but an impressive number of songbirds as well.

0.7 mile: Looking closely, you'll discover a genuine cattle underpass installed in the steam railroad days of long ago. This was built to allow cows get to the other side of the tracks.

0.89 mile: Grade crossing of County Route 20. This crossing also gives you a clear view of the sky to view the F-16 high-performance fighter jets that often fly out to the nearby military reservation at Fort Drum.

1.13 miles: Travel now on a fill about 10 feet tall. On each side former farm fields are being reclaimed by the forest. Look carefully and you'll see a few clinkers—unburned pieces of coal from the firebox of a steam locomotive—on the trail as well.

1.43 miles: Enter a small, short, hand-hewn rock cut that may be wet after a heavy rain.

1.49 miles: Note the wetlands here, which are host to a large number of ducks and other waterfowl.

1.83 miles: You're now going past ponds along the right-of-way. Look carefully and you may spot some antique railroad spikes and ties in the brush along the trail, and even some rare late-nineteenth-century bolts to join railroad tracks.

2.0 miles: Continue onto a cinder-based fill with ponds and other wetlands on each side. The ponds were most likely man-made during the construction of the railroad. In the railroad era they were called borrow-pits—the land was "borrowed" to make the fill, and the pits became filled with water from a high water table. Note the recent repair of the right-of-way from an apparent flood.

2.35 miles: Open farm fields lie on your left, while a young forest is starting to reclaim the meadow on your right.

2.67 miles: Cross another fill then head right into a short rock cut 15 feet tall. Note the genuine New York Central whistle marker here.

3.01 miles: Grade crossing at Elm Ridge Road. Note the evidence of an old milk transfer building on your left, just before the crossing. You'll also see three cattle guards in the trail. These are a special sort of grate that is uncomfortable for hoofed animals to walk on, keeping them from wandering down the trail. The grates are safe for bikes.

3.11 miles: A 30-foot deck-girder bridge over a small, unnamed stream.

3.62 miles: Head into a cut. Look around and you'll still see evidence today of the massive ice storm that devastated the area in the winter of 1998.

4.08 miles: Grade crossing of Schell Road. Look for the rail still in the road at the grade crossing.

4.52 miles: Cross the Indian River once again, this time on a 100-foot through-girder bridge with 6-foot-tall girders. Note the asphalt coating that protects the bridge timbers. County Route 46 is crossed immediately after the bridge.

5.33 miles: Rivergate Junction. The leg to the left is closed to

The Rivergate Trail passes under Route 136 in Theresa via this corrugated steel tunnel at 5.98 miles.

trail users because of right-of-way issues still to be solved. Turn right onto the leg that heads north to Theresa.

5.9 miles: Go through a series of meadows and pastures.

5.98–6.37 miles: The 100-foot tunnel here was designed not for trains, but to get trail users and cattle under (and across) County Route 136. Just out of the tunnel, you'll come upon the home of the farmer who owns the cattle that use the tunnel. Farther along the trail are wire gates; make sure to close them behind you after you pass through.

6.64 miles: Head steeply down a sandy embankment, across a small stream by way of a small bridge built by the Thousand Island Land Trust, then steeply up back onto the trail.

6.8 miles: If you park your bike here and head into the woods on the west side, you'll find a series of waterfalls that are a part of Black Creek.

6.84 miles: In this area you'll find a number of sand dunes on either side of the trail where ATV riders like to operate. In fact, much of this land is not open to ATVs—they're trespassing.

7.35 miles: Travel on a fill into a residential neighborhood along High Street in the town of Theresa.

7.46 miles: The large barn in this village setting seems to have had a relationship with the railroad for agricultural transfer. Just after this comes a rare old metal barn. This area also was the location for a small switching yard, as evidenced by the large area of cinder and three sets of ties. Bear left, going through the yard.

7.63 miles: Grade crossing of Route 26. This is a steep downhill, because the bridge over the road was taken down long ago. Once you're back up on the other side, you'll find a grass-covered trail.

7.82 miles: An unusual bridge here spans a small stream within a large wetland area that leads to the Indian River off to the east. This bridge was originally a military-owned movable ramp that was used to drive trucks up into the cavernous interiors of transport aircraft.

8.92 miles: Head back into the woods again and then alongside another wetland on your left, complete with beaver hutch.

9.4 miles: A short pressure-treated bridge is carried by concrete abutments that span a small stream.

9.65 miles: County Route 21 comes in from your left to run directly parallel as you continue to head north.

9.71 miles: Still adjacent to Route 21, you'll come upon an agricultural grade crossing and then a series of large rocky outcroppings. Some of these formations have small caves at the base.

10.43 miles: Grade crossing of Route 21 (English Settlement Road). Begin to swing more to the northwest.

10.74 miles: Cross over a small stream by way of a small, 6-foot bridge. A large amount of Chinese bamboo, an invasive plant, is seen here. Proceed into a cut about 12 to 15 feet deep. Trains have been stuck in this cut by snow and had to dig out.

10.93 miles: The trail ends at the grade crossing for Joyner Road. In years past the road crossed over the railroad by way of a bridge. Today the right-of-way on the other side of the road is totally grown in.

East-West Segment

0.0–0.28 mile: Start out in the village setting of La Fargeville, with a number of residences very close to the trail. Heading west, look for the slate sidewalk; all the backyards are mowed right up to the trail. In 900 feet you'll cross both Middle Road and NY Route 180, heading into large open farming areas. Note the large culvert, circa 1912, that spans the stream passing through.

0.65 mile: Agricultural grade crossing.

2.46 miles: Genuine New York Central concrete whistle markers are seen here. They feature a broad top with an embossed *W*.

2.77 miles: Grade crossing at Fox Hill Road.

3.19 miles: Stands of unusually large white birch trees. Check for signs of beavers near here.

3.23 miles: A very unusual railroad artifact is seen here: It's a New York Central Railroad section marker, denoting the border between the territories of two section gangs. Section gangs were the maintainers of the railroad right-of-way, which was built with two sections of rail planted vertically into the ground and sticking up 25 to 30 inches. Bolted onto them is one piece of timber. It stands 5 feet high and 4 inches thick, with a width of 16 inches. This used to be painted white with contrasting letters on it; it's even trimmed out with corner molding for a fine finishing touch.

3.29 miles: Beaver ponds are on both sides of the trail.

3.46 miles: Grade crossing at Black Creek Road, and then you emerge onto a grass-covered trail again.

3.64 miles: Interestingly, in a couple of hundred yards, the trail crosses Black Creek Road once more. Note that the rails are still in place below the road surface at the crossing; on the trail a few ties are still in place.

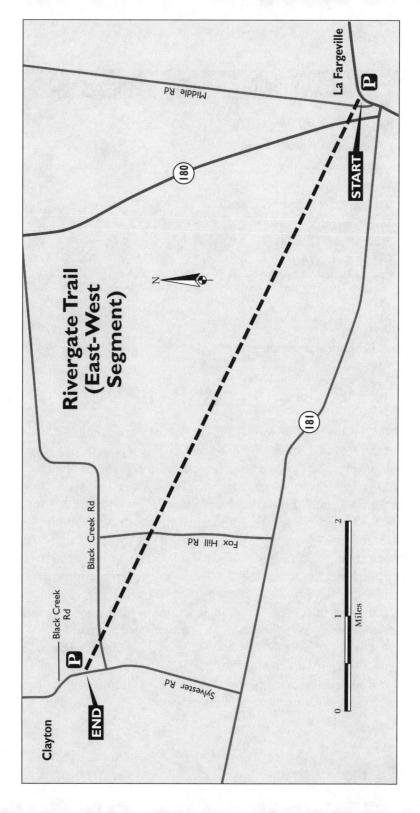

20 | South County Trailway

Endpoints: Elmsford, Yonkers.

Location: Westchester County.

Length: 6.29 miles.

Surface: Asphalt.

Uses: All nonmotorized uses.

To get there: The trailhead is located about 75 feet west of the intersection of NY Routes 119 and 9A in the village of Elmsford.

Contact: David DeLucia, Director of Park Facilities, Westchester County Department of Parks, Recreation and Conservation, 25 Moore Avenue, Mount Kisco, NY 10549; 914–864–7070.

For historical background see Trail 12, North County Trailway.

● ● ● ● ● ● ● ● ● ● ● ● ● ● ● ● ● ● ●

MILE BY MILE

0.0 mile: Heading south from the South County Trailhead, you'll find the first of a series of etched-metal signs that present the railroad history of the old Putnam line. In the 1920s the trolley tracks crossed the Putnam line at Tarrytown Road, where passengers from both modes could transfer to the other line. The Elmsford station is now the Lastazione Restaurant, one of only four station buildings—out of the twenty-two that once served the line—that still exist. The others are at Briar Cliff Manor (now a library), and the stations at Millwood and Yorktown Heights. (All these other stations can be seen on the North County Trailway—see Trail 12.)

0.01–0.3 mile: Various industries are backed right up to the right-of-way, but none seems to have any former railroad tie-in.

0.4 mile: Cross over a 40-foot-long railroad-era through-girder bridge that spans a stream.

0.6 mile: The large power transmission towers and lines here interrupt the canopy of trees overhead.

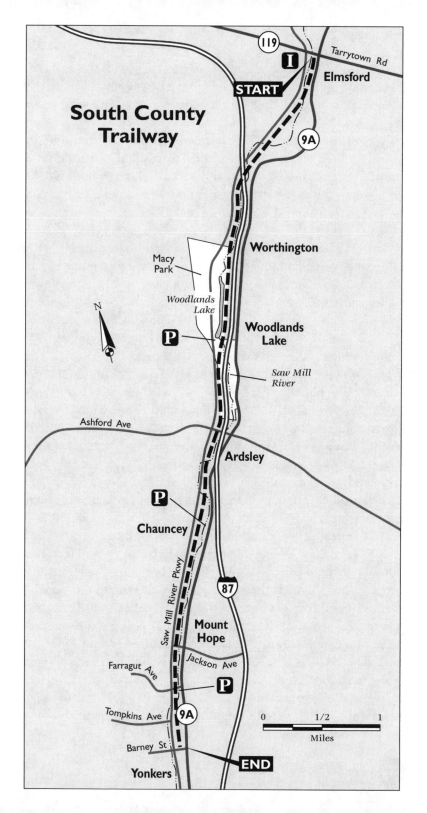

0.9 mile: The first of a series of emergency call boxes is seen here. These are solar-powered and bring peace of mind to those without a cell phone. Another through-girder bridge crosses a stream here.

1.1 miles: Here you'll find a modern box culvert/tunnel that swings the trail under a nearby access road and then back onto the railroad right-of-way. The Saw Mill River Parkway is very close by at the point; the road noise is evident. Right after you get back onto the right-of-way, you'll cross another railroad-era through-girder bridge.

1.65 miles: This is the location for Worthington Station. Originally called Aqueduct, the station was renamed for Henry Rossiter Worthington, a prominent local resident born in 1817. After inventing a steam pump, he invented a steam engine specifically for the kind of boats in use along the canal systems in New York. During the Civil War all U.S. naval forces were equipped with Worthington steam-powered pumps. The company went on to produce the prototype air compressor that is still in use today. Worthington Pump was later purchased by Studebaker, and then the production rights for all the old important Worthington compressors were bought by a Swedish firm, Atlas Copco, which still produces a variation of the original design by Mr. Worthington. The nearby Worthington estate was very large. The station was not a scheduled stop, but only a flag-stop station.

1.89 miles: Another 40-foot through-girder bridge over the meandering stream.

2.11 miles: Emergency call box.

2.5–2.7 miles: Reach a scenic vista known as Woodlands Lake. Picnic benches, a parklike atmosphere, a bridge to the other side of the lake, and a dam at the south end of the lake are the visual attractions here. The park across the lake is called Macy Park. This area was once part of the Philipsburg Manor. During the early part of the nineteenth century, grain and timber mill's powered by water from the Saw Mill River operated profitably here. After the railroad came through, a massive resort hotel, the Woodlands Lake Hotel, was erected on the far side of the lake. Nearly all the patrons came by way of the Put. Late in the nineteenth century, John Brown's dairy farm became the largest parcel of what is now Macy Park. J. P. Morgan was involved here as well: He owned part of the parcel, and one of his companies operated an icehouse that harvested ice from Woodlands Lake and stored it in a special building insulated with sawdust. The park was named for Everit Macy, who served as one of the first Westchester parks commissioners. It is also accessible by automobile from a direct exit off the Saw Mill River Parkway.

2.77 miles: Cross over the Saw Mill River again, this time by way of a modern bridge with a laminated wooden deck.

3.32 miles: A school bus parking lot and other light industries are on your left.

3.52 miles: Ashford Avenue overpass.

3.56 miles: Ardsley Station was here. Until the railroad came to town, this place was known as Ashford. When residents realized they wanted a post office as well as a train station, they had to choose another name for the community—New York already had an Ashford. Cyrus Field—the business partner of Samuel Morse, of telegraph and underwater cable fame—had a nearby estate with the name of Ardsley, from his ancestral home in England. The name change became official in 1896.

3.7 miles: Here you'll find some more light industry, and then a call box on the approach to another bridge. This is a modern prefabricated bike bridge; the others were rehabilitated railroad bridges.

4.08 miles: Reach another through-girder bridge, this one skewed to allow the railroad to cross the river at a bit of an oblique angle.

4.4 miles: Akzo-Nobel (formerly Stauffer) Chemical Company is on the left side of the trail. This older building obviously enjoyed rail service at one time in its history, as evidenced by the siding leading to the cemented-in, rail-served doors.

4.49 miles: Site of the old Chauncey Station. Interestingly, the entire central business district disappeared when the Saw Mill River Parkway came to town. Note the footings and stone retaining wall on the west side of the trail. Other bits and pieces of the station and its surroundings are still here as well.

5.3 miles: Mount Hope Station was here. This was a busy place with ticketing, telegraph, express package service, and a post office all contained in the building. A remnant of the pedestrian bridge over the tracks still exists, and a solitary iron beam guards nothing any longer. In the tall grass and brush on the east side of the trail lies a good amount of ties for the passing siding as well as a bit of foundation for the station. One of the best-known features of this community is the cemetery. It was constructed to serve the residents of New York City; for many years special funeral trains would bring mourners up from the city. This cemetery also has a 70-foot-tall memorial to Confederate army veterans.

5.5 miles: Travel under the Jackson Avenue Bridge.

5.9 miles: There's parking available here at Farragut Avenue.

5.93 miles: Cross over another stream by way of a through-girder bridge. Marion Road runs parallel and close to the trail. You're in Yonkers proper.

6.1 miles: Jason Street is now the parallel-running street. A number of houses face the street beyond the trail.

6.22 miles: Railroad Avenue. This is one of the most common street names in America, of course, but here there's no longer a railroad—only a trail.

6.29 miles: Grade crossing at Barney Street, which is the end of the trail. Note the old rail still in the street here.

21 | Wallkill Valley Rail Trail

Endpoints: New Paltz–Rosendale line, Gardiner–Shawangunk line.

Location: Ulster County.

Length: 15.8 miles.

Surface: Gravel, cinder.

Uses: All nonmotorized uses.

To get there: Take exit 18 off I–87, then follow NY Route 299 to New Paltz. Go into the downtown area; the rail-trail crosses the road. The New Paltz Passenger Station is just to your right. Park where it's safe and approved—which will most likely be on the street, not at the passenger station.

Contact: Eldeva Tofte, Wallkill Valley Rail-Trail Association, Box 1048, New Paltz, NY 12561; 845–255–5124; www.gorailtrail.org.

Accommodations: Country Meadows Bed & Breakfast, 41 Denniston Road, Gardiner, NY 12525; 845–895–3132; fax 845–895–1703; info@ countrymeadowsbandb.com; www.countrymeadowsbandb.com.

Bike repair/rentals: Bicycle Depot, 15 Main Street, New Paltz, NY 12561-1742; 845–255–3859; www.bicycledepot.com. TABLE Rock Tour & Bicycles, 292 Main Street, Rosendale, NY 12472; 845–658–7832; fax 845–658–7391; TABLERockToursandBicycles@yahoo.com; www. TABLERockTours.com.

Campgrounds: Hidden Valley Lake Campground, P.O. Box 1190, Kingston, NY 12402; 845–338–4616. Yogi Bear's Jellystone Park at Lazy River, 50 Bevier Road, Gardiner, NY 12525; 845–255–5193; fax 845–256–0159; yogibear1@msn.com; www.lazyriverny.com.

This is a special trail that combines history and natural beauty, yet is only 90 miles from New York City. Organized as the Wallkill Valley Railroad Company in 1866, with construction starting north from Montgomery in 1868, it opened to Kingston in 1872. This railroad was for a long time thought of as a separate entity from the parent roads of later years. Absorbed into the West Shore Railroad in 1881, it was made into a feeder line or branch of the West Shore's "High Iron" along the Hudson River. The West Shore Railroad itself was absorbed into the New York Central System (NYC) in 1885. Interestingly enough, the Wallkill was able to maintain a separate legal identity apart from both the West Shore and NYC until 1952. Conrail operated here in its early years but pulled the plug in 1977, when the last train came through.

Agricultural traffic provided much of the Wallkill line's revenue. Around the turn of the twentieth century, this meant milk. There were creamery complexes in most of the towns along the line, including one in Gardiner that was the first creamery ever built for Borden's. In New Paltz one of North America's oldest streets is seen: Huguenot Street, with its unusual stone houses, dates back to the late 1600s.

In 1983 the concept of the Wallkill Valley Rail-Trail was born in a report to the town of New Paltz by the New Paltz Environmental Conservation Commission. In 1991 the Wallkill Valley Rail-Trail Association (WVRTA) was formed by a group of private volunteers to develop, maintain, and promote the multiuse trail. In New Paltz, at the trail's northern end, it's owned by the village and town, while the southern section near Gardiner belongs to the Wallkill Valley Land Trust, Inc.

The goal was to have local governments and volunteers work together to bring the idea to fruition while limiting the costs to the taxpayers. This trail is an excellent realization of that aim, and the organization serves as a model for "Friends of the Trail" organizations around the county.

Volunteers are a big part of the Wallkill Valley Rail Trail. Major trail improvements, such as the redecking of the truss bridge over the Wallkill River, were accomplished with such labor. If you contact Eldeva Tofte of the Wallkill Valley Rail-Trail Association (see contact information above), she can provide you with information you need to join the organization.

This is also a very friendly trail for equestrians, who have a big presence in the valley; as you traverse the trail, you'll see some spectacular horse farms. In fact, equestrians had a hand in the design of the bridge railings, making them more comfortable from the point of view of a skittish horse.

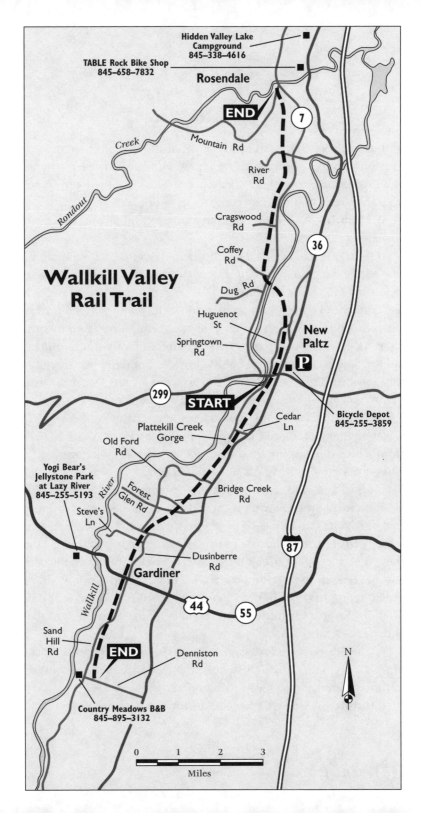

Wallkill Valley Rail Trail

Hidden Valley Lake
Campground
845-338-4616

TABLE Rock Bike Shop
845-658-7832

Rosendale

END

7

Mountain Rd

Creek

River
Rd

Rondout

Cragswood
Rd

36

Coffey
Rd

Dug Rd

Huguenot
St

New
Paltz

Springtown
Rd

P

299

START

Cedar
Ln

Bicycle Depot
845-255-3859

Plattekill Creek
Gorge

Old Ford
Rd

Yogi Bear's
Jellystone Park
at Lazy River
845-255-5193

River

Forest
Glen Rd

Bridge Creek
Rd

Steve's
Ln

Dusinberre
Rd

Gardiner

87

Wallkill

44   55

Sand
Hill
Rd

END

Denniston
Rd

N

Country Meadows B&B
845-895-3132

0   1   2   3

Miles

MILE BY MILE

Heading North from New Paltz

0.02 mile: This is an ornate, turn-of-the-twentieth-century station with a one-car-length train shed. A passing track used to be here to allow trains to approach one another. The station currently hosts an Italian restaurant, La Stazione—the station.

0.15 mile: An interesting cut-stone retaining wall lies on the east side of the trail.

0.4 mile: Grade crossing at Broadhead Avenue, with the remains of a NYC-type grade crossing signal cabinet. This structure used to hold the electrical components that powered the device. A creamery and tannery were some of the industries that provided traffic to the railroad from this location. The creamery shipped many of the old wooden reefer cars that carried hundreds of forty-quart milk cans apiece. The A. P. LeFevre Coal & Lumber Company was a community stalwart. The town's first electrical generating plant was located nearby; it's now the senior citizen housing adjacent to the trail.

This area is also home to the Huguenot Historical Society. The long building on the west side of the trail is the Deyo Assembly Hall, from which tours of the local historical district are organized. A fine glass producing facility was the original occupant here.

0.5 mile: Grade crossing of Mulberry Street, which is part of the Huguenot Historic District. Known as "the oldest street in America in continuous habitation," this place is worth a short detour. Many seventeenth-century homes are still here and easily observed from the street. Little Mill Brook is also seen here. In the 1800s the brook was harnessed to provide power to three mills that cut wood and milled grain. In times of high water on the Wallkill River, Mill Brook flows backward. Until the 1970s the surrounding land was used for agricultural purposes.

0.7 mile: A New York Central (NYC)—type battery box is seen here. This small, vaultlike structure housed the batteries used to power the grade crossing warning lights.

0.9 mile: A culvert allows Mill Brook to pass underneath.

The craggy precipices of the Shawangunk Mountains create interesting views to the west.

1.19 miles: Look for a NYC-type battery box, mile marker, and knocked-over signal control box.

1.2 miles: A good view of the Shawangunk Mountains opens up here as the trail widens and another culvert passes under it. A series of modern mile markers allows trail users to check their odometers. Marked in 0.25-mile intervals, they are constructed to look like old-style flanger signs. More battery boxes are here also.

1.8 miles: Enter a much more rural setting as the surrounding forest becomes marshy and the trail climbs onto a fill about 6 feet high.

1.9 miles: Head into a cut with gentle sloped earthen sides rising about 20 feet above the trail. NO TRESPASSING signs are seen here also.

2.0 miles: On a small fill, look for a culvert and some more railroad archaeology—namely a base for a signal standard on the west side and some telegraph poles on the east.

2.2–2.3 miles: SHOOTING RANGE signs appear on the approach to a deck-girder bridge, which in turn approaches a 400-foot, two-span, through-truss bridge over the Wallkill River. Nicely upgraded in 1993 with volunteer labor, pressure-treated decking and benches for sitting provide the perfect area for watching the scenic and slow-moving river. The north end of the bridge has a grade crossing for Springtown Road.

Here the Springtown Road Station once stood. This was a flag-stop station—one at which a waiting passenger would wave a white cloth or flag when the train approached, warning the engineer to stop and pick up passengers. Eight trains a day passed through here. The trail now is very rural with farms and horse paddocks. Great vistas of the Shawangunk Mountains are off to the west.

2.6 miles: Grade crossing at Coffey Road. Look for the flanger sign just southwest of this crossing; you might see some eighty-pound rail on the southwest side of the intersection. Rail is measured by the number of pounds per yard. By modern standards, eighty-pound rail is light, but by the standards of the turn-of-the-last century, it was on the heavy side.

3.27 miles: Grade crossing of Cragswood Road. Note that the rails are still in the road, though buried. A sign here notes that the size of the trees along the trail suggests that they began as seedlings after the last time the railroad cut brush here, from 1960 through 1964.

3.7 miles: An old NYC mile marker is here as well as the official end of the trail at the Rosendale town line. From this point on some trail sections that are privately owned are currently open and approved for trail users.

4.1 miles: Grade crossing at a gravel road; there's a whistle marker.

5.33–5.37 miles: A pretty impressive rock cut is seen here. Look closely near the bottom course of the cut and you'll see that it was widened in later years with pneumatically cut drill holes—evidence of more modern construction.

5.41 miles: Cross a small concrete bridge over a stream and the adjacent River Road. Just after that is an obliterated New York Central mile marker, which apparently sustained too many shotgun blasts.

6.15 miles: Look in the woods on your right and you'll see a large furnace and conveyor tipple system in the woods. It is reminiscent of times gone by when mineral mining was an important endeavor here in the East.

6.45 miles: The spur to the mine came off the mainline here.

6.7 miles: Head into a small cut, then continue onto a short concrete bridge.

6.9 miles: Grade crossing at Mountain Road, then go down a short hill at the approach to a high bridge.

7.02 miles: On the bridge at Rosendale. It's a 988-foot, deck-girder bridge with a curve to the right that takes it northerly as it

The high bridge at Rosendale is one of the most spectacular structures found on New York's rail-trails.

crosses Roundout Creek. It actually crossed the Delaware & Hudson Canal at this point as well—Rosendale calls itself Canal Town. The first bridge constructed in 1872 was a flimsy iron deck-truss bridge that placed severe weight and speed restrictions on trains that traversed it. Around the turn of the last century, the bridge was upgraded and strengthened, but it continued to have restrictions placed on it. With the coming of the lighter diesel engines in the 1950s, much of the concern about weight dissipated. When the line was abandoned and sold by Conrail in the early 1980s, the 11-mile segment from Rosendale to Kingston—including the bridge—was bought by John Wahl, who saw the possibility of a tourist train running from Rosendale or Kingston out onto the trestle. When that didn't pan out, he wanted to create a bungee-jumping park from the bridge, but the town refused to grant the necessary permission citing potential traffic concerns from startled motorists and other gawkers passing by. In 1991 Wahl's Wallkill Valley Railroad Company decked and opened the southern half of the bridge as a public walkway—but since this is privately owned, call the contact numbers provided above to make sure it's still open when you visit. Note that the hillsides near the bridge are largely covered with tailings from the many nearby cement mines.

Heading South from New Paltz

0.0 mile: An old drainage ditch is visible on your left as you head past Water Street. A gristmill and cooperage once occupied the complex on your left, but now you'll find shops and such. A brickyard flourished in this area in the early twentieth century.

0.1 mile: Head through a residential neighborhood on a small fill. A footpath on your right leads to a park overlooking the Wallkill River, on your right.

0.3 mile: Grade crossing of Plains Road. This area was once known as Hobo's Rock, because drifters camped out in the forest here during the Depression. A little farther south a switch came off the main to allow for a long lead to the various industries toward town. In the course of switching cars, train crews would occasionally spill coal, giving local folks free fuel. The marshy area now is home to nothing more exotic than salamanders.

0.5 mile: Travel on a fill above the marsh. A waterfall is visible on your left, with the water coming toward you—very scenic.

0.7 mile: In this area you'll see both cedar and black walnut trees.

1.45 miles: Grade crossing of Cedar Lane.

1.7 miles: Plattekill Gorge Bridge crosses over the stream at a height of 35 feet. This is a deck-truss railroad bridge, which features unusual differing types of abutments. The north end is built with "pudding stones," and the south end with poured concrete. It's likely that at one time a flood took out the south end's support, hence the more modern construction. A bench in the area is dedicated to the memory of Howard Buck.

2.5 miles: Grade crossing of a driveway as you pass by some beautiful apple orchards to complement the astounding views of the shag mountains.

2.7 miles: You're back on fill about 20 feet high. It'll drop off to about 40 feet, then abruptly come back to level ground.

2.85 miles: Grade crossing of Old Ford Road.

3.1 miles: A small cut is here, along with an agricultural grade crossing connecting some more orchards. You'll then reach another higher cut—15 feet tall.

3.4 miles: Another fill, this time about 20 feet tall. An interesting whistle marker is here, obviously of NYC design.

3.5 miles: Head slightly uphill and then into another small cut.

3.7 miles: Grade crossing of Bridge Creek Road. It was in this area that the Forest Glen Passenger Station once stood. Though a small and lightly visited station, it had an agent up until 1937, when passenger service ended. The Forest Glen Station also had a post office inside as well as a coalyard and general store nearby.

3.85 miles: Travel on a 15-foot fill as you approach a deck-girder bridge over Forest Glen Road.

4.1 miles: A little stream off to your right crosses under the fill by way of a typical NYC culvert made of preformed concrete slabs.

4.2 miles: The cut here can be wet and muddy at times.

4.5 miles: Look for remnants of ties bulldozed off to the side of the trail as you pass by a residential neighborhood.

4.6 miles: Grade crossing at Old Ford Road, where the rails are still in place.

Part of the panoramic view from the high bridge at Rosendale, north of New Paltz.

4.8 miles: Steve's Lane grade crossing. Dusinberre Road comes close to the trail.

5.0 miles: Concrete culvert; the trail widens. Horse paddocks are here, with some fine residents visible today. An interesting agricultural grade crossing leads to a beautiful meadow on your right.

5.2 miles: Residential neighborhood.

5.3 miles: The cinder base on the trail speaks of a history of washouts.

5.6 miles: A small industrial building on your left seems not to have a railroad heritage.

5.74 miles: Grade crossing at Route 44/55. This neighborhood is a hotbed of old railroad history. For example, off to your right, the red building is the former Borden Creamery complex. Built in 1881, it provided hundreds of cars of traffic to the railroad until it was closed in the 1920s. John Borden himself lived in the nearby town of Wallkill, and the Borden name in dairy products was born here. Smaller bits of railroad history include battery boxes and signal gear that powered the now-gone grade crossing apparatus.

The town hall, about 150 yards east of the trail, was once the one-room schoolhouse of Gardiner. Enlarged through the years, it has served in its current function since 1981.

Forgotten and torn-down history includes the site of the old Gardiner Hotel—a large structure that served as *the* place to stay for traveling salesman in days gone by. Rita's Restaurant stands there today. Also nearby was the usual coal and lumber complex to serve the needs of a growing community. The old depot itself, Gardiner Station, has been semirestored into an antiques store, Guilford Station. Back on the trail and heading south, you'll cross over Farmers Turnpike and then a small brook via a concrete-slab bridge.

6.2 miles: On your left is a large open area with signage warning people away from a hazardous environmental problem left over from the site's onetime use as a coalyard.

6.3 miles: Travel on a fill about 12 feet high, and then encounter an agricultural grade crossing along with a small cut. Gardiner Airport is nearby to your left; on weekends it does a good business with folks who like to jump out of planes. Keep a lookout for parachutists.

6.4 miles: The landscape opens up here to showcase a field on the left along with a residential neighborhood and another field on your right, past the hedgerow.

6.5 miles: Head onto a big fill here; it's 35 or 40 feet tall and only a few feet long, not much more than an interesting way to fill a gully.

6.78 miles: Grade crossing of Sand Hill Road. Look for the battery box on the southeast corner of the street.

7.0 miles: Travel on a slight 15-foot-high fill here, with parallel-running Sand Hill Road nearby on your right.

7.14 miles: The fill climbs to about 25 feet tall. Occasional ties can be found in this area also.

7.3 miles: Grade crossing. The trail widens up here with access for automobiles and farm vehicles, so be careful of a possible encounter.

8.0 miles: Travel on a small fill over a culvert; it's still wide enough for cars.

8.15 miles: Small cut with gently sloped sides.

8.16 miles: Denniston Road is the effective end of the line—the rail-trail is blocked by barbed wire at the south side of the road.

Endpoints: Platt Street in Glens Falls, Lake George Beach State Park in Lake George.

Location: The Warren County communities of Lake George, Queensbury, and Glens Falls.

Length: 9.42 miles.

Surface: Asphalt; the trail includes about 2 miles on city streets.

Uses: All nonmotorized uses.

To get there: Take I–87 to exit 19, head east on NY Route 254 for about 1 mile, and turn left onto Country Club Road. Parking will be on your left in less than a minute.

Contact: Patrick Beland, Director, Warren County Parks and Recreation Department, 4028 Main Street, Warrensburg, NY 12885; 518–623–2877.

Accommodations: The Glens Falls Inn, 25 Sherman Avenue, Glens Falls, NY 12801; 518–743–9365; fax 518–743–0696; info@glensfallsinn.com; www.glensfallsinn.com.

G lens Falls is an interesting small city in eastern New York, located on falls of the Hudson River near the resort community of Lake George. It's the site of the Hyde Collection—a museum containing European and American art—and the Chapman Historical Museum. Settled in the 1760s, the community, then known as Wing's Falls, was destroyed by British forces in 1780. The settlement was rebuilt in 1788 and named for Colonel Johannes Glen. Cooper's Cave and other places in the area are described in the James Fenimore Cooper classic, *The Last of the Mohicans.*

The Delaware & Hudson Railway came through town on the Fourth of July, 1869. The extension to the resort community of Caldwell (renamed Lake George in 1903) was not completed until 1882.

It was at this time a new combination rail/ship scenic excursion was marketed. Passengers could come down from Canada to the Plattsburgh area at the north end of Lake Champlain by rail, then board a steamship that would take them the length of both Lake

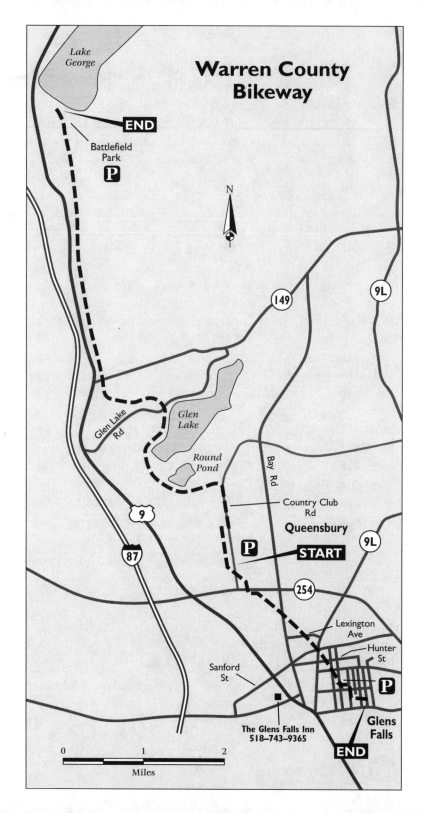

Champlain and Lake George to the south end at Caldwell. Here they could board the train again and be in New York in but a few hours more. This Adirondack excursion was the envy of the Catkills resorts; a ticket for this trip was one of the status symbols of the Gilded Age. In fact, the D&H, always searching for new sources of revenue, purchased the exclusive Fort William Henry Hotel in Caldwell. Indeed, the D&H acquired the steamboats and hotel *eleven years* before the rail line reached Lake George. This edifice, along with the ownership of the fleet of steamships that plied the lake, meant that the D&H could take care of all your vacation transit needs in the beautiful Lake George area. D&H also owned the Hotel Champlain at Bluff Point South of Plattsburgh and steamboats on Lake Champlain, locking up side-wheeler travel and hotel lodging there just as on Lake George. This lasted until the Great Depression when the D&H had to mothball the steamships in 1932 due to lack of patrons. They were later sold off in 1937, and the D&H was out of the lake-transit business.

There were a couple of interesting trackage features of this branch line. In the later years of operation (post-1925), the D&H had no turntable at the Lake George end. So to turn the steam engines around for the return trip, a "balloon" track turned the entire train at the lake. As the name implies, a balloon track is a track laid out in the shape of loop. So tight a radius was it that the train had to literally traverse at walking speed to ensure that it did not derail. After the turning procedure was completed, the train was usually backed out onto the same pier where the present Lake George Steamboat Company tour boat docks. That way, passengers could board the boat without much of a walk. This unusual track lasted until the time the line was abandoned.

The other interesting feature was a marine track or—as it was known locally—a "submarine track." If you were a wealthy yachtsman, you could have your boat transported to the lake by flatcar, and then put onto the special "marine" sidetrack that led directly into the lake so you could launch your boat. Such innovative marketing today would be worthy of the Golden Freight Car Award sponsored by the trade publication *Railway Age*.

The passenger station at Lake George is reminiscent of structures on the Santa Fe Railroad. Designed with a Spanish Mission motif and built of stucco with a tile roof, it looks somewhat out of place in upstate New York. Constructed in 1912, it still stands today, housing various small businesses. The station was renovated by the steamboat company in 2000, exposing and restoring some of the original interior features that had been covered up over the years.

Another attractive feature of this station is the representations of four people on the upper corners. These statues depict a Champlain-era soldier, a French and Indian War soldier, a backwoodsman, and an Indian warrior.

The freight business of the D&H at Lake George had dwindled so totally that by the early 1950s only about 120 cars a year were handled. Of this total, about forty cars carried origin lumber traffic from a smattering of local lumber mills. Passenger service ended to Lake George in November 1957, and in March 1958 freight service north of Glens Falls ended.

Parts of this trail right-of-way contains some street trackage where the Hudson Valley Railway Company—which provided both trolley and interurban services—and the Delaware & Hudson Railway ran near each other. This area became an official rail-trail in 1978.

In 2000 a new bike-pedestrian bridge was built over Quaker Road, Route 254, thus extending the trail south into the residential neighborhoods closer to the Hudson River and downtown Glens Falls. Accordingly, we describe the trail in two sections. The north segment travels 7.0 miles to the shore at Lake George, and the south segment heads 2.42 miles toward the downtown area, where an easy connection can be made to the Glens Falls Feeder Canal Trail. Much of the local railroad and industrial history here has been provided by Kip Grant, who lives in the area and is a great resource.

- -

MILE BY MILE

Heading North from Queensbury

0.1 mile: Country Club Road is on your right as you head north on the nicely paved trail. A small fill is here as you bend slightly to the east and pass through a hardwood forest. Look carefully and you'll see an occasional old telegraph pole with single and double cross arms (poles on the Lake George branch had two cross arms). These differ from the kind you'd see on the New York Central or even the various New England railroads in their extremely wide cross arms. The other railroads would certainly have used multiple rows of arms.

0.2 mile: Grade crossing of Sweet Road.

0.3 mile: Head past a residential neighborhood and a line of arborvitae that are about twenty-five years old. Unusual aquatic flowers are found growing in the marshy area to your left.

0.4 mile: An old barn is visible here, along with what was at one time an agricultural grade crossing. The trail bends to the right to avoid a new development of houses that were constructed after the railroad was abandoned.

0.7 mile: Back onto Country Club Road with a wide, nicely marked bike lane to navigate in.

0.8 mile: Go past Browns Path Road, which leads to your right.

1.0 mile: Travel past Glens Falls Country Club, where the surroundings are suburban and well kept.

1.2 miles: The bike route now takes a left onto Round Pond Road.

1.5 miles: In this area you'll share the right-of-way with golf carts.

1.8 miles: Go downhill past beautiful Round Pond on your right.

1.9 miles: The trail takes a right onto Birdsall Road and heads uphill. The Hudson Valley Railway (HVR) is on your right, on a fill. The New York Power and Light Company acquired the trolley right-of-way for its transmission lines.

2.3 miles: Head uphill (you'll see HVR fill off to your right), and then past Glen Lake.

2.5 miles: Cross a scenic bridge over a part of the feeder stream for Glen Lake. The interesting causeway found here is a perfect place to find aquatic birds up close and personal. The bikeway bridge is HVR; the adjacent bridge is D&H. The bikeway now follows the HVR right-of-way as far as NY Route 149.

2.7 miles: Run parallel to and then cross over Ash Drive.

2.9 miles: Zigzag downhill under the power lines and past some more wetlands and a small fill.

3.0 miles: Grade crossing of Glen Lake Road—which can be busy, so be careful.

3.2 miles: Go uphill once again. (The D&H climbs a gentler and longer grade off to the right, but that section is not in public ownership.)

3.4 miles: Continue uphill and then over a small bridge; a mountain stream passes underneath. A private campground, the Lake George RV Park, lies off to your right.

3.6 miles: Travel on a 20-foot-high fill—the tallest one yet. The right-of-way is steep in this area.

3.7 miles: Bikeway bridge over Route 149. The railroad used to cross over the highway at a grade (just east of the bridge), and if you look carefully you'll see some old ties still in place. A trolley company crossed as well.

3.9 miles: Head into the forest and back on the D&H right-of-way.

4.2 miles: A sign here indicates the trail to Colonel Williams Monument. Also in this area is a marshy, meandering stream that has the biggest dragonflies we've ever seen. These must show up on air-traffic control radar.

4.4 miles: The meandering stream crosses underneath again as you travel on a post-and-beam bridge.

4.5 miles: Heading uphill, a trail with blue markings appears on your right. This is an unofficial hiking trail that leads up to French Mountain.

4.8 miles: The trail opens up into a little glade area with a couple of picnic tables.

4.9 miles: Make a little zigzag as you get into a fenced-in area. A sand quarry is visible to your right. A rail siding is visible among the corrugated-metal-sided buildings. Formerly a lumber company, this is now a Wild West theme park.

5.3 miles: Seen here is an old-fashioned, 1940s-era cottage complex. A modern motel complex is on your right as you approach U.S. Route 9. You will parallel this busy highway for a short while.

5.4 miles: Grade crossing of Bloody Pond Road. You'll spot a tourist mecca advertised by the 30-foot-high "Uncle Sam"—this is the Magic Forest theme park.

5.8 miles: Pass a telegraph signal with the usual twin arms and five insulators per side. Head downhill: The right-of-way is on the side of a mountain.

5.9 miles: You're still on a shelf.

6.2 miles: Grade crossing onto Old Military Road. Follow the sign and take a sharp right. The trail tends to go downhill the rest of the way to the lake.

6.3 miles: Here can be found a genuine D&H mile wooden mile marker. Inscribed with "A69"—Albany, 69 miles—this marker is of a typical D&H design with its 10-by-10-inch wooden construction and pointed top. This is seen on many rail-trails of D&H heritage. Also here is a grade crossing of a driveway to a private residence.

6.5 miles: Go past a water theme park on your left. You're traveling on a small fill here, with some water pollution monitoring wells.

6.6 miles: Cross over NY Route 9L (American Legion Drive) via a through-girder bridge with the D&H logo still on it. On the north side of the bridge is an outlet to Stanton Drive. A Lake George school ball field is on your right.

6.8 miles: Go downhill as the ground drops away to your right; the right-of-way is on a shelf with a steep hillside going up the left side. Here the bikeway passes alongside the historic state-operated Battlefield Park picnic area, featuring the remains of Fort George.

7.0 miles: The trail swings around to your left, and the lake becomes visible. The trail then becomes parallel to Beach Road and ends a short distance ahead at the passenger station, which is across the street from the Steamship Dock. The village of Lake George is a modern tourist destination with a full smorgasbord of choices in restaurants, lodging, and family-oriented activities.

Heading South from Queensbury

0.1 mile: Heading out, the first notable feature is the beautiful new bike-pedestrian bridge built to carry trail users up and over busy Quaker Road. Observant users will note that there are actually two bridges. The first goes over a small stream called Halfway Brook,

while the second carries you over the road. On the far side of the bridge is the Aldi food store, connected directly to the trail. In years past a Grossman's building supply company was here; a dock adjacent to the rail line allowed cars of forest products to be unloaded directly on site. A second dock nearby was used for many years by the Woodbury Lumber Company to unload rail cars of lumber and building supplies. Woodbury advertised using a character called "Rapid Ralph," and people to this day can remember the "Rapid Ralph" sign identifying the site at what was the end of the track right next to Quaker Road. Woodbury and Grossman used their docks until track was removed, Woodbury predating Grossman by many years. Just south of the bridge, a railroad spur (the "brickyard spur") once veered off to the west, serving the Glens Falls Brick Company and a number of coal, oil, and lumber dealers.

0.25 mile: Head into a white pine forest; a smattering of formerly rail-served entities are found here as well. Dempsey Block & Steel was the former owner of the building with the vertical conveyor; it used to receive raw materials by rail. Note the old telegraph

This bridge over Quaker Road—opened in 2000—allowed for a new extension of the Warren County Bikeway to be built into downtown Glens Falls.

pole here, as well a gate in the fence where the siding entered the property.

0.35 mile: This is an interesting situation. You are now going through the center of the C. R. Bard Company's facilities—a medical hardware manufacturer. The trail bisects company property, and the employees use the trail extensively during lunch. Some even use the trail to commute to work by bike.

0.56 mile: Cross at Bay Road. This is a busy place, so be careful. It's interesting to note that the traffic signals above Bay Road are nonfunctional. In years past, the conductor on the train used to control this crossing; when the train needed to go through, he turned on the lights to stop traffic. They're still there, awaiting the train that isn't coming anytime soon.

0.72 mile: The expansive area on your left used to be the home of the Glens Falls Terra Cotta Company, one of the Northeast's largest manufacturers of decorative building trim components from terra-cotta. There used to be a large internal network of trackage; the company is believed to have operated its own narrow-gauge railroad using either a tiny steam locomotive or horse and mule teams to move small railcars of materials about the property. The company covered an area that would today be bounded by Bay, Ridge, and Quaker Roads. The only remaining part of the industry is the office—made entirely of terra-cotta—found at Ridge and Meadowbrook Roads, a few blocks northeast of here.

0.79 mile: Another footing for a relay box lies on the east side of the trail as you pass by more Glens Falls "Hometown USA" neighborhoods (see Trail 10).

0.95 mile: Grade crossing of Lexington Avenue. There are still more residential neighborhoods in this area.

1.05 miles: Grade crossing of Sanford Street. Just beyond this, you'll cross Ridge Street. Note the creative reuse of the former Borden Dairy Company building, a rail-served industry, into a local office and shop for Time Warner Cable Company. Also in this area, Dr. Russell A. Baker used to plant hundreds of flowers. The display adorned the triangular area traversed by the railroad between Ridge and Sanford Streets. This was a piece of Glens Falls that was seen by thousands of the region's residents from the 1950s all the way into the 1980s, and it seems that someone is carrying on the tradition here in a smaller way.

1.24 miles: Grade crossing of Hunter Street.

1.4 miles: Go past another formerly rail-served business. Note the sign starting to show beneath the paint across the front of the building—NATIONAL BISCUIT COMPANY BAKERY—better known today as Nabisco. This facility once made bread. A rail siding once primarily took in coal to feed an internal heating system. Today the north end of the plant is used as a furniture warehouse. Also adjacent to the trail is Cooper's Cave Ale Company, a local microbrewery that serves sandwiches as well as being a good place to stop and watch passersby. This building used to be the Trimbey Machine Works. Across the trail is another former dairy—Daisy Dairy. Cross both Dix Avenue and Walnut Street at an oblique angle. Be careful, as these are busy crossings.

1.55 miles: Cooper Street. The trail diverts from the railroad alignment here, because Miller Mechanical Services acquired the right-of-way for a building that sits directly on it. This site was the former facility of the Glens Falls Coal & Oil Company. The beautifully restored brick buildings on the Miller property are remnants of GF Coal & Oil. You will now jog left, then right onto Leonard Street.

1.71 miles: There's trailhead parking on Leonard Street for about fifteen cars alongside a small park. Some of the metal buildings here are owned by the local newspaper company, the Post Star. Ironically, they were the last rail served users in the area, and the reason why it kept on so long.

1.83 miles: The bikeway continues beyond this point: Cross Lawrence Street then, halfway down the next block, turn left onto the former railroad alignment once again. Just before you turn onto the bikeway, look on your right and you'll see the former D&H crossing tender's tower. This unusual two story building, constructed following World War II, housed rail employees. They could look south along the old yard area; when a train was coming across the numerous at-grade crossings, they would electrically lower the crossing gates. In later years the tower housed the Glens Falls freight agent. At the time of this writing, the tower and extant track are being restored to serve as a memorial to the railroad in Glens Falls. Call

Patrick Beland (518–623–2877) for information about this group.

2.42 miles: After passing by Prospect, Orchard, and McDonald Streets, the end of the trail is at Platt Street. Cohen and Son scrap yard is just beyond Platt; the track is still in place to serve it. Interestingly, there was once a tower at the McDonald Street crossing very similar to the brick tower at Lawrence Street (1.83 miles). The tower at McDonald Street was similar in architecture, but was made of wood. This tower was taken down sometime in the 1950s and moved to the big D&H Railroad facility at Oneonta, New York. Look for the foundation in the weeds at McDonald Street.

MORE RAIL-TRAILS

23 Allegheny River Valley Trail

Endpoints: A loop beginning and ending at Gargoyle Park in Allegany.

Location: Cattaraugus County.

Length: 5.6 miles.

Surface: Asphalt.

Uses: Walking, in-line skating, bicycling, running, fishing, cross-country skiing.

To get there: From NY Route 17 take exit 24 for the town of Allegany. Travel west 1 mile on 17th Street. Turn left onto NY Route 417 and travel south 1 mile to St. Bonaventure University. Take the first right entrance into the University and make an immediate right turn. Look for the track and football field parking lot; the trail is right next to the parking lot.

Contact: Joe Higgins, Trail Chairman, 716–371–4265 or 716–372–4433, joe@abbottwelding.com; or Greater Olean Chamber of Commerce, 120 North Union Street, Olean, NY 14760; 716–372–4433; www.oleanny.com.

The Allegheny Trail is an especially well-engineered and well-constructed trail. It is a loop trail, very unusual for rail-trails. About 40 percent of the trail is on the campus of St. Bonaventure University, and the trail is exceptionally well integrated into the college community and the towns.

A logical start is near the University's track and football field. From this point trail users can travel for more than 3 miles along the Allegheny River be-

The Allegheny River Valley trail is especially enjoyable on in-line skates.

tween Allegany and Olean and never cross a street. At the 2-mile
mark you will see Gargoyle Park on your left. Large shag bark hickory trees dominate the grounds, which include swings and a merry-
go-round. The St. Bonaventure campus ends at Gargoyle Park and
from here to the levee the land is owned by the Olean General Hos-
pital. It is more residential and has a few quiet street crossings. At 4
miles the trail parallels the Olean Rail Yards.

You'll also find many restaurants in downtown Olean and on
Route 417; contact the Greater Olean Area Chamber of Commerce
(716–372–4433; tourism@oleanny.com). There are no rest rooms
along the trail.

24 Allison Wells-Ney Trail

Endpoints: Thayer Road, Portland, to Prospect Station Road, Westfield.

Location: Chautauqua County.

Length: 3.3 miles.

Surface: Dirt, cinder.

Uses: All nonmotorized uses.

To get there: In the town of Brocton, take U.S. Route 20 west to Portland.
Then turn left onto Fay Street and continue all the way to a left turn onto
Ellicott Road. Then take a quick right onto Thayer Road.

Contact: Chautauqua Rails-to-Trails, P.O. Box 151, Mayville, NY 14757-0151;
716–483–2330.

The Pennsylvania Railroad's Chautauqua Branch ran from Mc-
Clintock, Pennsylvania to Buffalo, New York. The line entered Chautauqua County at Clymer and traveled northeasterly to Portland. At
Portland the line joined with the Nickel Plate and headed east to Buffalo.

The line followed the original route of the Buffalo, Oil Creek &
Cross Cut Railroad, which was chartered in 1865. The company was
later renamed the Buffalo, Corry & Pittsburgh Railroad. By the 1960s
freight loadings had fallen off; the line was abandoned in the early
1970s.

The trail today runs through woods, grape orchards, and agricultural fields.

Endpoints: NY Route 146A to Outlet Road and Powers Lane, Ballston Lake.

Location: Saratoga County.

Length: 3.35 miles.

Surface: Asphalt.

Uses: All nonmotorized uses.

To get there: Take exit 9 off I–87 (the Northway) and head west on NY Route 146. Take Route 146A north for about 6.5 miles until you reach the village of Ballston Lake. Shortly after crossing the railroad tracks, you'll spot the parking area for the Ballston Bike Path on your right.

Contact: J. D. Wood, Ballston Trail Committee, 518–399–6546.

Formed in 1902, the Schenectady Railway Company (SRC) was an interurban system—one traveling between cities rather than within a given community, like a regular trolley. In its early years, for a mere twenty-five cents you could travel from Schenectady to Ballston Lake and even beyond, to Saratoga Springs. This company operated the ubiquitous wooden cars right up to the eve of World War II, ceasing operations in 1940.

Much like trolley or interurban companies in New England and New Jersey, the SRC got into the amusement business to develop some weekend patronage. In this area, that meant spending nearly $75,000 to create a resort pavilion and other recreational facilities on the lake such as a beachfront, baseball fields, and oval tracks for bike and footraces. Sadly, virtually the only thing left from the days of the old amusement park is the carousel. This is being restored and housed locally. Someday it might be able to return to Ballston Lake.

After the interurban company went out of business, the corridor was sold off to the town, and it sat vacant for many years except for occasional visits by maintenance crews of both the railroad and the Niagara Mohawk Power Company (which has an underground gas pipeline parallel in the corridor).

In 1989 a mention of the corridor was included in the recreation sections of the town's master plan. After that, the town's recreation commission took the idea of a bike path from those master plan meet-

"Mr C.U.D." encourages trail users to keep the trail area clean.

ings and proceeded toward that goal. After lengthy negotiations with Ni-Mo regarding liability concerns surrounding the pipeline, the path became a locally funded reality in 1995. Though short in length, this project has been so successful that extensions and connections to neighboring towns are being considered.

26 Bog Meadow Brook Trail

Endpoints: Saratoga Springs.

Location: Saratoga County.

Length: 1.9 miles.

Surface: Dirt, original ballast.

Uses: All nonmotorized uses.

To get there: From the intersection of U.S. Route 9 and NY Route 29 in downtown Saratoga Springs, head east on Route 29 (Lake Avenue). At 2.5 miles the trailhead will be on your right.

Contact: Cynthia Beham, Project Director, Saratoga Springs Open Space Project, 110 Spring Street, Saratoga Springs, NY 12866; 518–587–5554.

27 Dryden Lake Park Trail

Endpoints: Dryden to Dryden Lake Park.

Location: Tompkins County.

Length: 4 miles.

Surface: Crushed cinder, grass.

Uses: Walking, mountain biking, horseback riding, cross-country skiing, fishing.

To get there: The Dryden Lake Park Trail is located near NY Routes 13 and 38, 10 miles to the east of Ithaca—an easy forty-five-minute drive from Binghamton, Elmira, or Syracuse. There is some parking (enough for two or three cars) at every crossroad. The midpoint of the trail, at Dryden Lake Park, can be found by following Route 38 south of Dryden to Keith Lane. Take this to Lake Road, which goes around the east side of the lake and past the golf course. The trail has a gravel parking area on the right, across the street from Tractor Service—a log-cabin-type house within the complex.

Contact: Larry Carpenter, Public Works Department, 607–844–8654. Equestrian resources: Lilley's Tack & Feed, 15 Livermore Cross, Dryden, NY, 13053; 607–844–9370. Pleasant Hill Tack Shop, Port Crane, NY, 13833; 607–648–4979.

The 4-mile-long Dryden Lake Park Trail is one of the several pathways in Tompkins County that are coming together to form a vast system of interconnected rail-trails, waterways, and other greenways. Located near Routes 13 and 38 about 10 miles east of Ithaca,

The Dryden Lake Park Trail provides access through a rich wetland landscape.

the trail begins in the charming small town of Dryden and has something for the whole family no matter the season.

The trail is elevated several feet aboveground for most of its length and affords some beautiful views of the adjacent farmland and hills, especially when the trees have lost their leaves for the season. Beaver activity is seen at the 2-mile mark. Use is frequent, even in wintertime, and most dog walkers are courteous in keeping their animals under control.

The main attraction, Dryden Lake Park, is located at 2.5 miles and has rest room facilities. This is the best place to park, being more or less at the trail's midpoint. Dams were rebuilt several times, each time changing the level of the lake, but it has always been a popular boating, fishing, and recreation site. For bird-watchers, this is one of the best sites in the Finger Lakes region. Even when the lake freezes, the inlet and the marshes are still open and used by a variety of waterfowl.

Dryden Lake was the site of an Indian camp because of its good hunting and fishing, and arrow flints can still be found. The Dryden Historical Society has done much to preserve the lake's story. To later settlers its water power was important. In 1820 a dam/sawmill was constructed until it was washed away in the flood of 1902.

In the summer the user is shaded by a full tree canopy as the trail passes alongside the lake. The trail ends 200 feet beyond the Tompkins–Cortland County line at Lake Road. Parking facilities are available. This last section of trail is also used as part of the Finger Lake Trail System and is being added to the North Country Trail System.

28 Gorge Trail

Endpoints: Clark Street in Cazenovia to Bingley. (Note that there is no trail access in Bingley. The trail drops straight down to the road and ends at the guardrail.)

Location: Madison County.

Length: 2.2 miles.

Surface: Crushed limestone, cinder, ballast with cinder on top, rough in some places.

Uses: Bicycling, fishing, horseback riding, walking, running, cross-country skiing.

To get there: From the intersection of U.S. Route 20 and NY Route 13 in downtown Cazenovia, head north on Route 13 for two blocks and then take a right onto Williams Street. There is a trailhead near the old passenger station. You can park behind the station.

Contact: Gene Gissin, Cazenovia Preservation Foundation, P.O. Box 627, Cazenovia, NY 13035; 315–655–2224.

This trail follows the original railroad bed established by the C&C Railroad in 1870; trains operated until 1967. At one time there were up to eleven train trips per day. The depot, now Gissin's Photography Studio, stands as a reminder as these past days. The depot was built in 1870 and remodeled in 1896.

29 East Ithaca Recreation Way/South Hill Recreation Way

Endpoints: Ithaca.

Location: Tompkins County.

Length: 2.2 miles in all.

Surface: Asphalt, gravel, cinder.

Uses: All nonmotorized activities; South Hill has a fishing access.

To get there: Take NY Route 366 east out of Ithaca. Turn right onto Game Farm Road and head south for about 0.5 mile to the trailhead. Parking is available on the west side of Game Farm Road.

Contact: George Frantz, Assistant Town Planner, Town of Ithaca, 126 East Seneca Street, Ithaca, NY 14850-4352; 607–273–1747.

Both these trails are part of an emerging system of trails soon to be realized in the greater Ithaca area. This system will include the longer Black Diamond Trail located along the east shore of Cayuga Lake, and even the Dryden Trail. Both trails are very close to Cornell University and Ithaca College and provide a link to surrounding neighborhoods and downtown Ithaca.

㉚ Hojack Trail

Endpoints: Redcreek, Hannibal.

Location: Cayuga County.

Length: 9 miles.

Surface: Cinder, ballast, grass.

Uses: All nonmotorized uses plus snowmobiles and ATVs.

To get there: From Fair Haven head south and east on County Route 94 for about 1.6 miles to County Route 95. Travel northeast on Route 95 for about 0.5 mile. This is where the Hojack and the Cayuga County Trail (Trail 7) intersect.

Contact: Michele Beilman, Director, Cayuga County Park and Trails Commission, Emerson Park Eastlake Road, Auburn, NY 13021; 315–253–5611.

㉛ Hudson Valley Rail-Trail

Endpoints: Town of Lloyd.

Location: Ulster County.

Length: 2.74 miles.

Surface: Asphalt, stone dust, grass.

Uses: All nonmotorized uses.

To get there: Take NY Route 299 in Ulster County, then head south or east on New Paltz Road (County Route 12) for about 0.75 mile. Turn north onto River Side Drive and continue 0.1 mile to Tony Williams Park, where the trailhead is located.

Contact: Hudson Valley Rail-Trail Association, 6 Main Street, Suite 3006, Highland, NY 12528. Greenway Conservancy for the Hudson Valley, Capital Building, Capital Station, Room 254, Albany, NY 12224; 518–473–3835.

The New York, New Haven & Hartford Railroad, usually called the New Haven Railroad, is among the most famous of northeastern railroads because of its scenic routes, fine trains—and ability to swallow up competing railroads. The New Haven Railroad's facility at the little town of Maybrook, not far from the start of this trail, was once the largest railroad yard east of the Mississippi River, and processed a large portion of the freight routed into New England.

The New Haven Railroad declined into bankruptcy in 1969 and was merged with the Penn Central, which maintained a single train on the old New Haven Railroad line. When the high bridge over the Hudson River at Poughkeepsie was damaged in a fire in 1974, the Penn Central declared the bridge unsafe, and the last working vestige of the New Haven Railroad was abandoned.

The trail corridor is now a right-of-way for a fiber-optic line. Because of the New Haven Railroad connection and the abundance of railroad infrastructure still visible along the trail, the Hudson Valley Rail-Trail is an especially interesting trail for railroad buffs. There is an interesting and informative Web site associated with this trail at highland.hvnet.com/articles/railtrail.htm.

32 Lehigh Valley Rail-Trail (Naples to Middlesex)

Endpoints: Naples, Middlesex.

Location: Ontario and Yates Counties.

Length: 6.5 miles.

Surface: Grass, dirt, some cinder.

Uses: All nonmotorized uses.

To get there: On the south end of Canandaigua Lake, follow NY Route 21 to the north side of Naples. Where County Route 12 intersects with Route

21, you'll find a large dirt parking lot. The railroad used to cross at this location. You can park here and head northeast along the trail.

Contact: New York State Department of Environmental Conservation, 6274, Avon-Lima Road, Avon, NY, 14414; 716–226–2466; www.dec.state.ny.us.

This line was once a component of the network that emanated from Stanley. Originally built for the farming industry to transport goods to market, it was also used to move coal, so the Lehigh Valley Railroad—one of the Northeast's best known coal-transporting railroads—purchased the old Middlesex Railroad in 1895 and integrated it into the system. It puttered along with declining success until 1970, when it was finally abandoned. Similar abandonments were taking place at this time in parts of the Midwest, where light-density branch lines were also being cast off. Many of New York's railroads in rural areas were those built of legally flimsy deed structures and when the railroads were abandoned, the rights-of-way were allowed to "revert" to adjacent landowners. This particular corridor is no different, but what allowed this trail to become publicly accessible makes an interesting story. It's all about how the Hi-Tor Wildlife Management Area came into being.

In the 1930s James Long, a local farmer, decided to get out of the dairy business. He offered to gift the land and an old farmhouse to the state. But the Great Depression was in full howl, and the state declined the offer unless the property came with an endowment to pay for maintenance. Long refused, and instead approached the federal government, which accepted his proposal. Later the federal government obtained other contiguous and nearby farms. After some years had passed, the federal government leased and eventually deeded all the properties to the state of New York for wildlife management and conservation land. One of the parcels came with the old abandoned railroad corridor that had reverted to one of the farmers, who in turn had sold it to the federal government.

All in all, Hi-Tor has about 6,500 acres in this reserve. Much of the areas nearest this old railroad corridor are wetlands, with some memorable vistas with the hills and farms of Naples for a backdrop. Don't forget, though, Hi-Tor is a wildlife management area—that means beware of hunters when hunting season arrives.

Because much of this rural route is adjacent to wetlands, be on the lookout for the great blue heron rookery. You are almost certain to see these majestic huge birds along the trail. A number of small bridges span the meandering streams and West River within the wetlands, some of them rare railroad-era bent-timber bridges. Be on the lookout for them. For a change-of-pace trip back to point A, consider riding back on NY Route 245, which parallels the trail a short distance southeast. The shoulders are decent, and the road isn't too heavily traveled. Best of all, it's mostly downhill back to Route 21.

33 Lehigh Valley Trail (Rush to Victor)

Endpoints: Rush, Victor.

Location: Monroe and Ontario Counties.

Length: 15.3 miles.

Surface: Grass, dirt, some chunky rock, railroad ballast.

Uses: All nonmotorized uses, but road bikes are not recommended due to the rough surface.

To get there: Take I–390 to NY Route 251. Follow Route 251 east to Mendon.

Contact: Victor Hiking Trails, Inc., 85 East Main Street, Victor, NY 14564; 716–234–8226.

This trail, still in development but open to public use, connects the towns of Rush and Victor. The surface is too rough for skinny-tire bikes, but that should change with planned resurfacing. Currently there is little use of this rustic, pleasant trail, most of which passes through woods, horse farms, open meadows, and wetlands.

34 Plattsburgh Bike-Ped Trail

Endpoints: Intersection of Jay and Hamilton Streets, and Nevada Oval East, which is within the former airbase at Plattsburgh.

Location: Clinton County.

Length: 1.55 miles.

Surface: Asphalt.

Uses: All nonmotorized uses.

The majestic railroad station at Plattsburgh is a short distance from the trailhead for the Plattsburgh Bike-Ped Trail.

To get there: Take exit 36 off I–87 and follow NY Route 22 for about 2.5 miles until you come to a fork. Take right fork at South Peru Street and follow this for about 0.8 mile to U.S. Route 9. Follow Route 9 north for about 0.5 mile and turn right onto Hamilton Street. Follow this for two blocks; the trailhead will be on your right. There's not much parking, so park where it's approved or safe.

Contact: Rosemary Schoomaker, Director of Community Development, City of Plattsburgh, 41 City Place, Plattsburgh, NY 12901; 518–563–7642.

This project was awarded funds for design and construction in 1999 and finally completed and opened in June 2001 as the Plattsburgh Pedestrian and Bicycle Bypass—better known as the Plattsburgh Bike-Ped Trail.

This is not a "rail-to-trail" project per se, but rather a "rail-with-trail" project in that it's built directly adjacent to the Canadian Pacific Railway's mainline along Lake Champlain. There are four to six trains a day, two of them Amtrak's premier name train, the Adirondack, named by *National Geographic* as one of the world's most scenic trains.

Though only 1.55 miles long, this trail passes by some scenic vistas of Lake Champlain, as well as the U.S. Oval National Register Historic District located within the old military installation at Plattsburgh. The town has a storied military history that stretches from the American Revolution and the War of 1812 to the Cold War.

35 Ralph C. Sheldon Nature Trail

Endpoints: Titus Road, Summerdale Road.

Location: Chautauqua County.

Length: 5.9 miles.

Surface: Dirt, cinder.

Uses: All nonmotorized uses.

To get there: From New York Thruway exit 60, take NY Route 394 south to U.S. Route 20. Drive west to County Route 21 and turn south. Go about 11 miles—the road turns into County Route 76—and turn left onto Titus Road. The trailhead will be on your left about 1.5 miles ahead.

Contact: Chautauqua Rails-to-Trails, P.O. Box 151, Mayville, NY 14757-0151; 716–483–2330.

Chautauqua County has miles of beautiful and scenic abandoned railroad corridors that wind through the most picturesque villages and hamlets imaginable. Two of these corridors—the Sheldon Trail and Allison Wells-Ney Trail—also have a wide variety of forest, meadow, and wetland habitats. That makes them especially attractive to birds and other wildlife. Bird-watchers have counted more than 175 avian species along the Sheldon.

For historical background on this trail, see Trail 24.

36 Remsen–Lake Placid Travel Corridor

Endpoints: Remsen, Lake Placid.

Location: Essex, Franklin, Hamilton, Herkimer, Oneida, and St. Lawrence Counties.

Length: 119 miles.

Surface: Intact rails and ties.

Uses: Snowmobiling.

Contact: Rick Fenton, Supervising Forester, New York State Department of Environmental Conservation, P.O. Box 458, Northville, NY 12134; 518–863–4545; rtfenton@gw.dec.state.ny.us. Jeff Johnson, President, New York State Snowmobile Association, 138 Old Forge Road, Illion, NY 13357; 315–894–5780; jeffj400yz@aol.com.

37 Rochester, Syracuse & Eastern Trail

Endpoints: Pannell Road in Perinton, Perinton–East Rochester village line.

Location: Monroe County.

Length: 6.0 miles.

Surface: Crushed limestone.

Uses: Bicycling, running, hiking, horseback riding, snowmobiling, cross-country skiing.

To get there: From I–490 take exit 26 to NY Route 31. Follow Route 31 east for 4.5 miles and then take a right onto Victor Road. Follow the road a short distance to the parking lot for trail users.

Contact: Dave Morgan, Director, Parks, Recreation & Parks Department, 1350 Turk Hill Road, Fairport, NY 14450; 716–223–5050; www.perinton.org.

It's not hard to see why Perinton was named "Trailtown USA" by the American Hiking Society and the National Park Service in 1996. The distinction of being one of the ten towns chosen for this award was a result of lots of hard volunteer work by the Crescent Trail Association and the town of Perinton. Together the Crescent Trail, the Rochester, Syracuse & Eastern Trail, the Perinton Bike Route, many individual park trails, and the Erie Canal Heritage Trail provide more than 45 miles of pathways for the town's lucky citizens. This trail, also called the Perinton Hike/Bikeway Trail, is a nice diversion from the Erie Canal Trail and a pleasurable connection to Lollypop Farms and the People's Soft Animal Care and Education Center.

Sometimes referred to as the Trolley Trail, the rail line was originally operated by the Rochester, Syracuse & Eastern Railroad from 1906 to 1931. Referred to then as the "On Time" Electric Inner Urban Railway, its two trolley tracks ran to the suburbs of Rochester.

The trail starts in the east on Pannell Road, but there's no parking there. A more convenient place to begin is 1 mile away at Egypt Park Trailhead, located at Victor Road and Route 31 next to the Lollypop Farm. You'll find rest rooms at Egypt Park and Perinton Park.

More than 40 percent of rail-trails perform double-duty as utility rights-of-way.

The crushed limestone surface is compact and will accommodate everything but in-line skates. There are some road crossings, so be careful and watch for traffic.

38 Uncle Sam Bikeway

Endpoints: City of Troy.

Location: Rensselaer County.

Length: 3.1 miles.

Surface: Asphalt.

Uses: All nonmotorized uses.

To get there: The trailhead is located on NY Route 142, one block east of Ninth Avenue in northern Troy, New York. The trail and parking are both found on the south side of the highway.

Contact: Robert Weaver, Commissioner, Troy Parks and Recreation Department, 1 Monument Square, Troy, NY 12180; 518–235–8993.

Directly across from Albany lies Troy, a port on the Hudson River and the eastern terminal for the New York State Barge Canal. Long known as a manufacturing center and a college town (Rensselaer Polytechnic Institute and Russell Sage College are here), Troy is also the hometown of one Samuel Wilson. He supplied the U.S. Army with food during the War of 1812 and was known to the troops as

"Uncle Sam." This nickname, of course, came to be better known as a caricature of the United States—hence the Uncle Sam Bikeway.

This trail was at one time known in railroading circles as the Passenger Main of the Boston & Maine Railroad (B&M). The B&M brought passenger traffic and a smaller amount of freight traffic to Troy, where folks could connect with trains of the New York Central and the Delaware & Hudson Railway for points elsewhere.

Today one of the country's premier model railroads is located in Troy, on the campus of Rensselaer Polytechnic Institute.

(39) Verona Beach State Park

Endpoints: Within Verona Beach State Park.

Location: Oneida County.

Length: 8.0 miles.

Surface: Cinder, gravel, grass.

Uses: All nonmotorized uses.

To get there: Take exit 34 (Canastota) off I–90, the New York Thruway, and proceed 7 miles north on NY Route 13. The park entrance will be on your left.

Contact: Al Gorton, Verona State Beach Park, P.O. Box 245, Verona Beach, NY 13162; 315–762–4463.

Appendix A

FOR FURTHER READING

This is a guide to some other resources that will expand your knowledge of the places described in this book.

Archer, Robert F. *Lehigh Valley Railroad—The Route of the Black Diamond.* Forest Park, Ill.: Heimburger House Publishing Co., 1977.

Beard, Howard D. "The B&M in Troy, New York, Circa 1945." *The B&M Bulletin* (Fall 1982).

Bednar, Mike. *Lehigh Valley Railroad.* Laurys Station, Pa.: Garrigues House Publishers, 1993.

Bernard, Vincent. "The West End." *The B&M Bulletin* (B&M Historical Society) Vol. XVI, No. 1 (1988).

Botzman, Harvey. *Erie Canal Bicyclist & Hiker Tour Guide, Second Edition.* Rochester, N.Y.: Cyclotour Guide Books, 2000.

Bridge Line Historical Society—Bulletin, Vol. 4, No. 4 (April 1994).

Cook, Richard J. Sr. *The Twentieth Century Limited—1938–1967.* Lynchburg, Va.: TLC Publishing, 1993.

Crist, Edward J. *Erie Memories.* New York City, N.Y.: Quadrant Press, 1993.

D&H Transportation Heritage Council. *Visit the D&H Heritage Corridor.* Hyde Park, N.Y.: National Park Service.

Drury, George R. *The Historical Guide to North American Railroads—Histories, figures, and features of more than 160 railroads abandoned or merged since 1930.* Waukesha, Wis.: Kalmbach Publishing Co., 1985.

Flanagan, Michael. *Stations—An Imagined Journey.* New York City, N.Y.: Pantheon Books, 1994.

Freeman, Rich and Sue. *Take Your Bike: Family Rides in the Finger Lakes and Genesee Valley Region.* Fishers, N.Y.: Footprint Press, 1999.

———. *Take Your Bike: Family Rides in the Rochester Area.* Fishers, N.Y.: Footprint Press, 1998.

Gallo, Daniel R., and Kramer, Frederick A. *The Putnam Division: New York Central's Bygone Route through Westchester County.* Westfield, N.J.: 1989.

Goddard, Stephen B. *Getting There—The Epic Struggle between Road and Rail in the American Century.* Chicago, Ill.: Basic Book, University of Chicago Press, 1994.

Grant, H. Roger. *Erie Lackawanna—Death of an American Railroad, 1938–1992*. Stanford, Calif.: Stanford University Press, 1994.

Grogan, Louis, V. *The Coming of the New York and Harlem Railroad*. Pawling, N.Y.: Grogan, 1989.

Harter, Henry A., *Fairy Tale Railroad—The Mohawk and Malone from the Mohawk, through the Adirondacks to the St. Lawrence—The Golden Chariot Route*. Utica, N.Y.: North Country Books, 1979.

Healy, Kent T. *Performance of the U.S. Railroads since World War II—A Quarter Century of Private Operation*. New York, N.Y.: Vantage Press, Inc., 1985.

Helmer, William, F. *O & W*. Hensonville, N.Y.: Black Dome Press, 2000.

Jones, Robert Willoughby. *Boston & Albany—The New York Central in New England—Volumes I & II*. Los Angeles, Calif.: Pine Tree Press, 1997.

Kudish, Michael. *Railroads of the Adirondacks—A History*. Fleischmanns, N.Y.: Purple Mountain Press, 1996.

———. *Where Did the Tracks Go*. Saranac Lake, N.Y.: The Chauncy Press, 1985.

Lilly, Douglas E. *The Lehigh and New England Railroad: A Color Retrospect*. Laurys Station, Pa.: Garrigues House Publishers, 1988.

Lowenthal, Larry, and Greenberg, William T. *The Lackawanna Railroad in Northwest New Jersey*. Morristown, N.J.: Tri-State Railway Historical Society, 1987.

Mabee, Carlton. *Bridging the Hudson: The Poughkeepsie Railroad Bridge and its Connecting Line*. Fleischmanns, N.Y.: Purple Mountain Press, 2001.

———. *Listen to the Whistle: An Anecdotal History of the Wallkill Valley Railroad in Ulster and Orange Counties, New York*. Fleischmanns, N.Y.: Purple Mountain Press, 1995.

Middleton, William, D. *Landmarks of the Iron Road—2 Centuries of North American Railroad Engineering*. Bloomington, Ind.: Indiana University, 1999.

Mohowski, Robert E. *New York, Ontario and Western Railway and the Dairy Industry in Central New York State*. Laurys Station, Pa.: Garrigues House Publishers, 1995.

Nehrich, John. *Milk Train Data Pack*. Troy, N.Y.: Rensselaer Student Union, 1993.

———. "The Rutland in Troy, 1989. The Year of Troy's Bicentennial." *The Rutland Newsliner* Vol. 3, No. 1 (March 1989).

Nielsen, Waldo. *Right-of-Way: A Guide to Abandoned Railroads in the United States.* Bend, Ore.: Maverick Publications, 1992.

Office of Parks, Recreation, and Historic Preservation. *Catharine Valley Trail Master Plan.* Trumansburg, N.Y.: 2000.

Phelps, George. *New England Rail Album: A Traveling Salesman Remembers the 1930s.* Glendale, Calif.: Trans-Anglo Publishing, 1990.

Regency House Publishing. *The Complete History of North American Railroads.* London: The Grange, 1996.

Roseman, V.S. *Railway Express—An Overview.* Denver, Colo.: Rocky Mountain Publishing, 1992.

Rossi, Louis. *Cycling along the Canals of New York.* College Park, Md.: Vitesse Press, 1999.

Schwieterman, Joseph P. *When the Railroad Leaves Town: American Communities in the Age of Rail Line Abandonment.* Kirksville, Mo.: Truman State University Press, 2001.

Shaughnessy, Jim. *Delaware & Hudson.* Berkeley, Calif.: Howell-North Books, 1967.

Sweetland, David R. *Lackawanna Railroad—In Color.* Edison, N.J.: Morning Sun Books, Inc., 1990.

Stillgoe, John R. *Outside Lies Magic— Regaining History and Awareness in Everyday Places.* New York City, N.Y.: Walker Publishing, 1999.

Van Diver, Richard B. *Roadside Geology of New York.* Missoula, Mont.: Mountain Press Publishing, 1985.

Wakefield, Manville. *Coal Boats to Tidewater.* Grahamsville, N.Y.: Wakefair Press, 1971.

———. *To the Mountains by Rail.* Grahamsville, N.Y.: Wakefair Press, 1970.

Walker, Mike. *Railroad Atlas of North America.* Kent, U.K.: Steam Powered Publishing, 1993.

Wilner, Frank N. *Railroad Mergers— History, Analysis, Insight.* Simon-Boardman Books, Inc., 1997.

Appendix B

RAILROAD HISTORICAL SOCIETIES

Camden & Amboy Railroad
Camden & Amboy Railroad Historical Society
P.O. Box 3277, South Amboy, NJ 08879

Central of New Jersey; Delaware, Lackawanna & Western; Lehigh & Hudson River; Lehigh & New England; Lehigh Valley; and Reading Railroads
Anthracite Railroads Historical Society
P.O. Box 519, Lansdale, PA 19446-0519

Conrail
Conrail Historical Society, Inc.
P. O. Box 38, Walnutport, PA 18088-0038

Delaware & Hudson Railway
Bridge Line Historical Society
P.O. Box 7242, Capital Station, Albany, NY 12224

Erie Lackawanna
Erie Lackawanna Historical Society
116 Ketcham Road, Hackettstown, NJ 07840

Fonda, Johnstown & Gloversville Railroad
Fonda, Johnstown & Gloversville Railroad Historical Society
115 Upland Road, Syracuse, NY 13207

Lehigh Valley Railroad
Lehigh Valley Railroad Historical Society
P.O. Box RR, Manchester, NY 14504-0200

Middletown & New Jersey Railroad
Middletown & New Jersey Railroad Historical Society
325 Collabar Road, Montgomery, NY 12549-1808

New Jersey Midland Railroad
New Jersey Midland Railroad Historical Society
P.O. Box 6125, Parsippany, NJ 07054

New York Central System
New York Central System Historical Society
P.O. Box 81184, Cleveland, OH 44181-0184

New York, Chicago & Saint Louis
Nickel Plate Road Historical & Technical Society
P.O. Box 381, New Haven, IN 46774-0381

New York, New Haven & Hartford
New Haven Railroad Historical & Technical Association
P.O. Box 122, Wallingford, CT 06492

New York Susquehanna & Western
New York Susquehanna & Western
Railroad Historical Society
P.O. Box 121, Rochelle Park, NJ
07662-0121

Ontario & Western Railway
Ontario & Western Railway Historical Society
P.O. Box 713, Middletown, NY 10940

Pennsylvania Railroad
Pennsylvania Railroad Technical &
Historical Society
P.O. Box 389, Upper Darby, PA 19082

Pennsylvania-Reading Seashore Lines
Pennsylvania-Reading Seashore
Lines Historical Society
P.O. Box 1214, Bellmawr, NJ 08099

Ulster & Delaware Railroad
Ulster & Delaware Railroad Historical Society
P.O. Box 404, Margaretville, NY
12455-0404

GENERAL RAILROAD ASSOCIATIONS

National Railway Historical Society
P.O. Box 58547, Philadelphia, PA
19102-8547

New York Railroad Enthusiasts
P.O. Box 040320, Staten Island, NY
10304

The Railroad Enthusiasts Inc.
3 Durham Lane, Gonic, NH 03839

Railroad Station Historical Society,
Inc.
430 Ivy Avenue, Crete, NE 68333

Railroadians of America
P.O. Box 6125, Parsippany, NJ 07054

Railway & Locomotive Historical
Society
P.O. Box 215, East Irvine, CA 92650-
0215

Appendix C

LIST OF SERVICES

1 BRONX RIVER PATHWAY
Bike Repair/Rentals
Bronx River Bicycle Works
6 North Bond Street, Floor 1
Mt. Vernon, NY 10550-2551
914–667–7417
bronxriverbicycleworks@msn.com

2 ERIE CANAL HERITAGE TRAIL
Accommodations
Adams Basin Inn
425 Washington Street
Adams Basin, NY 14410
716–352–6784
halya@adamsbasininn.com
www.adamsbasininn.com

Country Cottage Bed & Breakfast
7745 Rochester Road
Gasport, NY 14067
716–772–2251
www.countrycottagebandb.com

Liberty House Bed & Breakfast
131 West Main Street
Palmyra, NY 14522
315–597–0011; fax 315–597–1450
info@libertyhousebb.com
www.libertyhousebb.com

Twenty Woodlawn Bed & Breakfast
20 Woodlawn Avenue
Fairport, NY 14450
716–377–8224
conniebf@frontiernet.net
www.nycanal.com

The Victorian Bed & Breakfast
320 Main Street
Brockport, NY 14420
585–637–7519
sk320@aol.com

Bike Repair/Rentals
Bicycle Outfitters
45 North Main Street
Brockport, NY 14420-1648
716–637–9901; fax 585–637–8909
fattirejunkie@aol.com
www.bicycle-outfitters.com

Freewheelers
1757 Mount Hope Avenue
Rochester, NY 14620
716–473–3724

RV & E Bike and Skate
40 North Main Street
Fairport, NY 14450
585–388–1350; fax 585–377–4510
rvebike@frontiernet.net
www.rvebike.com

Scooter World
3752 South Main Street
Marion, NY 14505
315–926–0707; fax 315–926–0415
scooter@rochester.rr.com
www.scooterworldonline.com

Sugar's Bike Shop
2139 North Union Street
Spencerport, NY 14559-1261
716-352-8300.

3 OLD ERIE CANAL TRAIL
Accommodations
Beard Morgan House Bed &
  Breakfast
126 East Genesee Street
Fayetteville, NY 13066-1302
315-637-4234; fax 315-637-0010
beardmorgan@yahoo.com

Bike Repair/Rentals
Wayne's & Meltzer's Bicycle Shop
2716 Erie Boulevard East
Syracuse, NY 13224
315-446-6816; fax 315-446-1156
dwv1218@aol.com
www.waynesbikes.com

4 MOHAWK-HUDSON
BIKEWAY
Accommodations/Food
The Mansion Hill Inn & Restaurant
115 Philip Street
Albany, NY 12202-1731
518-465-2038; fax 518-434-2313
inn@mansionhill.com
www.mansionhill.com

6 CATSKILL SCENIC TRAIL
Accommodations
Boncranna Bed & Breakfast
13 Maple Avenue
Hobart, NY 13788
607-538-1129
boncranna@aol.com
www.boncranna.com

7 CAYUGA COUNTY TRAIL
Campground
Shon's Boat Basin & Campground
14678 Lake Street
Fair Haven, NY 13064
315-947-6635; 800-523-9878;
  fax 315-947-6343
shons@zlink.net
www.fairhavenny.com/shons

8 D&H CANAL HERITAGE
CORRIDOR
Accommodations
Baker's Bed & Breakfast
24 Old Kings Highway
Stone Ridge, NY 12484-5713
845-687-9795; fax 845-687-4153
dbakersbandb@aol.com
www.bakersbandb.com

Captain Schoonmaker's Bed &
  Breakfast
913 State Route 213
High Falls, NY 12440-5717
845-687-7946
info@captainschoonmakers.com
www.captainschoonmakers.com

Inn at Lake Joseph
400 St. Josephs Road
Forestburgh, NY 12777-6240
845-791-9506

Bike Repair/Rentals
TABLE Rock Tour & Bicycles
292 Main Street
Rosendale, NY 12472
845-658-7832; fax 845-658-7391
TABLERockToursandBicycles@
  yahoo.com
www.TABLERockTours.com

Campgrounds

Catskill Mountain Ranch
538 Mount Vernon Road
Wurtsboro, NY 12790
845–888–0675; fax 845–888–0216
info@catskillmountainranch.com
www.catskillmountainranch.com

So Hi Campground
425 Woodland Road
Accord, NY 12404-5232
845–687–7377; fax 845–687–7723
sohicampground@aol.com
www.sohicampground.com

Food

Depuy Canal House
Route 213
High Falls, NY 12440
845–687–7700; fax 845–687–7073
lfraser@ulster.net
depuycanalhouse.net

9 GENESEE VALLEY GREENWAY

Accommodations

Country Inn and Suites by Carlson
130 North Main Street
Mount Morris, NY 14510
585–658–4080; fax 585–658–4020
cx_mtmo@countryinns.com
www.countryinns.com/
    mountmorris.ny

Glen Iris Inn
7 Letchworth State Park
Castile, NY 14427
585–493–2622; fax 585–493–5803
mltnwt@aol.com
www.glenirisinn.com

Bike Repair/Rentals

Massasauga Bike Rentals and
    Tours
2139 Mill Street
Nunda, NY 14517
716–468–5964
massasaugabikes@aol.com
www.massasaugabikes.com

Campground

Woodstream Campsite
5440 School Road
Gainesville, NY 14066
585–493–5643; fax 585–493–5643
camp@woodstreamcampsite.com
www.woodstreamcampsite.com

Food

Broman's Genesee Falls Inn
P.O. Box 238
Portageville, NY 14536
585–493–2484; fax 585–468–5654
lynneygirl@juno.com
www.10kvacationrentals.com

10 GLENS FALLS FEEDER CANAL TRAIL

Accommodations

The Glens Falls Inn
25 Sherman Avenue
Glens Falls, NY 12801
518–743–9365

11 HARLEM VALLEY RAIL TRAIL

Campgrounds

Camp Waubeeka Family
    Campground
133 Farm Road
Copake, NY 12516-1601
518–329–4681; fax 518–329–5781
waubeeka@taconic.net
www.campwaubeeka.com

Oleana Family Campground
2236 County Route 7
Copake, NY 12516-1433
518–329–2811; fax 518–329–0703
ole@taconic.net
www.oleanacampground.com

12 NORTH COUNTY TRAILWAY
Bike Repair/Rentals
Bicycle World
7 East Main Street
Mount Kisco, NY 10549-2203
914–666–4044; fax 914–666–4049
IMARCOS@ALTAVISTA.COM

The New Yorktown Cycling Center
1899 Commerce Street
Yorktown Heights, NY 10598-4409
914–245–5504; fax 914–245–5263
tom@yorktowncycle.com
www.yorktowncycle.com

13 OLD CROTON AQUEDUCT TRAIL
Accommodations
Alexander Hamilton House
49 Van Wyck Street
Croton-on-Hudson, NY 10520
914–271–6737; fax 914–271–3927
alexhous@bestweb.net
www.alexanderhamiltonhouse.com

Bike Repair/Rentals
E/T Cycle Center
75 South Riverside Avenue
Croton-on-Hudson, NY 10520-2648
914–271–6661; fax 914–271–6803
etcycle@verizon.net
www.etcyclecenter.com

Tarrytown Cycles
11 North Broadway
Tarrytown, NY 10591-3201
914–631–1850; fax 914–631–1853
bikemaniac@aol.com

14 ONTARIO PATHWAYS RAIL TRAIL
Accommodations
Sutherland House Bed & Breakfast
3179 State Route 21 S
Canandaigua, NY 14424
585–396–0375; fax 585–396–9281
goodnite@frontiernet.net
www.sutherlandhouse.com

15 ORANGE HERITAGE TRAIL
Accommodations
Caren House Bed & Breakfast
1371 Orange Turnpike
Monroe, NY 10950
845–782–0377; fax 845–782–7449
carenbb@warwick.net
www.carenhousebb.com

16 OSWEGO RECREATIONAL TRAIL
Campground
Lazy K-RV Ranch Camping
965 Stone Barn Road
Cleveland, NY 13042-3203
315–675–8100; 888–381–6415;
    fax 315–675–8860
www.lazykrvranch.com

17 OUTLET TRAIL
Accommodations
Wagener Estate Bed & Breakfast
351 Elm Street
Penn Yan, NY 14527-1446
315–536–4591; fax 315–531–8142
wagenerestate@wagenerestate.com
www.wagenerestate.com

21 WALLKILL VALLEY RAIL TRAIL

Accommodations

Country Meadows Bed & Breakfast
41 Denniston Road
Gardiner, NY 12525
845–895–3132; fax 845–895–1703
info@countrymeadowsbandb.com
www.countrymeadowsbandb.com

Bike Repair/Rentals

Bicycle Depot
15 Main Street
New Paltz, NY 12561-1742
845–255–3859
www.bicycledepot.com

TABLE Rock Tour & Bicycles
292 Main Street
Rosendale, NY 12472
845–658–7832; fax 845–658–7391
TABLERockToursandBicycles@
    yahoo.com
www.TABLERockTours.com

Campgrounds

Hidden Valley Lake Campground
P.O. Box 1190
Kingston, NY 12402
845–338–4616

Yogi Bear's Jellystone Park @
Lazy River
50 Bevier Road
Gardiner, NY 12525
845–255–5193; fax 845–256–0159
yogibear1@msn.com
www.lazyriverny.com

22 WARREN COUNTY BIKEWAY

Accommodations

The Glens Falls Inn
25 Sherman Avenue
Glens Falls, NY 12801
518–743–9365; fax 518–743–0696
info@glensfallsinn.com
www.glensfallsinn.com

Get Your Rail-Trail Guidebooks

- Florida   • California   • Wisconsin
- Washington & Oregon
- New England States (CT, RI,VT, MA, ME, NH)
- Mid-Atlantic States (MD, DE, VA, WV)

"An invaluable guidebook to some of the country's best rail-trails… quick and easy-to-read details get us on the trail fast, while the historical mentions add spark."

— Linda Frahm, *Walking Magazine*

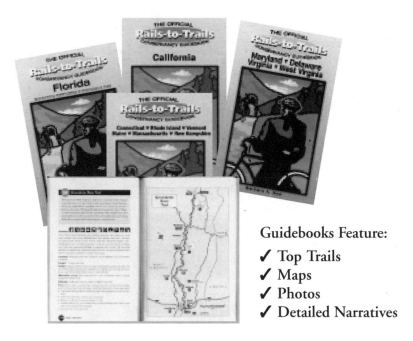

Guidebooks Feature:

✓ Top Trails
✓ Maps
✓ Photos
✓ Detailed Narratives

3 Easy Ways to Order:

1. Mail form on the next page with your check or credit card information.
2. Call 1-800-888-7747, ext 11 with your Visa, MasterCard or American Express card.
3. Visit www.railtrails.org to order online.

RAILS
- to -
TRAILS
CONSERVANCY

Please send me the following RTC Guidebooks!

❏ Florida ❏ Washington & Oregon
❏ California ❏ Mid-Atlantic States (MD, DE, VA, WV)
❏ Wisconsin ❏ New England States (CT, RI, VT, MA, NH, ME)

Item #	Guidebooks	Member Price	Non-Member Price	Qty	Total
GPG1	Mid-Atlantic	$12.95	$14.95		$
GPG2	New England	$12.95	$14.95		
GPG3	California	$12.95	$14.95		
GPG4	Florida	$10.95	$12.95		
GPG5	Wisconsin	$12.95	$14.95		
GPG6	Washington & Oregon	$12.95	$14.95		
GRT1T	1000 Great Rail-Trails *(Directory)*	$12.95	$14.95		
			Order Total		$
	Sales Tax (CA, FL, MA, MI, OH, PA & DC see chart below)				$
	Shipping & Handling Charge *(Please allow 6–8 weeks for delivery)*				$ 5.95
			Total Enclosed		$

❏ I want to join Rails-to-Trails Conservancy. My membership contribution is enclosed (amount checked below). As a member I will receive one year of *Rails to Trails*, the colorful, quarterly magazine that celebrates trails and greenways, as well as discounts on publications and merchandise.

❏ $18 Regular ❏ $25 Supporting ❏ $50 Patron
❏ $100 Benefactor ❏ $1,000 — Trailblazer Society level includes invitations to exclusive rail-trail excursions.

❏ My check, payable to Rails-to-Trails Conservancy, is enclosed.
❏ Charge my credit card: ❏ MC ❏ VISA ❏ American Express
Card # _____ Exp. _____
Signature _____
Name on card *(please print)* _____

Ship to *(please print)*:
Name_____
Street _____
City _____
State, Zip _____
Phone _____
Email _____

SALES TAX CHART		
	CA	8.50%
	FL	7.00%
	PA & MI	6.00%
	DC & OH	5.75%
	MA	5.00%